WHAT DOES THE LORD REQUIRE?

WHAT DOES THE LORD REQUIRE?

A Guide for Preaching and Teaching Biblical Ethics

Walter C. Kaiser Jr.

Baker Academic

a division of Baker Publishing Group

Grand Rapids, Michigan

© 2009 by Walter C. Kaiser Jr.

Published by Baker Academic
a division of Baker Publishing Group
P.O. Box 6287, Grand Rapids, MI 49516-6287
www.bakeracademic.com

Printed in the United States of America

Library of Congress Cataloging-in-Publication Data
Kaiser, Walter C.
    What does the Lord require? : a guide for preaching and teaching biblical ethics / Walter C. Kaiser, Jr.
      p. cm.
    Includes bibliographical references (p.   ) and indexes.
    ISBN 978-0-8010-3636-1 (pbk.)
    1. Ethics in the Bible—Study and teaching. 2. Christian ethics—Biblical teaching—Study and teaching. 3. Preaching. I. Title.
    BS680.E84K35 2009
    241—dc22
                                     2008046647

For
Richard A. and Miriam Armstrong
Gracious friends,
Faithful prayer warriors,
And generous and wise counselors,
Who led Gordon-Conwell Theological Seminary board
During most of my years as president.
1 Corinthians 2:9; Isaiah 64:4

CONTENTS

Dana

7

INTRODUCTION

Living and Acting as God Would Have Us Live and Act (Psalm 15)

E thics is not a distinctively Christian enterprise, for Paul argued that even pagans, who show no outward knowledge of the law, demonstrate that the work of the law has been written on their hearts (Rom. 2:14–15). One's perspective, or world/life view, provides the starting point for all ethics. Thus one's ethical actions could begin from a humanistic, Islamic, Buddhist, or atheistic frame of thinking, as well as a biblical one.

The Use of the Bible for Ethical Decisions

A biblical ethic begins with the light of Scripture: "Your word is a lamp to my feet and a light for my path" (Ps. 119:105). Thus for Christians, biblical ethics is the reflection on human acts and conduct from the perspective given to us in Holy Scripture from our Lord. Though it contains sixty-six books written by some forty human authors, the Bible itself speaks of this compilation as one book (John 10:35; 17:12; 1 Tim. 5:18). The apostle Paul claimed that "all Scripture is God-breathed and is useful for teaching, rebuking, correcting and training in righteousness, so that the [person] of God may be thoroughly equipped for every good work" (2 Tim. 3:16–17)—including such works as ethical and moral living that are pleasing to our Lord.

But just how does a person use Scripture in making or evaluating ethical decisions? Scripture is the "norm" (a word coming from the Latin word *norma*, which originally meant "a carpenter's square," a tool that determined whether a corner or line was square and straight) we can use to show that an action or a decision is right or wrong, just or unjust. Scripture can be used in four different ways in this connection; it can act (1) as a guide, (2) as a guard, (3) as a compass, and (4) as a principle. Accordingly, *guides* point out the route we should take, while *guards* warn us against wrong decisions or paths. *Compasses* help us gain our orientation, and *principles* gather the abstract ideas that encapsulate a number of examples found in Scripture.

Our knowledge, then, with which to evaluate ethical issues is gathered from Scripture. It is our only authoritative source for hearing God's direction for acting properly and justly. But we must also use our understanding, as well as our hearts and consciences, in applying that word of God for action. There is the understanding we have received at our birth, often called common sense. But we also have an erroneous understanding due to the fall of Adam and Eve in the Garden of Eden and the result of our own sin. Fortunately, there is also the third understanding, by which we are led in a proper way using the light of Scripture. The Psalmist rightly cried out, "Give me understanding, and I will keep your law and obey it with all my heart" (Ps. 119:34).

The Complexity of Life

Life, however, can get very complicated, as we are reminded daily through our newspapers, television newscasts, and stories of human tragedies around the globe. For example, in the postelection violence that erupted in Kenya, Africa, in 2007, an eyewitness described how he dashed in and out of a crowded church building in Kenya that had been set ablaze by the insurgents. The eyewitness, on his last dash into the flaming church to rescue a few more, heard a cry for help that came from the burning inferno, "Uncle! Save me uncle, save me!" These were the pleas of the rescuer's young nephew trapped in the burning church building. In a moment of hesitation, the man looked at the flames, perhaps thought of his own family he had to care for, and decided he could not make one more charge into the building to rescue his dying nephew.[1] Should he have attempted to rescue his nephew, even if it endangered his own life, or should he have recalled his obligation to provide for his own immediate family as a prior commitment over that of saving another life? How does one decide what to do in situations such as these that are so filled with opposing demands? Which action takes precedence over another when they seem to conflict or when they place opposite demands on us? Not all ethical situations in life involve such contrary and conflicting ethical absolutes as this story (between saving a life and providing continuing care for one's family), but in every situation, we daily must make decisions that either reflect well on what our Lord has taught us or reflect badly on our obedience to God's word.

Is the Bible Useful for Twenty-First-Century Ethics?

All of this raises questions for the believer: How applicable is the Bible's moral standard in our own day, especially as the moral and ethical dilemmas seem to be getting more and more complicated? Is biblical truth still the valid measure for what is right, wrong, good, just, and fair? Is the character of God still the basis for affirming that there is an ethical absolute in the universe, or must we go (as in the hymn "Break Thou the Bread of Life") "beyond the sacred page" in order to meet the new demands made on us?

These questions, and a whole series of others like them, are raised by Bible-believing Christians as often as they are raised by secular citizens around the globe trying to make their way ethically and morally in the twenty-first century. Sadly, in all too many situations, we who teach, preach, and lead in the church have offered, at best, a minimal amount of help from the Scriptures. If we do not live by bread alone, as Scripture reminds us, but by every word that proceeds from the mouth of God (Deut. 8:3), then there is a serious need for instruction from Scripture at the lay and pastoral level in order that we might offer help to meet the challenges of our day ethically, doctrinally, and morally. We must help God's people to see where the dilemmas they are facing stand as discussed in fact or in principle in Scripture. Too many teachers and preachers, not to mention parents and other caregivers, shy away from helping others understand the Word of God for making moral decisions in life because they believe ethics is too complicated and too personal, or they are just unaware of the biblical teaching. They think it will engender division, because people's minds are already made up as to what they will do or not do. And if they haven't made up their minds already, pretty soon they will, and they surely don't want anyone telling them that God's word says differently!

But will those excuses and realities pass the test of the final day when we stand before the Lord? For too long now we have given all too little guidance from the lectern, pulpit, and home. This must change—or we who should have taught will be directly responsible to our Lord for our society's moral decay because of our failure to let God have his say on all the current matters of ethics and morals that afflict our culture so directly. Even ignorance of God's Word is no excuse for not doing what is right! (Prov. 24:12).

The Importance of Biblical Ethical Teaching Texts

Because of the urgent need for sound biblical ethics, I have attempted to combine insights from my study and teaching on the ethics of the Old and New Testament with some of the key teaching passages in the Bible. I have provided expositional outlines and the authoritative teaching-blocks from God's word as possible primers of the pump, as it were, for shaping living that is pleasing to God. It is my hope that these helps can be translated into a series of Bible studies, such as elective college or adult Bible studies, in-home Bible studies, and studies used in the educational program of the church, Christian college, or seminary. They may even end up as a series of messages that will demonstrate that the Bible is able to help us where the rubber meets the road, that is, in the tough ethical and moral decisions of real life. If it is too risky to do a series of Sunday morning messages, then what about a Sunday evening set of messages, or a special week of meetings on these themes by the pastoral staff, possibly with some help from outsiders? The important issue that must not be lost is that these messages must be expositions on the word of God. Service clubs like Kiwanis, Elks, Lions, and other civic organizations can highlight and analyze societal ills, but what is needed is a demonstration of the power of the word of God as the only possible source that stands a ghost of a chance at impacting and changing these problems.

How Does God Expect Us to Live? (Psalm 15)

What better place to introduce this series of studies than Psalm 15:1–5, a veritable summary of those who have fixed their lodging place and solid confidence in the Lord God? In the preceding psalms, David described the intensity of evil in his day, which does not seem to be all that different from our own day, for in Psalm 12:8 he advised, "The wicked freely strut about when what is vile is honored among men [and women]." But over against the corrupted humanity of that day, and ours, God was seeking out "the company of the righteous" (Ps. 14:5).[2] In the face of a blatant atheism that sassily challenged, "There is no God" (Ps. 14:1), accompanied by a "corrupt" lifestyle and "vile deeds" (Ps. 14:1c), God was still bent on presenting to that culture, as in our day, a people who were conformed to his will and held together by God himself, rather than by the spirit of the age in which they lived.

Psalm 15 is a wisdom psalm that has three parts, with the middle part presenting a tenfold structure on the moral conditions God is seeking. The structure is as follows:

I. The Question (15:1)
    What does God expect of us if we are to live in his blessed presence?

II. The Tenfold Set of Moral Conditions as the Proper Response (15:2–5a)

Positive Conditions	Negative Conditions
1. Living blamelessly	4. No slander
2. Doing what is right	5. No wrong
3. Speaking the truth	6. No reproach
7. Despises hardened sinners	8. No usury
9. Keeps his promises	10. No bribery

III. The Promise (15:5b)
    All who do these things shall never be shaken!

When David asks the question about qualifications for living and dwelling in God's holy presence in his tabernacle and on his holy hill in Zion, one might have expected a list of ritual requirements for such an entrance to worshiping and living for God. Instead, there were ten conditions, not developed as commands that were parallel to the Ten Commandments, but easy enough that a young person could tick them off on their ten fingers in recalling their substance and import. Even though there were no prohibitions against dishonoring one's parents, divorce, stealing, or murder, this list had much in common with that in Psalm 24 and Isaiah 33:15, which, though shorter, contained some guidelines that were similar along with others that were different:

Psalm 24:4

1. Has clean hands	2. Has a pure heart
3. No worship of idols	4. No falsehood = idolatry

Isaiah 33:15

1. Lives righteously	2. Speaks what is right
3. Rejects gain from extortion	4. Doesn't accept bribes
5. Shuts his ears to murder plots	6. Shuts his eyes to evil plots

It is fair to say, then, that what David places in front of us are some godly examples and representations of wise living to the glory of God. Even though all of the Decalogue is not represented, it would appear that an absolute standard that is based on the character of God stands behind this tenfold list in Psalm 15. Therefore, since that list was given in a day "when the foundations [were] being destroyed" (Ps. 11:3), so similar to our own troubled times, the ten conditions of Psalm 15 are worth examining for our own edification as well.

A Godly Lifestyle

First up in this list is the one "whose walk is blameless" (Ps. 15:2). This does not mean that the godly person must be perfect to enjoy the presence of God but that his or her "lifestyle" (our modern equivalent for the Hebrew concept of "walk") must be marked by "integrity," for the Hebrew word *tamim* signals a moral way of life. To render this word as "blameless" may focus too much on the negative aspect, for it implies wholeness and soundness. Even prior to the arrival of the law under Moses, "Noah found grace in the eyes of the LORD" (Gen. 6:8 NKJV), as did Abraham (Gen. 17:1). These men of God aspired to making integrity the goal and mark of their lives. The outward mark of integrity toward God is strengthened by the fact that this person "does what is righteous" (Ps. 15:2b). And that in turn has an inward aspect as well, for this one "speaks the truth from [the] heart" (v. 2c). The wise person is one who expresses what is in the very core of their being by the speech that proceeds from the center of their innermost self. All three of the activities mentioned here are in the Hebrew text in participial forms in Psalm 15: "walking/living," "doing," and "speaking," just as a similar triad appears in Psalm 1:1, in which the three actions also form a figure of speech known as a hendiatris, that is, one total idea of practicing the presence of God by calling on all three aspects of life. As Franz Delitzsch summarized it, "We have three characteristics here: a spotless walk, conduct ordered according to God's will, and a truth-loving mode of thought."[3]

An Ungodly Lifestyle

The preceding three positive conditions are followed by three negative acts that the person dwelling in the presence of God does not commit. First of all, such a person does not "gossip," or "has no slander on his tongue" (v. 3).[4] The unusual verb (Hebrew, *ragal*) has the meaning in the intensive stem "to spy out," in the sense of "going around" to spread things abroad. But the meaning of avoiding slander and gossip seems established well enough to be retained here (cf. 2 Sam. 19:27). Therefore, just as the first three positive conditions called for wholeness and soundness in one's character, now a negative condition calls for restraint in one's vocabulary. That concept is brought out further in the second and third negative conditions in verse 3. The wise person purposefully does not lay traps for his friend or neighbor. He just plain refuses to give credence to evil reports about others. In fact, the Hebrew text makes a little word play on the word for "neighbor" (*rea'*) and the word for "wrong/evil" (*ra'ah*). That is matched by a third negative where this righteous person "casts no slur on his fellow [person]." Here too, unnecessarily raking up anything of a negative nature just to load (Hebrew, *nasa*) reproach on someone is to be rejected summarily.

Over against the wise actions of those who walk with God is the "rejected" or "scorned/vile" person who is characterized by the evil deeds that he or she does. This is not the occasional practitioner of evil but one who is determined to do evil and as a consequence earns the scorn of the man or woman who "honors those who fear the LORD" and "keeps his oath/promise even when it hurts" (v. 4b–c). This sense of integrity and honor does not mean that such rash promises as those of Jepthah (Judg. 11:31, 34–39) or Herod (Matt. 14:6–11) must be kept to the detriment of innocent people. It is possible to beg for release from such improperly thought-out oaths, as in Proverbs 6:1–5 and Leviticus 27:1–33. But for valid promises and vows, wise persons remain loyal to their word (Eccles. 5:1–7; Matt. 5:33–37).

Usury—that is, charging a high rate of interest in such a way as to extort money from a brother's misfortune—is roundly condemned in Scripture.[5] The Law and the Prophets returned to this topic frequently (Exod. 22:25; Lev. 25:37; Deut. 23:20; Ezek. 18:8). The passage here (Ps. 15:5a) objects to charging a poor person an exorbitant rate of interest instead of helping the individual with loans of money at no interest. If charging interest in general were being condemned here, then Matthew 25:27 (which allows it) would not make sense; so this has nothing to do with modern forms of commercial trading and charging interest—so long as it is not exorbitant. Instead it is aimed at those who loan money at interest to avoid offering help to a brother free of charge, an act of mercy that Scripture requires. The well-to-do must not take advantage of the poor, nor must they thwart justice by offering a bribe in court (Exod. 23:8; Deut. 16:19). Again, while the word for bribery can also mean any kind of compensation, what is being decried here is accepting compensation from the hungry or discriminating against the poor in favor of the well-to-do or the influential.[6]

Those heeding the injunctions found in these ten commands will find a solid sense of security, for the one "who does these things will never be moved/shaken" (Ps. 15:5b). That is the promise of God. That person may experience adversity, but God's affirmation is that he or she will never be shaken or moved from the love of God. Was this not the emphasis Jesus gave in his Sermon on the Mount? Accordingly, the ethical system does not stand apart from the Lord himself, but it is grounded in the theological teaching of the Scriptures.

Conclusions

1. God is now calling you and me to live without blame, to do what is right, and to speak the truth. We need to respond to him if we are going to stand in his holy presence one day in the future.
2. God is calling you and me to stop all forms of slander against everyone, to do no wrong, and to live without reproach. We can trust our Lord to help us rise to these challenges, for he is able to help us refrain from doing any of these three things.
3. You and I need to keep our promises as we avoid the social company of hardened sinners.
4. You and I should not avoid giving our money to the poor by using our money for reprehensible forms of bribery. God can help us to act differently even in such matters as these.

Bibliography

Bahnsen, G. L. *Theonomy in Christian Ethics*. Nutley, NJ: Craig, 1977.

Baker, David L. *Two Testaments, One Bible: A Study of Some Modern Solutions to the Theological Problem of the Relationship between the Old and New Testaments*. Downers Grove, IL: InterVarsity, 1977.

Birch, Bruce C., and L. L. Rasmussen. *Bible and Ethics in the Christian Life*. Rev. ed. Minneapolis: Augsburg, 1989.

Kaiser, Walter C., Jr. *Toward Old Testament Ethics*. Grand Rapids: Zondervan, 1983.

Lalleman, Hetty. *Celebrating the Law? Rethinking Old Testament Ethics*. London: Paternoster, 2004.

Ruler, A. A. van. *The Christian Church and the Old Testament*. Translated by G. W. Bromiley. Grand Rapids: Eerdmans, 1971.

Stott, John R. W. *New Issues Facing Christians Today*. Rev. ed. London: Marshall Pickering, 1999.

Wilson, R. R. "Approaches to Old Testament Ethics." In *Canon, Theology, and Old Testament Interpretation: Essays in Honor of B. S. Childs*, edited by G. M. Tucker, D. L. Petersen, and R. R. Wilson, 62–74. Philadelphia: Fortress, 1988.

Wright, Christopher J. H. *Living as the People of God: The Relevance of Old Testament Ethics.* Leicester, UK: Inter-Varsity, 1983; published in the US as *An Eye for an Eye: The Place of Old Testament Ethics for Today.* Downers Grove, IL: InterVarsity, 1983.

————. *Walking in the Ways of the Lord: The Ethical Authority of the Old Testament.* Leicester, UK: Apollos, 1995.

Discussion Questions

1. If society changes, are we as believers not also obligated to modify our actions to some degree to fit in with society? If that is so, how can we keep to such high standards as God sets?
2. If Jesus approved of charging a fair rate of interest, what is so wrong with usury?
3. If we all sin daily, how can we approach a holy God in worship knowing our hands, hearts, and bodies are already unclean? What can make us clean again?
4. How important is the Old Testament for understanding what a believer must be and do and how he or she must act toward others?

1

THE POOR, OPPRESSED, AND ORPHANS

Isaiah 58

It is estimated that in 2003, twelve million children became orphans in sub-Saharan Africa as a result of the HIV/AIDS epidemic on that continent. It is likewise estimated that sixteen thousand children die of hunger-related complications each day—one death every five seconds. Moreover, in 2004, an estimated one billion people earned less than the subsistence level. [1]

The Christian Response to the Disenfranchised

Tender, loving care toward those in the throes of poverty and oppression and those who were recently widowed, deprived, or orphaned are repeatedly identified as the real hallmarks of the Christian church down through the centuries. Thus, to cite an early example, when the Athenian philosopher Aristides was summoned to defend his fellow believers in front of the Emperor Hadrian in AD 125, he testified as follows: "[We] love one another. The widow's needs are not ignored, and [we] rescue the orphan from the person who does him violence. He who has, gives to him who has not, ungrudgingly and without boasting."[2]

That same Christian influence can be traced historically through the life of the church as believers placed a priority on bringing the little children to Jesus (Mark 10:14) and providing care for the fatherless (Deut. 26:12). Christians, for example, influenced the legal protection of children in the Roman Empire of the fifth and sixth centuries. The reformer Zwingli transformed several monasteries in Switzerland into orphanages. And another Christian statesman, Ashley Cooper, led the fight against child labor practices in Britain in the nineteenth century.

No less significant was the Christians' concern for those who were economically deprived, those individuals who were also the focus of specific provisions contained in the Mosaic law (Exod. 23:11; Lev. 14:21; 19:10). While these persons were not to receive favoritism just because they were poor (Lev. 19:15), neither were they to be avoided and overlooked by the rest of God's people or by society itself. When they were exploited, their cry to God for help (Ps. 34:6) was often answered by those who showed a helping hand to them by the grace and mercy of God (Ps. 41:1; Prov. 14:21).

Usually the word *poverty* is used for those who are "income-deficient." Three definitions are used to show what we mean by "income-deficient": (1) those who live below the "poverty line," an "absolute" minimum income needed for an urban family of four to "get by"; (2) those whose income is below 50 percent of the national median income of all workers, ; and (3) those who possess the smallest percent of a "share of the national income." Regardless of which of these three definitions is used, the "poor" still represent "an island of deprivation in a sea of affluence."[3]

Add to this group in the poverty level the class of the orphans, the widows, and those who are subjected to all forms of injustice and tyranny as a result of direct oppression, and the need for the Christian ethic of help and a call for action by believers is all the more dramatic. The Bible constantly calls for social justice (e.g.,

Exod. 3:9; Deut. 23:15–16; 24:14; Ps. 10:17–18; Jer. 7:5–7; Amos 4:1; Ezek. 45:8; James 2:5–7). In the divine scheme of things, God demanded rulers and those in leadership to exercise fairness, justice, and oversight to make sure that what was right was done for all their citizens and followers. But no less responsible for strong resistance to oppression and help for the poor were God's people vis-à-vis the whole fabric of society itself. No person or group was to use its power to exploit another (Deut. 16:18–20; Ps. 82:1–4; Prov. 21:15; Amos 5:7–15). Accordingly, the cry of the poor and the fatherless was clear; most people agreed on the need to end all oppression and injustice. How to attack such problems, however, was a point of disagreement. In many instances, what was needed was the phrase used on the original Great Seal of the United States: "Rebellion to Tyrants is Obedience to God."[4]

The biblical way to tackle these ills in our American society and around the world is first of all to examine one or more of the great teaching passages on this problem. One of the best for our purposes is found in Isaiah 58:1–12. While at first the passage seems to address another issue more directly (the problem of religious ritualism and formalism, or to be more accurate, phony spirituality), this text goes on to give one of the most explicit directives to believers who wished to demonstrate the reality of their professed faith by fighting oppression and poverty and by taking responsibility for the needs of the poor, the orphan, the widow, and those in society who had been disenfranchised and deprived of loving concern.

The Social Responsibilities of God's Family

The Christian ethical action proposed to help remedy some of these ills can be found in Isaiah 58:1–12, one of the great teaching texts of the Bible on this issue:

> Text: Isaiah 58:1–12
>
> Title: "The Social Responsibilities of God's Family"
>
> Focal Point: verse 6, "Is this not the kind of fasting I have chosen: to loose the chains of injustice and untie the cords of the yoke, to set the oppressed free and break every yoke?"
>
> Homiletical Keyword: Responsibilities

Interrogative: What are the social responsibilities of God's family
in bringing the love of God to answer the cries of the oppressed,
the poor, the widow, or the orphan?

Outline:
  I. We must stop our religious pretensions (58:1–2)
     A. To correct habits
     B. To correct doctrines
     C. To correct practices
     D. To correct wishes
     E. To correct liturgies
 II. We must allow God to expose our shallowness (58:3–5)
     A. Our wool-gathering on religious days
     B. Our irritability on religious days
     C. Our devising oppressive tactics on religious days
     D. Our pretense at piety on religious days
III. We must respond to our Lord's redirecting of our service
     (58:6–12)
     A. To loosen all unjust bonds
     B. To relinquish all fraudulent contracts
     C. To release the crushed
     D. To break every yoke
     E. To share our bread
     F. To shelter the homeless
     G. To clothe the naked
     H. To assist our own needy relatives

There is no question that the primary responsibility of believers
of the living God is to spread the good news of the gospel. But that
gospel—centered on the Messiah's death, burial, and resurrection as
the grounds for all who would come by faith to trust him—is the same
gospel that carries the corollary of our social responsibilities as well.
It is to this corollary that we now turn in this Scripture passage.

I. We Must Stop Our Religious Pretensions (Isa. 58:1–2)

God commanded the prophet Isaiah to raise his voice to threaten
divine action against all religious hypocrites and phony pietists, who
pridefully hoped to gain favor and esteem from God because they

were so correct in their outward ritualistic forms of worship, to the disregard of matters of neighborly love and concern for the needy. Therefore, God directed the prophet to reprove these religionists as severely as possible with a loud voice that would sound like a trumpet blaring out an alarm that something was out of kilter with those who pretended such devout piety. These phonies must be dragged into the light, since their values were more than slightly distorted. The alarm must be sounded vehemently, for the consciences of these people had been lulled to sleep, and awakening them to action required more than the usual sort of gentle talk. All bases for excuses must be removed from these sorts of people who seemed to have a ready answer for any type of charge.

In their own eyes they had (1) *correct habits*, for did they not "seek [God] out" "day after day" (v. 2a)? They also alleged that they had (2) *correct doctrines*, for they were "eager to know [God's] ways" (v. 2b)—or so it seemed to them. They also judged they were "a nation that does what is right and has not forsaken the commands of its God" (v. 2c–d); that is, they felt they had (3) *correct practices*. Add to that pretense the fact that they felt that they had "ask[ed God] for just decisions" (v. 2e); therefore, they felt they also had (4) *correct wishes*. Finally, they felt theirs were the (5) *correct liturgies*, for "they seem[ed] eager for God to come near [usually a liturgical term, "to draw near" or "come closer"] to them" (vv. 2–3). Their assumption was that their outward performance in their services at the temple had appeased God so that he had to show his favor toward them. They appeared to be saying: "We just love the temple services. We would never miss an opportunity to hold another fast (or meeting) before our God!" What else could God wish from them? But it was all for show. Moreover, it was selective in its areas of service without involving evidence of any social ministries to those hurting physically.

But our Lord had only authorized one day of fasting in the Bible: the Day of Atonement (Lev. 16:29), Yom Kippur. On their own, the people had later added four other times of fasting to remember the tragic events of the siege and fall of Jerusalem, as Zechariah 7–8 informs us. What the other fasts mentioned in Isaiah were all about, who knows? Given these additions (and others like them), they wanted to know if God hadn't indeed been impressed by their religious fervor and liturgical formalism. Surely God had seen all the times when they denied themselves food and water; surely he had seen all their expensive sacrifices, and without a doubt he had witnessed their long prayers. For all this, they felt entirely self-satisfied. Likewise, God must have been extremely proud to have worshipers such as them, wouldn't you think?

But God had not viewed all of their efforts in the same light as these worshipers had. The prophet was to remind Israel of its "rebellion" and "the house of Jacob [of] their sins" (v. 1). That is why the prophet had to sound out his message louder in his clarion call, to show them and to show us what was wrong with what outwardly seemed to be so commendable.

II. We Must Allow God to Expose Our Shallowness (Isa. 58:3–5)

The question of Isaiah's audience was twofold: (1) "Why have we fasted . . . and you [Lord] have not seen it?" and (2) "Why have we humbled ourselves and you [Lord] have not noticed?" (v. 3). God was supposed to be grateful and fully impressed by such ardor and devotion to himself and the worship of his person. So what was wrong?

Their attitudes and the state of their hearts had exposed the motives of all the hard work they had put into their worship of God. Not only had they fasted in order (falsely) to atone for their sins, such as cheating and robbing others (cf. Jer. 7:9–11), but even during the time of their fasting they were contriving ways to improperly gain control of property that was not rightfully theirs. Instead of focusing on God and their need for repentance and change, they were busy thinking about how they could pull off other business schemes that would enrich their pockets to the disadvantage of the poor and the disenfranchised. It was necessary, then, for the prophet to bring up the injunctions of the second tablet of the law of God to help them see that what was being done in the temple was more show than it was real substance.

It is verses 3b–4 that exposed the shallowness of their liturgies in worship. Did not this congregation do as they pleased (v. 3c) even on the day of their fasting? It was not a day for concentrating on God and their sin, but one of having quiet times to reflect on how to be more aggressive in their businesses. Was that not enough to expose the emptiness of their formalism? Did that not show that their hearts were not pure and that they were not living rightly or abstaining from deceit and injustice? How could such double-standard living be the basis for God's acceptance of any or all of their proposed fasts (v. 5)? It was not, in fact, what God wanted, and it was not what their neighbors needed either. The only thing that happened on their fast days was that they grew irritable and quarrelsome. They were pugnacious and ready to start a fight at the drop of a hat. So how could they expect their voices to be heard in prayer with all of that going on (v. 4d)? Of course God could see that they walked around with their heads bowed down and their backs bent over like a bunch of reeds in pretended humility. Sure, God could see that they were "lying on sackcloth and ashes" (v. 5d), but the question remained: "is that what you call a fast, a day acceptable to the LORD" (v. 5e–f)?

The lack of purity from the heart and the lack of concern for others polluted all their efforts at serving and worshiping God. The link between fasting and all acts of helping was that both required doing without something; it meant restricting their lives, as we must also restrict our rights and our desires for the sake of others. But it was easier to limit that restriction to their days of fasting, even if they were self-imposed, than to reach out to others in need of help.

III. We Must Respond to Our Lord's Redirecting of Our Service (Isa. 58:6–12)

If Isaiah's audience was so hidebound on fasting, then here was another kind of fast that God was now proposing. It was a type of "fast"[5] that was accompanied by love for other mortals. These too were acts of self-denial, but they called for positive actions: (1) "loose the chains of injustice," (2) "untie the cords of the yoke," (3) "set the oppressed free," and (4) "break every yoke" (v. 6).

Over against the people's sole, but false, dependence on cultic or ritualistic behavior, God calls for a practical rearrangement of their priorities. All four verbs of verse 6 call for some type of liberation from all sorts of "hard bargains," "perverted judgment," and economic or political "treachery." Any or all of these attempts to render some form of liberation and release from the metaphorical "yoke"—a heavy wooden device that went around an animal's neck (e.g., an ox's neck) and could be attached to the tongue of an implement that the animal was to pull, such as a plow or a wagon. The yoke was a metaphor for all the improperly imposed burdens that had been put over the necks of those who were poor, oppressed, widowed, or orphaned.

But there were more ways of showing what real religion was like. That encouragement is recorded in verse 7. It is not enough to say that we have never injured our neighbor in any way. Neighbor-love also calls for an active work on our part to meet the needs of the poor and the oppressed. The act of denying ourselves food for the sake of a fast seems hollow when (1) we show little or no regard for those going hungry around us (vv. 7, 10). Moreover, what about (2) the presence of the homeless in our midst? And what about (3) those poorly clothed? And it is not always a case of going into the inner city to find those who are starved, homeless, or naked; what about (4) our own relatives—our "own flesh and blood" (v. 7d) who often are just as deprived, yet left abandoned despite our possessions? Sometimes it seems easier to try to help some unknown person on skid row or in the tenements of the inner city than to help our own Uncle Louie, the tragic person in our own family!

With a surprising shift from these suggested eight duties for helping others in verses 6–7, there come seven promises in verses 8–12 (interrupted in verses 9c–10b once again with four more conditions). Instead of the earned favor that the people were seeking through their cultic formalism, God promises favor only for those who seek to follow God's agenda for heeding his ways (v. 2a). He will give that group of believers an incredibly rich assortment of blessings: light, healing, guidance/protection, and his very own presence (vv. 8–9).

First of all, our "light will break forth like the dawn" (v. 8a), our Lord promised. That is, the light within and around us will burst forth like the sunrise itself. In contrast to the wrath of God, his love is called "light," because God's love is able to flood over and stamp out the darkness of our pessimistic times and general outlook. A quiet and cheerful life lived in the love of God was much to be preferred over the wild trouble of the upsetting entanglements of life. Moreover, sudden recovery would come to those "sick" of all the hurry and bustle of life. It is as if new skin were stretched over the wounds and the infections of life healed. The very stress factor that so frequently is injurious to our health will be relieved and the pressure will be lifted when life is lived in the way God ordered it to be lived (v. 8b). And what is more, "righteousness" itself will go before us, and the very presence of God (his "glory") will protect us as our "rear guard" (v. 8c–d). The imagery here is that of the wilderness march of the Israelites years ago under Moses, where there was a "pillar of cloud by day" that became a "pillar of fire by night" (Exod. 13:21–22; 14:19–20) that went before the nation. In like manner, God himself (here called the very essence of the quality of being "in-the-right," i.e., "righteousness") will give the individual and group the guidance that is needed, as he walks in our vanguard and rear guard, that is, before and behind us. Thus, when Israel was diligent in performing works of compassionate love, it was like an army that had righteousness for its leader and guide and that also left in its train evidences of the presence of God ("glory" of God, coming from the Hebrew verbal root "to be heavy," i.e., the sheer weight or gravity of God's presence in all of his majesty and power).

The fourth promise is most amazing. For those who act compassionately toward those in need, God will answer their prayers (v. 9a–b). Usually it is said when God calls mortals, we should best respond with "Here am I!" But surprisingly, God promises that under these conditions, when we mortals cry out to him in prayer, after attending to the needs of those around us, he, God, will answer this time with, "Here am I!" (v. 9b). What a marvelous promise! It is as if God responds to our prayers with something like, "Did you call out to me? I am ready to act on your behalf right now."

But it is important to remember the conditions for such sensational promises of God to which, before the other three promises are announced, the prophet returns to remind us of three more forms of behavior and conditions that we must comply with. The first two conditions are negative and the third is positive. First of all, remember that we must "do away with the yoke of oppression" (v. 9c). In addition to what we have already said about this metaphor of the "yoke," we can add that this word "yoke" points to all the annoyances and irritants directed toward the poor and the afflicted as described in verse 6. In this second case a new aspect is added: we must do away "with the pointing of the finger and malicious talk" (v. 9d). This no doubt is a reference to all forms of mockery, contempt, false accusation, spreading of vicious rumors, and the like. The poor and the oppressed must no longer be the objects of highbrow scorn or contempt, or be the brunt of our jokes or snide contrasts between them and us. They too are made in the image of God and are deserving of our respect, love, and help.

The third condition is put in a positive form: we must "spend [our] selves in behalf of the hungry and satisfy the needs of the oppressed"

(v. 10a–b). Therefore, instead of making ourselves hungry at our self-proclaimed spiritual fasts, what about alleviating the hunger of those who are starving? This passage calls once again for action on behalf of all the oppressed, and again, the action is directed away from the self and toward others. First Corinthians 13:3 in effect says, "If I give all my goods to the poor and have not love—forget it" (cf. 1 John 3:17).

With these three further reminders of the conditions God sets as the proper prelude to all sincere and devout worship of himself, he returns to three more promises in the set of seven found in this passage. Once again our "light will rise in the darkness" (v. 10c). Present darkness and adversities will give way to the glorious light of God's presence on our pathway and lives, as promised already in verse 8a. The sixth promise about the Lord's guidance and satisfaction (v. 11) describes more fully and emphatically the promise made in verse 8c–d. God's promise of his guidance rejuvenates and invigorates all the days of our lives. How could it be less? For "in him there is no darkness at all" (1 John 1:5).

The seventh and final promise (v. 12) assures rebuilding and restoration of the deserted ruins. Even our bones, which previously trembled and shook because of the sorrows and guilt that were causing a wasting away of our frames (Job 4:14; Ps. 31:11; Jer. 23:9), will now be strengthened (v. 11c). God's grace is greater than all our sin. He can restore years that the locusts have swallowed up. But what is called for is a response of obedience and a love that comes from God.

Conclusions

1. A religion that has self-gratification as its main purpose is a false and vain religion. It just will not fit the task of bringing glory to God nor will it meet our own needs to be fulfilled and happy in the service of God.
2. What pleases God is not our own pleasure but doing what he has commanded us in his Word. We do not live by bread alone or by any other form of competing substitutes offered ostensibly to God, but only by every word that comes from the mouth of God.
3. The church of our Lord Jesus dare not remain silent on the issues of the poor, the widowed, the orphaned, or the oppressed. Nor dare we to imagine that the government must now carry

this responsibility, and thus we are let "off the hook." If we've taken this route, perhaps that is why we do not seem to bask in the love/light of God, why we have little or no healing for the soul or the body, why we find little or no guidance personally or corporately, and why we find that our prayers go unanswered.

4. This emphasis on the poor, the oppressed, and the orphan is not a "social gospel" that *only* shows acts of neighborly kindness to those who are hurting; it must also be accompanied with salvation in Christ—along with soap and soup, as the Salvation Army slogan goes. Society cannot be redeemed, but individuals can be redeemed. There are social laws, but no social gospel.

5. Our social responsibilities are large, but the same Lord who called us to announce the gospel will be with us to help the hurting as well.

Bibliography

Blomberg, Craig L. *Neither Poverty Nor Riches: A Biblical Theology of Material Possessions*. Grand Rapids: Eerdmans, 1999.

Cotton, Bill. "Biblical Priorities: The Cry of the Oppressed." *Evangel* 11 (1993): 13–16.

Fensham, F. C. "Widow, Orphan and the Poor in the Ancient Near Eastern Legal and Wisdom Literature." *Journal of Near Eastern Studies* 21 (1962): 129–39.

Gillingham, Sue. "The Poor in the Psalms." *Expository Times* 100 (1988): 15–19.

Gowan, Donald E. "Wealth and Poverty in the Old Testament: The Case of the Widow, the Orphan, and the Sojourner." *Interpretation* 41 (1987): 341–53.

Hanks, Thomas D. *God So Loved the Third World: The Biblical Vocabulary of Oppression*. Translated by J. C. Dekker. Maryknoll, NY: Orbis, 1983.

Levin, Christoph. "The Poor in the Old Testament: Some Observations." *Religion & Theology* 8 (2001): 254–73.

Lohfink, Norbert. "Poverty in the Laws of the Ancient Near East and of the Bible." *Theological Studies* 52 (1991): 34–50.

Mooneyham, W. Stanley. *What Do You Say to a Hungry World?* Waco: Word, 1975.

Neville, Richard W. "The Relevance of Creation and Righteousness to the Intervention for the Poor and Needy in the Old Testament." *Tyndale Bulletin* 52 (2001): 307–10.

Patterson, Richard D. "The Widow, the Orphans and the Poor in the Old Testament and Extra-Biblical Literature." *Bibliotheca Sacra* 130 (1973): 223–35.

Pleins, J. David. "How Ought We to Think about Poverty? Rethinking the Diversity of the Hebrew Bible." *Irish Theological Quarterly* 60 (1994): 280–86.

Porteous, Norman W. "The Care of the Poor in the Old Testament." In *Living the Mystery*, edited by J. I. McCord, 143–55. London: Blackwell, 1967.

Sider, Ronald J. *Rich Christians in an Age of Hunger*. Nashville: Thomas Nelson, 1997.

Whybray, R. N. *Wealth and Poverty in the Book of Proverbs*. Journal for the Study of the Old Testament Supplement Series 99. Sheffield: Sheffield Academic Press, 1990.

Willis, John T. "Old Testament Foundations of Social Justice." *Restoration Quarterly* 18 (1975): 65–87.

Discussion Questions

1. What is my main purpose as a believer?
2. What value do I put on the Word of God by the way I actually use it in my daily life?
3. Do I want my prayers to be answered? Do I wish God would give me guidance more frequently and meaningfully? To what degree is my lack in these areas attributable to the very omissions mentioned in this passage?
4. Do I and my church exhibit a good balance between the gospel of salvation and help to those who are hurting?

2

RACISM AND
HUMAN RIGHTS

Genesis 9:18–27; James 2:1–13, 25–26

The factors that form the differentia of race are incidental and
more relative to skin color, cultural origins, and features of
bodily shape, skills, languages, and heritage than to any real
criteria that can be scientifically measured. Racism has manifested
itself in more recent times, for example, in Nazi Germany as anti-
Semitism. Germany's Hitler absolutized Nordic origins and culture
and thereby arrogated to himself a humanly devised form of election.
In so doing, he demeaned the image of God in men and women and
demonically elevated one form of the races as a superrace over all
others.

Racism takes many different forms, but each attempt is self-de-
structive and in direct violation of what God has taught. For example,
African Americans have in recent memory been denied equal access
to education, employment, voter registration, and the use of public
facilities. But none of this type of vaunting one race over another is

a distinctively recent phenomenon; it can be found throughout the pages of history in almost every culture in the past. However, Christian believers are sternly warned to have no part in this type of Archie Bunkerism, which uses all sorts of derogatory words about every race other than one's own.

The Bible itself consistently talks about only one human race. It argues that God made "of one blood all nations of men" (Acts 17:26 KJV). There is no difference between the various peoples on the earth even though there are differences in hair color and texture, skin tones, or eye shapes. But none of such differentia is the basis for declaring one group of people to be superior or inferior to another.

In fact, as Kerby Anderson has noted:

> Race is also an imprecise term in large part because it is not based upon scientific data. People of every race can interbreed and produce fertile offspring. It turns out that the so-called differences in the races are not very great. A study of human genetic material of different races concluded that the DNA of any two people in the world would differ by just 2/10ths of one percent.[1] And of this variation, only six percent can be linked to racial categories. The remaining 94 percent is "within race" variation. . . . In other words, all racial differences are statistically insignificant from a scientific point of view. These differences are trivial when you consider the 3 billion base pairs of human DNA.[2]

Some of the greatest harm on the ethical issue of racism has come from an improper interpretation and handling of the "Curse on Canaan" in Genesis 9:18–27. In fact, this text is often referred to as the "Curse on Ham." This text does not provide in the least any justification for the ridiculous claim that with this curse the African was eternally condemned by God! A careful examination of this Scripture will show once and for all that no such claim is found in the biblical text. After examining Genesis 9:18–27, we will turn from the negative aspect of teaching on race to the positive form in James 2:1–13, 25–26.

The Curse on Canaan (Gen. 9:18–27)

It is all too embarrassing to relate that as recently as the last century it was not uncommon for some churches and some Sunday school literature to teach that the reason that the skin of African Americans was black was due to the curse on Ham and his descendants. This audacious teaching was used in the nineteenth century to justify slavery and racial discrimination of all types, to the disgrace of many of the churches. There are not words strong enough to properly rebuke attributing such an incorrect meaning to this text. It simply is not so, and the text of Scripture will not sustain such poor exegesis.

Noah is introduced in Genesis 9:20 as a worker of the soil and as one who planted a vineyard. As a new vintner, he apparently over-imbibed and consequently became intoxicated (v. 21). The result was that he "lay uncovered inside his tent" (v. 21b).

The Genesis text does not pause to moralize on his drunkenness, either in approval or in disapproval, as is often the case with many such narrations in Scripture. Wine itself was not forbidden in Israel, for later on we are told that Samson, as a Nazirite, was to be dedicated to the Lord and therefore both he and his mother were forbidden to drink wine (Judg. 13:3–5). This restriction would have been meaningless if the whole nation also was similarly restricted. Nevertheless, the Bible was not hesitant in condemning wine-bibbing (Prov. 23:29–35) or in equating it with its use in acts of harlotry (Hosea 4:10–11) even though there are other texts that support its moderate use as a sedative (Prov. 31:6) or to cheer the heart (Judg. 9:13; Ps. 104:15; see our discussion in chapter 13).

Whether Noah was the discoverer and innovator of viticulture is uncertain. Even if he were, I doubt if that would fully absolve him of his drunkenness. But the point of the story is not Noah's culpability. The fact is that in his drunken stupor he removed his clothes in his tent and, now naked, apparently passed out. What the narrative is concerned about is what happened subsequent to this and the part each of the three brothers played in the resulting infraction.

The culprit of our story is Ham, but he is also immediately identified as the "father of Canaan." His offense was this: he "saw his father's nakedness and told his two brothers outside" (v. 22). Noah's act of "uncovering" himself is paralleled in this text by "seeing." While some Jewish interpreters thought this was some type of euphemism for castration or even sodomy, there is nothing to support either of these views except the verb "had done" (v. 24), which is not much to go on.[3] Others have tried to suggest, based on the uses of *galah*, "to uncover," and "to see" (Hebrew, *ra'ah*), that Ham slept with his mother and she bore Canaan as a result. But this view does not seem to fit with the fact that Ham's two brothers, Shem and Japheth, "walked in backward" with their faces away and "covered their father's nakedness" (v. 23). Both of them acted honorably and commendably in this matter.

When Noah regained his sobriety and somehow (the text never tells us how) learned "what his youngest son [Ham] had done to him" (v. 24), he said, "Cursed be Canaan!" (v. 25). Therein lies the conundrum: Why was Canaan cursed when his father Ham had done whatever he had done? We are not told directly.

Canaan is identified in Genesis 10:6 as the last and presumably the youngest son of Ham. Their line is spelled out in further detail in verses 15–19 of the Table of Nations chapter (Gen. 10). Thus it was this Canaan who was to be "the lowest of slaves" (Hebrew, *'ebed 'ebadim*, Gen. 9:25). But what was the causal linkage between the father Ham's act and this curse on his youngest son, Canaan? We are only left to guess from what happened in the next centuries in the land of Canaan. It is a well-known fact that no matter where archaeologists dig in the layers belonging to the early Canaanites, especially up until the time of the Hebrew conquest of the land under Joshua, the soil yields hundreds of fertility-rite pottery pieces, all with exaggerated sexual portions of the female figure (and occasionally the naked male form as well). It would appear that what Noah saw was that this son of Ham was, as we say, "a chip off the old block," having the same sexual perversions as his father Ham. Ultimately, after something like two millennia of waiting to see if there was any repentance and change, God finally deeded the land of Canaan over to Israel, for the "cup of iniquity" of the Canaanites (and Amorites) had by then "reached its full measure" (Gen. 15:16).

So the judgment fell on the occupants of the land of Canaan, which was eventually ceded over to Israel after their exodus from Egypt. But in no way can this text be used to infer or directly teach God's judgment on anyone from Africa. If that were anywhere near being close to the correct teaching, the curse should have indicated one or more of Ham's other three sons, who were "Cush," (Hebrew, *kush*), which may be "Ethiopia," "Egypt" (Hebrew, *mitsrayim*), or "Put" (Hebrew, *put*), which refers to North Africa. Canaan, however, is the well-known occupant of what became the Holy Land itself.

But let us turn to a more positive teaching found in the New Testament. There we have direct teaching that men and women are to refrain from showing favoritism or making any sort of class distinctions between various people groups.

God's Rejection of Partiality and Racial Discrimination

James, the half-brother of our Lord, writes a whole chapter in the Bible to urge us: "Don't show favoritism" (2:1). Such unjust and false discrimination is a real scandal wherever it happens, but this is especially true in the house of God. We propose to examine portions of the second chapter of James in the following exposition:

Text: James 2:1–13, 25–26

Title: "God's Rejection of Partiality and Racial Discrimination"

Focal Point: verse 9, "But if you show favoritism, you sin and are convicted by the law as lawbreakers."

Homiletical Keyword: Demonstrations

Interrogative: What demonstrates that we are lawbreakers and that we are showing partiality and discriminating against others?

Outline:
  I. The way we give preference to some and not others (2:1–4)
 II. The way we favor the wealthy and insult the disenfranchised (2:5–7)
III. The way we refuse to follow the royal law of love (2:8–13)
IV. The way we refuse to imitate Rahab's reception of strangers (2:25–26)

I. The Way We Give Preference to Some and Not Others (James 2:1–4)

The topic that dominates the second chapter of James is the helping hand we all owe to the needy. When believers start to judge others by worldly standards, which is where *partiality* begins, we are in trouble. James illustrates his point by having two different visitors show up at the church, one who is "gold fingered" (Greek, *chrysodaktylios*) with an expensive ring (or two?) and the other with "shabby clothes" (Greek, *rhypara*), tattered and lacking in what is accepted in that situation as having class. The way each is treated calls for the stern rebuke of Scripture.

The believer must not adopt the standards of the culture of the world that favors the rich man by giving him the best seat in the house and discriminates against the poor man, assigning him the lowliest of places in the house of worship! This probably was not a hypothetical example but was an actual happening among the believers, which James knew had taken place. Nor was this example from the early church the last time this would happen, for in the eighteenth-century Church of England, some had become so elitist and so ungracious that John Wesley had to resort to the open fields and graveyards to proclaim the good news to coal miners and the poor. Wesley founded the Methodist group, which opened its doors to all irrespective of their social standing or their status or wealth. However, more than a century later William Booth had to found the Salvation Army once again over the same principle. This need to relearn the same lesson all over again was not limited, of course, to the Anglican or the Methodist churches, for all too frequently the story has been repeated in church after church regardless of its denominational affiliation.

Does not Scripture teach us that "To show partiality is not good" (Prov. 28:21), for "Rich and poor have this in common: the LORD is the Maker of [us] all" (Prov. 22:2). Moses likewise taught, "Do not pervert justice; do not show partiality to the poor or favoritism to the great, but judge your neighbor fairly" (Lev. 19:15). In place of all forms of partiality, James reckons all believers as part of "our glorious Lord Jesus Christ" (James 2:1).

II. The Way We Favor the Wealthy and Insult the Disenfranchised (James 2:5–7)

If we are to live as God wants us to live, we must reflect the mind of God as he has demonstrated in our salvation. Did not all of us who are believers—rich, poor, or otherwise—begin with the choice of our Lord (v. 5)? This choice went back long before the creation of the world, so how could it have been grounded on our present social status or race? In fact, the materially poor are often those who more quickly realize their spiritual needs. Did not Jesus teach, "Blessed are the poor in spirit, for theirs is the kingdom of heaven" (Matt. 5:3)?

It has often been said that "the ground is level at the foot of the cross." If that is so, and it is, then favoritism, social ranking, discrimination, and demeaning jokes and slurs against those not part of our group or race are all totally out of bounds and unbecoming in every way of a believer in Jesus.

Not only do such actions insult the poor but they also fail to realize that it is often, though not always, true that it is the rich who are the ones guilty of exploiting others (vv. 6–7). All such decisions to fawn over the rich to the disadvantage of the poor make no sense in this light. Our focus cannot be a materialistic one, but it must always be a spiritual one instead. To act in a worldly way is to bring disrepute on the majestic name of the Lord who called us and to whom we belong (v. 7).

III. The Way We Refuse to Follow the Royal Law of Love (James 2:8–13)

The "royal law" is the law found in Leviticus 19:18, "Love your neighbor as yourself." Thus, the issue is no longer merely one of partiality, disregard for the poor, or a racist mentality; it is a matter of following a life of obedience to Christ, which sets the standard for all proper action in these critical areas as well as in other areas.

It should be noticed that not only did James quote directly from the Septuagint version of Leviticus 19:18b, but as Luke T. Johnson observed, six other verbal or thematic allusions also exist between the book of James and Leviticus 19:12–18. They are as follows:[4]

James	Leviticus
"Do not show favoritism" (2:1).	"Do not show partiality" (19:15).
"If you show favoritism . . ." (2:9).	"Do not show partiality" (19:15).
"You shall love your neighbor as yourself" (2:8).	"Love your neighbor as yourself" (19:18a).
"Do not slander one another" (4:11).	"Do not go about spreading slander among your people" (19:16).
"Behold! The wages you failed to pay the workmen who mowed your fields are crying out against you" (5:4).	"Do not hold back the wages of a hired man overnight" (19:13).

James	Leviticus
"Don't take out your resentments on each other, brothers" (5:9).	"And your hand shall not avenge you, and you shall not be angry with the children of your people" (19:18a).
"Do not swear . . . so that you will not be condemned" (5:12).	"Do not swear falsely by my name and profane the name of your God" (19:12).
"Remember, whoever turns a sinner away from error, lo, he will save him from death and cover a multitude of sins" (5:20).	"Rebuke your neighbor frankly so you will not share in his guilt" (19:17b).

Note that only verse 14 of Leviticus 19:12–18 is without a parallel in the book of James. It surely appears that James was giving an exposition on that section of the Holiness Code (Lev. 17–26) in the book of James.

In James 2:8, the writer has singled out one particular law from the whole context of Leviticus 19:12–18 and called it a "royal law." He may have named it by this term because it is the law of the "kingdom," which he has just mentioned in verse 5, or it may be so named because it is the law that rules all the other laws, perhaps as Paul argues in Romans 13:8, 10 (NRSV)—"Owe no one anything, except to love one another . . . therefore, love is the fulfilling of the law." Thus, with this law all the other laws are hammered home. This law is preeminent, for if we are not willing to obey God in the way we act toward other peoples of other social strata or race, then how can we say we love God? If we loved God we would do what he says and we would keep his commandments (John 14:15)—this being more indicative of our way of life than a good number of more subtle commands that are more internal.

All too frequently the claim is heard: "Of course, we are not under the law; we are under grace, so why should we have to obey any law, including this one?" In principle, it is correct that we are under grace and not under law, and thanks be to God that it is so. But to leave the matter there is to invite a misunderstanding. We are "to be judged by the law" (James 2:12). This is not a judgment in order to be saved and redeemed, but since that law of God reflects his very character and being, "all the principles which exist in the divine nature have been translated by God into precepts and given to His children for their obedience. We cannot pick and choose, therefore. God has given us a law."[5]

Surprisingly James is even more explicit. If we do not respect other persons, regardless of their race, education, status, or possessions, we might be judged without mercy (James 2:13). Both Jesus (Matt. 6:14–15; 18:23–35) and James make the same point. As Motyer put it, "It is not that our mercy towards others has purchasing power [for our salvation], but it has evidential value. . . . Without a merciful disposition towards others we can neither realistically seek nor effectively receive God's mercy for ourselves."[6] Just as we are taught in the Lord's Prayer to pray for those against whom we have sinned/trespassed as well as for those who have sinned us, so we too realize that "mercy triumphs over judgment" (2:13). The same mercy that led us to redemption is the mercy that continues to accompany us in situations, such as these times of refusing to show partiality.

James wraps up his argument for mercy and kindness toward all regardless of any worldly markers by urging us to see that following the implications of the preceding argument demonstrates what genuine faith is all about. There is no conflict in James (or with Paul) between faith and works. His concern, instead, is with the potential abuse of faith. Can a believer shut up his or her response to those who are lacking in food, clothes, and the necessities of life and then still say he or she is saved by the grace of God? James doubts it very strongly, for such a spurious faith cannot affirm love for God and be devoid of a love for one's neighbors—regardless of their present status, color, or achievements. Real faith will expose itself, either positively or negatively, by the way it reacts to those in need (2:14–18). Where faith has no action in this area, it is probably dead (2:17). But if faith is accompanied by deeds, then it is genuine.

IV. The Way We Refuse to Imitate Rahab's Reception of Strangers (James 2:25–26)

To make sure we see how practical this can be, James appeals to a regular mortal, Rahab the prostitute, who reached out in a sacrificial and self-giving way to persons who were total strangers to her. She hid the Hebrew spies who came to her establishment to learn from the inside what was the state of affairs in Jericho, which was about to be attacked by Israel. If the example (which we have omitted in our discussion here) of Abraham (James 2:19–24) seems to single out a figure who is too towering for us to follow, then Rahab clearly shows how ordinary persons could, and did, demonstrate exactly what is desired in our relations to those in need.

The text does not specifically approve of Rahab's lie to the king of Jericho's men, who asked her the whereabouts of those who came to her rooming house. In Scripture, approval of a character in one area of their life (e.g., here of Rahab's faith and fear of the Lord over against her fear of the king of Jericho) is not thereby an approval of all areas. David was a man after God's own heart, but that did not give him a free pass in the Bathsheba story. Solomon was declared Jedidiah, "Loved by the Lord," but there were perhaps a thousand reasons why God found fault with him (his multiple wives and concubines!). Rahab did give "lodging to the [Hebrew] spies and sent them off in a different direction" (James 2:25). Therefore she too shows that "faith without deeds is dead" (2:26). She put her faith in the Lord more than she put her trust and fear in the king of Jericho; that is how she got into the Hall of Faith in Hebrews 11.

Therefore, just as Abraham held back nothing from God (not even his beloved son Isaac; see Gen. 22; James 2:21), so Rahab risked everything in receiving the spies since she saw that there was no other God like the God of heaven and earth—the God who had worked so miraculously for Israel at the Red Sea and in the battles against Sihon and Og on the other side of the Jordan River. Both of their lives were lives of obedience that began inwardly with faith, but a faith that expressed itself outwardly in active concern and love for all those in need.

Conclusions

The questions that we must ask of ourselves, then, are:

1. How culturally sensitive am I as a person, and as a member of the body of Christ, toward those of other races, social status, education, and financial achievement? As the nations of the earth are brought to our front door, are we accepting and receptive and helpful to them, or would we rather send missionaries to them "in their own contexts"?

2. How well do we empathize with others whose viewpoints and position in society are different from our own?
3. To what degree do I withhold judgment and show tolerance in the biblical sense of the word to others outside my race, class, social standing, and education? Do I build bridges and tear down barriers that all too often separate races and cultures, or do I put up roadblocks mentally, emotionally, and actually?
4. To what extent do I consider myself and my standing in society to be superior to others? Does this not violate Romans 12:3 (NRSV) that we are "not to think of [ourselves] more highly than [we] ought?"
5. To what extent do we take a stand when we or others tell ethnic jokes that demean and tear down other races and those from different cultures than our own?

Bibliography

Adams, E. Lawrence. *Going Public: Christian Responsibility in a Divided America.* Grand Rapids: Brazos, 2002.

Conde-Frazier, Elizabeth, S. Steve Kang, and Gary A. Parrett. *A Many Colored Kingdom: Multicultural Dynamics for Spiritual Formation.* Grand Rapids: Baker Academic, 2004.

DeYoung, Curtis Paul, et al. *United by Faith: The Multicultural Congregation as an Answer to the Problem of Race.* New York: Oxford University Press, 2003.

Edwards, Jefferson D. *Purging Racism from Christianity: Freedom and Purpose through Identity.* Grand Rapids: Zondervan, 1996.

Emerson, Michael O., and Christian Smith. *Divided by Faith: Evangelical Religion and the Problem of Race in America.* New York: Oxford University Press, 2000.

Volf, Miroslav. *Exclusion and Embrace: A Theological Exploration of Identity, Otherness, and Reconciliation.* Nashville: Abingdon, 1996.

Washington, Raleigh, and Glen Kehrein. *Breaking Down Walls: A Model for Reconciliation in an Age of Racial Strife.* Chicago: Moody, 1993.

Discussion Questions

1. Not since 1890 has the United States seen such large numbers of immigrants landing on our shores. What attitude should the believer take to this huge influx of internationals? What does Scripture say about the alien and the resident alien? Is there a difference between legal entry and illegal entry?
2. Where have you seen racial discrimination in the church, and what did you do about it? Must there be a homogeneous unit principle of one class or one race in a church in order to have the church grow as some church growth experts now advocate?
3. How do we as believers tend to show partiality to those of greater wealth, class, education, and the like?
4. How can the book of James be used to combat some of these ills in our midst?

3

GAMBLING AND GREED

Matthew 6:19–34

Kenneth S. Kantzer defined gambling in a 1983 *Christianity Today* article as:

> an artificially contrived risk, taken for selfish gain at another's expense, with no constructive product or social good as its goal.[1]

Henlee H. Barnette defined gambling this way:

> Gambling involves the transfer of something of value from one person to another on the basis of mere chance.[2]

Usually this form of "chance" is distinguished from the risks that are involved in buying stocks on the stock market by the fact that the money in the stock market is used for the development of industry.[3] Likewise, the purchase of all forms of insurance also involves some risk, but neither in the stock market nor in the insurance industry is chance the controlling factor.

History of Gambling

Gambling is not the new kid on the block, for it has been practiced in the history of most nations as far back as most records go. Pompeii's ruins, for instance, yielded gaming tables, as the discovery of dice with numbers on all six sides in ancient Egypt also confirms. The Roman historian Tacitus (about AD 100) observed that gambling was common among the German tribes.

Even in the history of the United States of America, Kantzer noted the early hold gambling had on this nation:

> America began as a gambling nation. Columbus' sailors whiled their time away crossing the Atlantic by playing cards. In 1612 the British government ran a lottery to assist the new settlement of Jamestown, Virginia. . . . George Washington declared, "Gambling is the child of avarice, the brother of iniquity, and the father of mischief"—but he kept a full diary of his own winnings and losses at the card table. In 1776 the First Continental Congress sold lottery tickets to finance the Revolution. From 1790 to 1860, 24 of the 36 states sponsored government-run lotteries. Many schools and hundreds of churches conducted their own lotteries to raise funds.[4]

Puritans like Cotton Mather preached against gambling and were supported later on by Methodists and Baptists, until many states rejected government lotteries, with the state of Louisiana being the last to end its lottery at the end of the nineteenth century. But the twentieth century reopened the state-run lottery once again, led by the Roman Catholic use of lotteries, and by 1985 most states had followed the lead of New Hampshire (1964) of setting up a public lottery.

The Social Effects of Gambling and Lotteries

Now that various forms of legalized gambling have once again come to the United States, it would appear that the fever has affected the greater part of our population. At times in the past, gambling was thought to be something that centered on organized crime and was indulged in only by the few. Now, almost every state and the District of Columbia feature gambling as a way to supplement state income, often for such stated worthy projects as public education.

Gambling now comes in all sorts of varieties. As one gets off the airplane in Las Vegas, what one sees instantly are the slot machines and an assortment of other amusing ways to get rid of your money. But that Las Vegas scene is now repeated in all sorts of truck stops, bars, and convenience stores.

The preferred form of gambling for many is in the state-sponsored lotteries, with their weekly or daily lottery numbers and scratch-off tickets. The second most popular form of gambling can now be found in the casinos, usually operated by Native Americans. Often the initial attraction to these casinos is found in the economically priced dinners that are available. The hope is that the diner will just see if Lady Luck is with him or her as they pull the handles on one or two slot machines or try out the casino card games at the poker or blackjack tables or play roulette.

There is still another category or two to entice the gambler: sports betting or pari-mutuel betting on horses, dogs, and other sporting events. Many business office pools place bets on some upcoming well-advertised sporting events with the bet going on the point spread, the winner, or even against the bookmaker's odds. And forty-three states have legal horse racing with some one hundred and fifty racetracks in the United States.

Now there is even online gambling, which makes the temptation all the more accessible on the Internet and offers a real enticement for those who are severely addicted to all forms of gambling.

Why Is Gambling Bad for Society?

Just as there is an Alcoholics Anonymous, so there is a Gamblers Anonymous. The latter organization estimates there are some twelve million compulsive gamblers in the United States. The pity of the whole matter is that the *Gambling Awareness Action Guide* estimated in 1984 that 96 percent of the compulsive gamblers began making bets when they were not yet fourteen years of age![5]

Whereas most state lotteries were introduced with the promise that they would bring in an enormous cash flow for the welfare and educational needs of each state, the results have not followed that predicted pattern. The social costs that show up in other areas were not cost-accounted against this income. Some of the negative results have been embezzlements, theft, family poverty, marital disharmony, substance abuse, spousal abuse, suicide attempts, and many other unrecognized costs. Instead of gambling being an easy way to raise a type of tax money painlessly, it turns out that the costs were just transferred to another area with even more devastating results than the original shortfall of money in one or another state-supported activity.

The worst result was that those who could least afford to gamble, the poor and the disadvantaged, spent three times as much money gambling (as a percentage of their income) as those at the higher end of the spectrum. The largest number of those who purchase gambling tickets are poor, black, or Hispanic. [6] Moreover, the more uncertain the times, the larger the number of those who play in order to make the big hit that they hope will solve all their problems. No final figures are available for the real social costs of gambling, but it is clear that there are enough indicators to warn the state and society that they are playing Russian roulette with the lives and minds of their citizens.

Many have pointed out in defense of gambling that the "casting of lots" was very common in the Bible (Num. 26:52–56; 1 Sam. 10:20–21; 1 Chron. 24:5; Acts 1:26). In fact, after Judas hanged himself, his successor was chosen by lot, and later decisions in the church were also made in a similar manner. But the basis for this usage was anchored in God's sovereignty and his control over what seemed from mere observation to be only a matter of chance. As the book of Proverbs taught, "The lot is cast into the lap, but its every decision is from the LORD" (Prov. 16:33).

The act of transferring something of value from one person to another on the basis of pure chance and at the cost of many others losing (many who could ill afford to lose what they bet) stirs the Bible's desire for justice, fairness, and concern for the poor. It also violates the doctrines of work, of love for one's neighbor, and of a careful stewardship of all that God has entrusted to each one of us.

The ante has continued to rise as persons hoping to become instantly rich and to have the thrill and excitement of seeing Lady Luck favor them have poured more and more money into the coffers of these modern money-changers. To put one's trust in Lady Luck is to launch an attack on God's sovereignty and his providential care over us for our good. It says in effect that I am not happy with what God has allotted to me, or that I believe I am able to help myself much better than God has been able to do so far. But the biblical text teaches that "godliness with contentment is great gain" (1 Tim. 6:6; Heb. 13:5). Where contentment lags, so does godliness! Why have so many believers lost their sense of contentment with who God is and what he has given to them?

The lure of gambling is the lure of materialism. However, believers are invited instead to have a distinct calling, or vocation, from God. Of course, this calls for diligence and zealousness in our work (Prov. 6:10–11), but it also calls us to avoid stealing (Eph. 4:28) and any kind of laziness that looks for an instant windfall from a lucky break.

Wealth has not always made its possessors happy. John D. Rockefeller said, "I have made millions, but they have brought me no happiness." Cornelius Vanderbilt agreed: "The care of millions is too great a load . . . there is no pleasure in it." John Jacob Astor complained, "[I am] the most miserable man on earth." Even Henry Ford observed, "[I] was happier doing a mechanic's work." When we trust money rather than God (Job 31:24–28; Prov. 11:28; 1 Tim. 6:17–19), we are led to a false sense of security and we end up being deceived (Matt. 13:22; Mark 4:19; Luke 8:14) as we build on an unstable foundation (Prov. 23:4–5), while becoming proud (Prov. 28:11). In addition, we also risk the possibility of stealing from God (Mal. 3:8) and then stealing from others (1 John 3:17).

The best teaching passage against gambling and greed is found in Matthew 6:19–34.

In God We Trust; All Else Is Rust

Text: Matthew 6:19–34

Title: "In God We Trust; All Else Is Rust"

Focal Point: verse 21, "For where your treasure is, there your heart will be also."

Homiletical Keyword: Principles

Interrogative: What are the principles that show we must trust in God alone?

Outline:
    Introduction (6:19–20)
  I. We are what we think about (6:21)
  II. We are what we fix our eyes on (6:22–23)
  III. We are, and become, what we are slaves to (6:24)
  IV. We are what we care most for (6:25–34)

Already in Matthew 6:1–18, Jesus had described the Christian's *private* life as it touched on the areas of praying in one's own closet, giving, and fasting. Then Jesus turned to the believer's *public* life in the world as it affected his or her money, possessions, food, drink, clothing, and ambition. For our Lord, it was not simply a matter of jettisoning our goods or downscaling our lifestyle, but it was a matter of the whole heart and a matter of our eyes. Verse 21, our focal point or big idea of the passage, is matched by verse 22: "The eye is the lamp of the body. If your eyes are good, your whole body will be full of light." The Greek word for "good" is *haplous*, "sound," or more literally "single." Here is a metaphor for a person wholly devoted in his or her service to God. Not infrequently in Scripture, the "eyes" are used as an equivalent for the "heart." Thus "to fix the eye" is equal to "to set the heart" steadfastly on the Lord (cf. Ps. 119:10 with Ps. 119:18), as it is in Matthew 6:21–22.

We need to examine four principles that say "in God we trust; all else is rust." So what really defines us: Our possessions? Our values? Our goals? Our loyalties? Our basic drives?

I. We Are What We Think About (Matt. 6:21)

In Malachi 3:16, "a scroll of remembrance was written . . . concerning those who feared the LORD and honored [thought on] his name." These God-fearers put their highest stock, values, and esteem in the "name of the LORD." In this context, the "name" of God counted as his person, his doctrine, his ethics, and his character. In the judgment of the God-fearers of Malachi's day, the name of God ranked as their prized possession above all other values, goals, and estimations. So his name must also be our chief possession, delight, and aspiration of worship.

That is why our hearts are exactly where we put our most treasured possession—either stayed on the Lord or on coveting all sorts of fantasies that the lottery or the sports pool is going to fulfill for us. Some just think about their treasure, or their possible treasure, and that defines them pretty well. If there is not a prior loyalty to our Lord and a willingness to detach ourselves from all our material and external concerns as ultimate goals, then we will be shaped and molded into looking and acting exactly like our imagined worldly treasures.

Of course, Scripture nowhere forbids our owning possessions, owning private property, saving for a rainy day, or buying life insurance policies. In fact, Scripture praises the little old ant who crawls along the ground storing up food for the winter months (Prov. 6:6–8), yet it scolds the believer for making no provision for his own family (1 Tim. 5:8). All the stuff of life is given to us by our Creator to enjoy. As 1 Timothy 4:4–5 taught:

> Everything God created is good, and nothing is to be rejected if it is received with thanksgiving, because it is consecrated by the word of God and prayer.

First Timothy 6:17 adds this teaching:

> Command those who are rich in this present world not to be arrogant nor to put their hope in wealth, which is so uncertain, but to put their hope in God, who richly provides us with everything for our enjoyment.

Therefore God forbids the selfish accumulation of goods. It is a fantasy to think that my goods will define me and tell me who I am and what I am worth. So we must not lay up only for ourselves or become hardhearted to the needy. Martin Luther wrote:

> Wherever the Gospel is taught and people seek to live according to it, there are two terrible plagues that always arise: false preachers who corrupt the teaching, and then Sir Greed, who obstructs right living.[7]

"Secularism" essentially means "of this age." Another word for this same concept is "worldliness," which takes two forms: positively, a love for the world, and negatively, an anxious care for the things of this world. Thus, "the world" is an outlook, a mentality, a way of looking at life that places anything or everything equal to or above God. Accordingly, we must not center on the world but on Christ, his kingdom, and his righteousness. Centering on our worldly possessions will end up bringing us moths, rust, decay, and break-ins. However, it is the things that are not seen that are the really eternally lasting things (2 Cor. 4:18). The unseen things contain an inheritance that is incorruptible, undefiled, and one that does not fade away, reserved in heaven for us (1 Pet. 1:4).

II. We Are What We Fix Our Eyes On (Matt. 6:22–23)

The result of a "single-eye," a "good, sound eye," is a well-illuminated body, or one in which a person is open to God. This wholehearted devotion to Christ enables us to find our way in life, directing us to a true goal. But an evil, bad eye leads to a life of blindness and darkness, because selfish materialism gives no light on life.

Our gaze toward God must be an exclusive and steady look that is undisturbed by worldly aims and goals. The eye is often regarded as the soul that opens up to the body. Psalm 123:2 expresses this in the form of a simile that compares the eyes of a slave looking for the slightest gesture of their master with our eyes looking to the Lord our God for his direction and provision.

That is the problem with coveting money easily gained from gambling. If we fix our eyes solely on the goal of the big winning, then it begins to define us in ways that lead away from God and turn us into being thoroughly materialistic and concerned totally with externals. We deny that God is in charge of all of life and that he runs the world providentially. We invent a new verse not in the Bible that says: "God helps those who help themselves."

III. We Are, and Become, What We Are Slaves To (Matt. 6:24)

It is a true saying that "no one can serve two masters. Either he will hate the one and love the other, or he will be devoted to the one and despise the other. You cannot serve both God and Money [Mammon]." While one can perhaps satisfactorily serve two employers, he cannot have two owners. Indeed, the essence of slavery is single ownership.

The prophet Elijah in 1 Kings 18:21 asked the people: "How long will you waver between two opinions? If the LORD is God, follow him; but if Baal, follow him." Likewise, one cannot divide their allegiance between God and "Mammon," which is the Aramaic word for "wealth." But the living Lord demands exclusive and entire devotion from all those who believe in him and worship him.

This matter of serving two masters is significant and worthy of an illustration. The story is told of a farmer who announced to his wife that their best cow had given birth to twin calves, one red and one white. "We must dedicate one to the Lord," he proudly declared to his wife. "Which one?" she asked. "Let's wait," he said, "for when we sell them, then we will say which one is the Lord's." A few months later the farmer burst in the farmhouse with bad news: "The Lord's calf died!" This story is all too true of much so-called wholehearted dedication. When things get tough, often the first place to cut and to economize is what we had said was dedicated to the Lord or to the Lord's work. That sounds like such persons have two masters, not just one. Isaiah 42:8 and 48:11 make it clear: "I am the Lord, that is my name! I will not give my glory to another."

When Matthew 6:24 uses the words "to hate" and "to love," they are used in a comparative way, not as an active hatred or a psychological hatred. It is a displacement of one thing for a higher loyalty.

IV. We Are What We Care Most For (Matt. 6:25–34)

Repeatedly Jesus urges "do not worry" (vv. 25, 31, 34) about the trinity of the cares of this world: (1) What are we going to eat? (2) What are we going to drink? and (3) What are we going to wear? Gentiles seek all those things, but our lives in Christ must be a whole lot more than the dread concern over only temporal matters.

Our word "worry" comes from an old Anglo-Saxon root meaning "to choke." The Old English word translated as "worry" is *wyrgan*, meaning "to strangle." In Middle English the verb gave rise to the meaning "to choke, to tear." That is what worry will do. It is the Greek word used of Martha, who was "worried" (*merimnao*, Luke 10:41) with the tasks of serving Jesus while Mary was sitting at Jesus's feet learning. All the preparations she was making for dinner had "distracted" her (Luke 10:40). Philippians 4:6 warns, "Do not be anxious [Greek, *merimnate*] about anything." Anxiety does not sound like contentment or trust in the Living God!

Some want to know what is wrong with worry. Some like to worry. They would worry if they didn't have anything to worry about. But here's what is wrong with worry: it is incompatible with faith and belief. By worrying we will not increase the production of our food, drink, or clothes. The only thing that worry will do, as a matter of fact, is shorten our lives. Martin Luther taught:

> You see, [God] is making the birds our teachers. It is a great and abiding disgrace to us in the Gospel that a helpless sparrow should become a theologian and a preacher to the wisest of men. . . . Whenever you listen

to a nightingale, therefore, you are listening to an excellent preacher. . . . It is as if he were saying, "I prefer to be in the Lord's kitchen. He has made heaven and earth, and he himself is the cook and the host. Everyday he feeds and nourishes innumerable little birds out of his hand."[8]

The doggerel also had it straight:

Said the robin to the sparrow: "I should really like to know why these anxious human beings rush about and worry so." Said the sparrow to the robin: "Friend, I think it must be that they have no heavenly Father, such as cares for you and me."

Worry is also incompatible with seeking first the kingdom of God and his righteousness (Matt. 6:33a), for then "all these things will be given to you as well" (6:33b). For all who have repented of their sins, God's kingdom has begun in their lives already. Therefore, what these believers seek above all else is to see the success of that kingdom as a matter of number one importance. This is not sinful imperialism or evangelical triumphalism; it is Christ's triumph, his kingship and conquest over all evil, which is the final and ultimate goal of all who know him. This success both for him and his people can come without the intervention of any of our dependency on luck, chance, or selfish stealing of an other person's hard-earned money.

Conclusions

To answer God's call in this passage merely by downscaling tends to deal only with the symptoms and not with the root issue. When our eye focuses on the self rather than God, we feel that, with luck and money as our savior, we can extricate ourselves from almost any kind of difficulty.

Instead, with our eyes fixed on the singular goal of seeking first the kingdom of God and his righteousness, we need to reorient our values, our goals, our loyalties, and our priorities.

If we have just toyed with placing a bet here or there, we need to do a 180-degree turn and ask God for his forgiveness. We need to lobby the state and those promoting pools, number chances, lotteries, and pari-mutuel betting games in sports and other areas to stop creating a social blight on the poor, the undereducated, and the oppressed. Seldom has the story for those who have won ended in a positive way, for not having been accustomed in most cases to handling so much money at once, it wreaks havoc on them morally and socially. Nor has it always been a gain for the Native Americans who run the casinos, for just as we brought a blight upon them two centuries ago with liquor and gunpowder, so we may be once again blighting a whole people with such enormous wealth that it is almost inconceivable that they will emerge in any other way except in a total disaster such as sudden wealth often fosters.

Greed has an appetite that is bottomless, for once it has grabbed hold of us, it will not let up unless, in the mercy of God, we ask for his deliverance.

Bibliography

Anderson, Kerby. *Christian Ethics in Plain Language*. Nashville: Thomas Nelson, 2005, especially pp. 166–73.

Henderson, J. Emmett. *State Lottery: The Absolute Worst Form of Legalized Gambling*. Atlanta: Georgia Council on Moral and Civil Concerns, n.d.

Mann, James. "Gambling Rage: Out of Control." *U.S. News and World Report* 30 (May 1983): 30.

Petersen, William. *What You Should Know about Gambling*. New Canaan, CT: Keats, 1973.

Thompson, William Norman *Legalized Gambling: A Reference Handbook*. 2nd ed. Santa Barbara, CA: ABC-CLIO, 1997.

Discussion Questions

1. Should Christians play the lottery or go to the casinos with a prayer that God will help them win so they can make a huge gift to the church to get a new building or some other worthy project?
2. Why does the Bible argue so strenuously against all forms of coveting and greed when we are also told to "covet earnestly the best gifts" (KJV) or in the NIV "eagerly desire the greater gifts" (1 Cor. 12:31)?
3. If the devil is going to collect all that money in lotteries and the like, should not Christians also try to get their hands on it, since the devil has had it already too long?

4

MEDIA, ENTERTAINMENT, AND PORNOGRAPHY

Philippians 4:4–9

Few things impact our daily lives more than the modern media. Newspapers, magazines, movies, television, iPods, the Internet, and devices such as BlackBerries have all had an enormous influence on us as they shape our values, opinions, and what is judged to be the latest fashion in talk, acting, and taste. For some, the strongest influence seems to be coming from television, for according to an oft-quoted 1980 report, "By the time the typical American school child graduates from high school he or she will have spent [close to] 11,000 hours in school and 15,000 in front of the television tube."[1]

While the media has enormous potential for uniting humanity around the globe by means of satellites and the Internet (by broadcasting such things as royal weddings, presidential inaugurations, Super Bowl football games, and the Olympics), it also has an equal power for evil and negative effects on society, depending on the quality of its content.

Television is regularly blamed for its constant use of violence and its exploitive way of featuring sex. Since both sex and violence usually attract larger audiences for those who are paying for these programs, the fallout effect on the morality and the demeanor of those watching is startling. As a result, traditional values from the home, family, church, and society are often attacked and depicted as passé and part of a fleeting neurotic generation. The minds of the younger people are being manipulated so that they "conform" to the new morality and new ethic, instead of being "transformed" by God's renewing of the mind (Rom. 12:1–2).

Neil Postman, in his widely discussed book, *The Disappearance of Childhood*, observed that

> the maintenance of childhood depended on the principles of managed information and sequential learning. But the telegraph [which continues its extension today with television, Internet, and instant messaging] began the process of wrestling control of information from the home and school. It altered the kind of information children could have access to, its quality and quantity, its sequence, and the circumstances in which it would be experienced.[2]

The point is that there is a new source of values, which is not the home, school, or church. The pastor, schoolteacher, mom, dad, or grandparent are replaced as the fountainhead and source of values and culture.

The New Music

By all odds, however, nothing can claim the role of being the most influential change agent of the youth culture but music. Allan Bloom, professor of philosophy at the prestigious University of Chicago, dramatically made this point:

> This is the age of music. . . . A very large proportion of young people between the ages of ten and twenty live for music. It is their passion; nothing else excites them as it does; they cannot take anything alien to music. . . . Rock music is as unquestioned and unproblematic as the air the students breathe.[3]

He continued:

> But rock music has one appeal only, a barbaric appeal, to sexual desire—not love, not *eros*, but sexual desire undeveloped and untutored. . . . Young people know that rock has the beat of sexual intercourse.[4]

Music, not the parents, the schools, or the church, has captured the minds and souls of the young today. It has also brought in its wake a revolutionary view of sex and has transformed most of life and living. Whether young students are jogging, studying, or just lounging around, the beat of modern music drums into their brains at a volume level that is a recipe for early deafness. It is undeniable that not only the music but also some of the lyrics are way beyond the boundaries of what is proper for a civilized society, much less a godly one.

The News Media

In "The Statement of Principles of the American Society of Newspaper Editors," Article V states:

> Sound practice, however, demands a clear distinction for the readers between news reports and opinion. Articles that contain opinion or personal interpretation should be clearly identified.[5]

But this distinction is almost totally missing in most of our news reporting today. Usually those in the news business tend to be more secular and more liberal, if not more humanistic, than the rest of society. The ways this bias shows up were listed very nicely by Kerby Anderson.[6] The "tricks of the trade" include:

1. *Language.* Words and labels can be powerful tools. Accordingly, abortionists turn out to be "pro-choice," "family planning consultants" while those opposing abortion are labeled "anti-abortionists" or "militant moralists" instead of "pro-life" or "advocates for the lives of the unborn."
2. *Inclusion and Exclusion.* The amount of coverage given to an event increases or decreases its importance over against other

events featured. Thus, pro-life rallies are ignored in favor of a march for the environment or a parade for homosexuals.

3. *Placement*. Journalists and broadcasters set the impression for the public either by making a story a headline, or lead report, or by burying it in the back of the paper or broadcast.

4. *Interviewing*. Usually only a small part of the interview appears in the story. Often the same question is asked numerous times until a quotable "sound bite" (from the media's point of view) can be extracted from all that was said.

5. *Selectivity*. Often the persons interviewed are those with whom the press agrees. By using these folks as sources, a story can be turned into a platform for the paper or station's own views.

6. *Use of Experts*. Often when both sides of an issue are presented, be it ever so rare, many stories will end with an "expert" whose bias leaves the final impression on what is "best" thought on this issue.

Startling research on the media by professors Robert Lichter and Stanley Rothman showed that 86 percent of the media either seldom or never attended religious services, while 50 percent had no religious affiliation at all.[7] Later surveys and polls only strengthened these observations, such as the ones conducted by the Pew Research Center, The Freedom Forum, Roper Center, and the like.[8]

Sex and Violence in the Media

Surveys have found that 75 percent of Americans feel that television exposes viewers to "too much sexually explicit material," yet that has had little effect on the advertisers that support those programs. Continued exposure to graphic violence against women, for example, has had the effect of making its viewers less sensitized to violence against women and less sympathetic to rape victims. Irving Kristol, a social commentator in a *Wall Street Journal* column, asked:

> Can anyone really believe that soft porn in our Hollywood movies, hard porn in our cable movies and violent porn in our "rap" music is without effect? Here the average, overall impact is quite discernable to the naked eye. And at the margin, the effects, in terms most notably of illegitimacy and rape, are shockingly visible.[9]

It is no different in the area of violence. It would appear that the normal fare of an anchorperson on the television news is something like two murders, three rapes, one mugging, a fire in a nightclub killing one hundred, and a twelve-year-old boy or girl being kidnapped. Newspaper and television station owners try to argue that a half hour to an hour exposure to all of this has little impact on the young eyes watching the five o'clock news before the parents get home, yet they argue on the other hand that a thirty-second commercial will really influence persons to buy their product. Which way do they wish to argue? Does television have an observable effect or does it not?

Add to this the violence seen in the movies and on television, and the case for alarm becomes rather mind-boggling. Psychological studies on the impact of sex and violence on viewers of all ages have not been encouraging, to say the least.[10]

Pornography

By definition, pornography is the portrayal of sexually oriented material, either in written or in visual form, that is deliberately designed to stimulate a person sexually. This is nothing short of a call for inducement to lust, when judged from biblical standards. Such salacious viewing is harmful not only to the person but eventually to society itself in the effects it often reaps. Few sins, if any, are strictly private; they bear fruit and have an effect on the rest of society.

The 1967 controversial Presidential Commission on Pornography concluded that there were no adverse effects on youth or adults from viewing pornography. Therefore, they recommended that all legal restrictions on pornography be lifted. But a blue-ribbon panel of experts in the Attorney General's 1986 Commission on Pornography reversed almost every conclusion of the 1967 Commission. Instead, they gave detailed documentation for the link between hard-core pornography and many forms of crime and social ills the country was facing. It also denied that any First Amendment rights were violated when those who peddled "kiddie porn" were deprived of this form of making money.

While secular society has often been selectively quiet on certain forms of the use of children in pornography, such as on the Web (not to mention the church's long silence as well), interestingly enough, in

Denmark the humane society has decried the use of animals in portraying bestiality! Will it take animal rights activists to bring Western culture back to its senses about the abusive treatment of women and children?

The Marquis de Sade (1740–1814), whose name lives on in our vocabulary in the word "sadism"—the inflicting of pain on another for personal pleasure—viewed every woman as a legitimate object for any act desired by men. In his own hideous words he proclaimed:

> It becomes incontestable that we have received from Nature the right indiscriminately to express our wishes on all women. . . . It cannot be denied that we have the right to decree laws that compel women to yield to the flames of him who would have her; violence itself being one of that right's effects, we can employ it lawfully. Indeed! Has Nature not proven that we have that right, by bestowing on us the strength needed to bend women to our will? The issue of her well-being, I repeat, is irrelevant.[11]

Rousas J. Rushdoony, in his 1974 book entitled *Politics of Pornography*, argued that the flood of pornography permitted by the Supreme Court decisions between the 1950s and 1960s is strikingly similar to the blueprint outlined by de Sade two centuries prior to these two recent decades. If any further evidence is needed, it must be noted that organized crime now dominates the porn industry of our day.

A Whole New Mindset

In a world filled with distorted sexuality, violence, and abusive sexual actions, particularly against children and women, the apostle Paul's injunctions in Philippians 4:4–9 are most relevant.

Text: Philippians 4:4–9

Title: "A Whole New Mindset"

Focal Point: verse 8, ". . . think about such things."

Homiletical Keyword: Excellencies

Interrogative: What excellencies should I fill my mind with instead of the distorting images from the entertainment industry of our day?

Outline:
I. We must rejoice in the Lord (4:4–7)
  A. Four admonitions
    1. Do rejoice
    2. Use self-restraint and gentleness
    3. Do not be anxious
    4. Present your requests to God
  B. Applications
II. We must fill our minds and practices with all that is excellent
    (4:8–9)
  A. Six ethical terms plus two injunctions
    1. Whatever is true
    2. Whatever is noble
    3. Whatever is right
    4. Whatever is pure
    5. Whatever is lovely
    6. Whatever is admirable
       a. Anything that is excellent
       b. Anything that is praiseworthy
  B. Four Practices
    1. Whatever you have learned
    2. Whatever you have received
    3. Whatever you have heard
    4. Whatever you have seen

I. We Must Rejoice in the Lord (Phil. 4:4–7)

The keynote of this book of Philippians is "Rejoice in the Lord" (also 1:18; 2:17, 18). Therefore, it comes as no surprise that this same command is repeated. Rejoicing in the Lord did not call for fitful moments of spiritual highs induced by some type of spiritual bromides, nor was it a case of "I'm OK and you're OK." Despite any hardships in Paul's culture or ours, all people should be joyful in our Lord himself.

Paul's second admonition was that believers should be marked by self-restraint and gentleness of action and spirit that would be evident to all. This was not to argue for an easygoing pliability that could be shaken like a reed in a breeze. But it did include a generosity of heart and mind that would be slow to take offense and swift to forgive others who may have offended us. Where one would normally expect retaliation, Paul urged an attitude of kindness and gentleness.

Even for those who were naturally zealous, enterprising, pure, and upright, the admonition was to express the joy of the Lord in a spirit that was personally cheerful and open to others. This still has ramifications in the way we treat those in the culture of the news business and in our seeing the defects in the way that we go about our business. Even if we don't approve of many of the media's shortcomings, we can approach them, and what they stand for, with self-restraint and gentleness. We are to respond honorably rather than responding in kind to how we have been treated as believers or holders of some of the positions the press and media demean.

The third admonition is one that calls for a refusal to worry and be overly anxious about the state of affairs in the world of entertainment or any of the modern media outlets of our day. Yes, these must be matters of deep concern and often need appropriate action, but we must not fret as if wrong is always going to sit on the throne, and as if the work of God's men and women will have little or no effect. Such a small view of God must be squelched immediately and decisively. We should not give up and adopt an attitude of indifference, but neither should we fret about what is going on (Ps. 37:1).

The fourth and final admonition is that we should present our petitions to our Lord. The peace of God that results from casting all our cares on him goes way beyond any kind of homegrown therapies. This is what will set up a military guard over our hearts and minds. Such guardianship takes place only in Christ Jesus our Lord.

The application of these admonitions is almost self-evident, for as we have examined each one, we have paused long enough to put our modern day into the ancient picture and have sought to apply many of the same actions to new challenges from our culture.

II. We Must Fill Our Minds and Practices with All That Is Excellent (Phil. 4:8–9)

We are given things to think about in this list of six or eight virtues, depending on how one reads the list. Paul uses the indefinite adjective (Greek, *hosa*) to introduce six ethical terms. To be sure, this is not a distinctively Christian list of virtues that is unrepresentative of any other times or places, for such lists were not uncommon in ancient literature. For example, Professor Frank Thielman has pointed to the Stoic philosopher Cleanthes (331–231 BC), who defined "the good" as that which was "well-ordered, just, holy, pious, self-controlled, useful, honorable, due, austere, candid, always secure, friendly, precious, . . . consistent, fair-famed, unpretentious, caring, gentle, keen, patient, faultless, permanent."[12] That is not a bad list, especially from a secularist. Would that similar lists emerge from our secular culture and times.

The word *virtue* comes from the root *vir*, meaning "to be strong"; thus, what is most becoming of a person of strength, one's valor, is wrapped up in "virtue." Romans located virtue in military courage; Italians placed it in knowledge of antiquities; the English placed it in chastity; and the Scottish, in thrift and industry.

But our Lord and Creator wants our hearts and minds to be filled with much more than the media tends to offer in our day. Rather than filling our minds with trash and that which debilitates us as persons made in the image of God, the list begins, not by accident, with truth. Everything that is "true" is to command the top of our thinking and being. Whatever is true about God, mortals, the church, the world, the arts, and the beautiful—that is where we are to begin. In many cases easy and quick kinds of mindless entertainment cannot begin to measure up to this standard of truth. Truth is where we begin in our pattern of thought and action.

In like manner, we are to focus on whatever is "noble" or "honest" and "fair." The things that are being opposed here are double talk, slander, avarice, and unbecoming conduct. Those things that are honorable and noble thereby possess dignity and are opposed to the frivolous and indecorous. That is what commends them as the proper objects of thought and reflection.

From there we move on to all that is "right": those things having an unchanging and abiding rectitude about them; those are the next things worth thinking about and pondering. Some things are right in that they are the real immutables of life.

Those things that are "pure" appear next on our list of the best things to think about. Here we mean those things that are not tainted or corrupted, but are clear in nature, transparent in purpose, leaving no blot on the conscience or stain on the character. All too many things in the world of the media do just that: they leave us feeling dirty and with blots and stains on our character. That is not what is worthwhile or uplifting for any of us.

Next, we find a call to focus on all the "lovely" things in the world. There are things in this world that not only stimulate a sense of endearment, but that cause a sense of homage to spring up within one's being. There is true loveliness. Beauty is too precious a gift to overlook or to take a philistine attitude toward.

The topic of lovely things is followed by whatever things are "admirable" or "of a good report." The stuff that is worth watching and enjoying from the media is that which causes those who view it to exclaim, "terrific," "well done!" The things contemplated here are vindicated by the judgment and approval of the heart and the soul after being nourished, and thus should be applauded.

Accordingly, if the previous six things exhibit any "excellence" or any "praise," then those are the things that ought to fill our days and our thoughts to the glory of God. That is where moral excellence demonstrates what is best for those who are the real *mensches* of our day. So if anyone is going to be worthy to have "praise" bestowed on them, they should ponder seriously the six virtues of the previous list.

Paul concludes with four verbs. All those things that the Philippians, and now that we, have learned, received, heard, and seen in the apostle, these we must do. The full form of the formula is not just "imitate me [Paul]," but rather it is: "Imitate me as I am imitating Christ Jesus." It begins with instruction and what we have "learned." But it also goes on to tackle the result of instruction, which is the appropriation and embracing of that knowledge (1 Cor. 15:1; Gal. 1:12; 1 Thess. 2:13). This was also to be joined with the report that had circulated in the church about Paul's character—what people had "heard" and "seen."

The point was this: those are the "things" that we should "practice." Paul wants us to reproduce his lessons and example as our own.

Conclusions

The diet offered in many of the media forms of entertainment today are the sorts of things that debase and tear down the greatness for which mortals were created. Instead, the challenge of our text is to fill our minds with everything that is at once true and has value and worth. Therefore, all that we have learned from the gospel, received as our own, heard as the message over and over, and seen in its powerful action, we must reflect on these things, for they are the worthwhile things of life that build a person up and give them real joy.

To exchange all of this for salacious porn, titillating sexual scenes, or violence on massive scales is to shrink one's soul and to exchange what is noble, right, pure, lovely, and admirable for junk and sewage. Instead, let us think on higher things.

Bibliography

Anderson, Kerby. *Christian Ethics in Plain Language*. Nashville: Thomas Nelson, 2005, especially pp. 188–200.

Bloom, Allan. *The Closing of the American Mind*. New York: Simon and Schuster, 1987.

Kristol, Irving. "Sex, Violence and Videotape." *Wall Street Journal*, May 31, 1994.

Lichter, S. Robert, Stanley Rothman, and Linda S. Lichter. *The Media Elite*. New York: Adler and Adler, 1986.

Mander, Jerry. *Four Arguments for the Elimination of Television*. New York: Morrow, 1978.

McQuilkin, Robertson. *An Introduction to Biblical Ethics*. Wheaton: Tyndale, 1989, especially pp. 232–37 and 488–93.

Muggeridge, Malcolm. *Christ and the Media*. Grand Rapids: Eerdmans, 1977.

Postman, Neil. *The Disappearance of Childhood*. New York: Vintage, 1994.

Rushdoony, Rousas J. *The Politics of Pornography*. New Rochelle, NY: Arlington, 1974.

Discussion Questions

1. In your experience, is there any truth to the assertion that television, movies, and the Internet have a bad impact on you personally in your attitudes toward women, violence, and sexuality? On others? On children?

2. Is it true that soft, as well as hard, porn has a deleterious effect on your own sexual urges and desires? On society in general? On the ministry?

3. Do you feel that most newscasters do their level best to make sure that they separate fact from opinion, or do you think that there is an agenda behind the way material is presented, the substance of what is presented, and the conclusions they leave you with in the day's news?

4. Over the span of your life, have you seen a decline or a rise in the ethical and moral standards of the entertainment industry as seen in Hollywood's films, television's programming, and what is available on the Internet?

5

ADULTERY

Proverbs 5:15–23

Robertson McQuilkin stated the case against adultery most succinctly and accurately when he taught:

> God's standards on human sexuality are treated in Scripture as the most important of all rules for relations among people. In the Old Testament, teaching against adultery is emphasized second only to teaching against idolatry. . . . Sexual fidelity, more than most virtues, clearly demonstrates the purpose of the law: man's welfare. Human sexuality is one of God's most delightful gifts. But the sordid record of human history and the anguish of personal experience highlight the basic reality that this joy is reserved for those who "follow the Manufacturer's instructions."[1]

Defining Adultery

Adultery is voluntary sexual intercourse, or voluntary thoughts of such activity, between a married person and someone other than his

or her marriage partner.[2] While there is nothing new about the act
of adultery, since it has been committed down through the corridors
of time, it has accelerated its presence and activity in our day more
than ever. In the past there was shame connected with the discovery of adultery, along with public ridicule, but in our day television,
feature films, and much novel writing features adultery almost as a
celebrated cause.

The exact prevalence of adultery is difficult to determine, but none
of the figures are reassuring or hopeful in the least degree. The Janus
Report on Sexual Behavior stated that one-third of the married men
and one-quarter of the married women in the United States admitted
to having at least one extramarital sexual affair.[3] The National Opinion
Research Center from the University of Chicago gave lower percent-
ages (25 percent of the married men and 17 percent of the married
women), but "even when these lower ratios of men are applied to the
current population, that means that 19 million husbands and 12 million wives have had an affair."[4] The obvious remark is that adultery
is becoming all too common and all too accepted in society.

It is doubtful if the United States will ever go back to putting adul-
terers in stocks and publicly humiliating them, or even forcing them
to wear a huge capital "A," as employed in Nathaniel Hawthorne's
Scarlet Letter, as a means of shaming some who would otherwise
unthinkingly participate in this sin. However, the sad news is that
society appears no longer able to enforce a rule against adultery on
any large scale because the behavior has become so common.

The Statistics on Affairs

There is little doubt on the part of the pollsters that sex outside of
marriage is increasing year by year. Statistics from ten years ago have
shown that adultery has increased by 5 percent or more in each of the
last three decades. The largest increase comes from women who are
employed full-time and are working outside the home. This, however,
may also change as women get into chat rooms on the Internet and
find a friend who is at first stimulating, then flirtatious, only to suddenly lead to discussing sexual questions, often with intimate details
of their marital relationships. These online virtual affairs are just as
seductive as real, live contact, for they tend to be as addictive as alcohol. Cyberspace affairs seem to offer the protection of a safe distance

from these invisible parties, but they can grab hold of a person just as firmly as physical affairs.[5]

Marital infidelity is also a great destroyer of homes and marriages. Statistics say that 65 percent of those who engage in an adulterous affair will end up divorced. Only 35 percent of the couples who go through the trauma of such marital infidelity remain together. There is no reason, however, why a divorce must take place as a sequel to such disruptive events. One counselor claimed that 98 percent of her clients remained together after going through counseling.[6]

The amazing fact is that somewhere near 80 percent of Americans disapprove of adultery. Nevertheless, even knowing that adultery is wrong and that it can have disastrous effects on the children from that marriage and on the marriage itself, they are still drawn to this form of infidelity like a moth to a flame.

If adultery were strictly a private affair that left no scars except on the one who initiated it, that might lead to a more mitigated estimate of its damage; alas, it now seems to be evident that adulterous behavior in one or more of the parents can have lasting effects on their own children when they reach adulthood. If children from divorced families are also likely to divorce, it now seems apparent that adulterous behavior in a parent can beget similar adulterous behavior in their children as well. The sins of the fathers (and mothers) are thereby visited on the next generations too!

Preventative Maintenance against Infidelity

Adultery is never therapeutic, despite what some magazines and pop-psychology books imply. Affairs do not revive a dull or boring marriage; instead, the marriage develops an air of secrecy, and we create a whole string of lies to our partners as a necessary cover-up for what is going on. As Frank Pittman observed, "The infidelity is not in the sex, necessarily, but in the secrecy. It isn't whom you lie with. It's whom you lie to."[7] This last part is true, but in my estimation the infidelity is in the sex as well.

Marriages take work. The best way to prevent marital infidelity is to do preventative maintenance before a breakdown in relations takes place. Frank Pittman claims he has counseled over ten thousand couples in the last forty years with some seven thousand experiencing infidelity. He gave a list of nineteen suggestions that would help couples to avoid affairs. My list is shorter, though influenced somewhat by his. Here is my list:

1. Like Job (31:1), make "a covenant with [your] eyes not to look lustfully" at a woman or a man. Sexual fantasies must be dealt with in one's heart, mind, and eyes before they mature into a scenario or a role that wants to be played out.
2. Never be alone in the presence of a member of the opposite sex other than your spouse. Always leave the door open when working with or counseling such an individual.
3. When on the road away from home, always have a stated time to call home every day so that you do not start to develop a separate life or leave yourself open to what might at first be innocent conversation with another to relieve your loneliness, but could snowball into more intimate talk.
4. Do not expect your marriage to make you happy every day and in every way. Let your spouse be a source of comfort to you instead of requiring him or her to always make you happy.
5. Christian marriage is a covenant not only between the husband and wife but also between the couple and God (Prov. 2:17; Mal. 2:14). As such, it is not a social contract that can be revoked if one or the other breaks it; there still is the consideration of how to get God out of the contract, which he is loathe to do!
6. Let scriptural teaching instruct you and make you wiser on how to act in your marriage. Christian couples who study God's Word together and pray together have a better chance of staying together.

Don't Compromise Your Marital Love

Let us turn, therefore, to a positive teaching passage found in Proverbs 5:15–23 for just such help from the Word of God. Even though it is in the form of an allegory, the significance of its teaching is enormous. It must also be said that the secular community often accuses the Christian community of being very prudish and negative about sex within the married estate. Secularists love to mock Christians as being puritanical and unable to state what they should do about the sexual side of their nature. But nothing could be further from the truth, for the Scriptures have a good deal of material on just this topic.

When God created Adam and Eve, the first order of business in the Bible was to teach them about their sexuality, that is, after doing their "leaving" of home, the man and the woman should "cleave" to each other. It is amazing that it was not the gospel that came first, but rather this teaching on the two becoming "one flesh." Add to this the fact that Jesus took time out of his busy life, in which he had only three years to teach everything that his disciples would need to know after he left them, to attend the marriage at Cana (John 2). And what the living Word did for the institution of marriage at Cana, the written Word of God did in the book of Song of Solomon as it taught the joys of marital bliss. In fact, the passage we now turn to in Proverbs 5:15–23 was written by the same author, Solomon, who wrote the song called the "very best song" (Hebrew uses the genitival relationship, "Song of Songs," as it does for the "King of kings," the "Lord of lords," to express the superlative) about this relationship between a man and a woman. The allegory we are about to study, in fact, is a good entrée to the whole book of Song of Songs/Solomon.

Text: Proverbs 5:15–23

Title: "Don't Compromise Your Marital Love"

Focal Point: verse 18, "May your fountain be blessed, and may you rejoice in the wife of your youth."

Homiletical Keyword: Reasons

Interrogative: What are the reasons why we must rejoice in the wife of our youth?

Outline:

I. Our spouse is the source of our enjoyment (5:15)
   A. The enjoyment is in the tasting
   B. The beauty is in the faithful and exclusive preservation of the relationship
II. Our relationship to our spouse must be protected by us (5:16–17)
   A. Our intimate lives must be kept private and exclusive
   B. Our special marital acts of sharing are to be reserved for each other
III. Our spouse must be our delight (5:18–20)
   A. We must take special pride and joy in the spouse of our youth
   B. We should always be captivated by his/her love

IV. Our relationship to our spouse is exposed to the gaze of God
(5:21–23)
A. All our ways are in full view of God
B. Wicked deeds only entrap us

This passage is one of the most delightful sections in the Wisdom literature of the Old Testament.[8] In contrast to the warning given in Proverbs 5:1–14 against companionship with an adulteress, the teaching in Proverbs 5:15–23 celebrates the comforts and joys of true marital love. Instead of facing the "utter ruin" (v. 14) that comes from sexual liaisons outside of marriage, Proverbs invites us as readers to contemplate the pure joy of divinely intended marital love.

Proverbs 5 fits quite well within the category of instruction that is so characteristic of wisdom materials. This chapter opens with the familiar address, "My son" (v. 1). The student is warned to "pay attention" and to "listen well" (v. 1), for the aim will be to "maintain discretion" and to "preserve knowledge" (v. 2). The reason for this alert is given in verses 3–6. It is this: adultery may appear sweet and smooth, but in the end it is "bitter as gall" (v. 4) and deadly in every way (vv. 5–6).

That same warning is enlarged in verses 7–8 by the introductory "Now then" in verse 7. Again, briefly stated, it is this: "Keep to a path far from her, do not go near the door of her house" (v. 8). A longer motivational statement is given in verses 9–14, but simply stated again it warns: "lest you give your best strength to others and your years to one who is cruel" (v. 9).

But the two warnings in verses 1–14 only tell us what not to do; what is needed is a positive encouragement of what we should do. And that is what the allegory of Proverbs 5:15–23 gives to us. Unfortunately, some biblical scholars have failed to see the straightforward unity and plan in this chapter and have instead tended to separate this latter portion of the chapter from its frontpiece.

I. Our Spouse Is the Source of Our Enjoyment (Prov. 5:15)

Rather than settling for a negative description of what it is we are not to do within the marriage bond, the wisdom teacher Solomon will now teach us positively on the subject of sexual morality. He will use poetic metaphors from a land that is characteristically hot, where the climate always raises one's level of thirst. That will suggest to him the metaphor for enjoying one's spouse: it will compare to a good, cold drink of refreshing water that quenches one's thirst on the sultry, hot day. It is clear that the singular forms of the "cistern" and "well" are symbols of the wife, for the enjoyment meant here is sensual and refreshing. There is no attempt to compare the anatomy of the female form, but only to symbolize the enjoyment and attachment each has for the other in the marriage situation. Thus, the metaphor commands us to be faithful to our spouses. Every clandestine affair or attraction violates God's clearest injunction, for in the original divine plan God intended for us to have only one marriage partner; yes, even in the midst of what otherwise was a disapproved Old Testament polygamy.[9] The basis for the figure is found in Isaiah 36:16, where "every one of you will eat from his own vine and fig tree and drink water from his own cistern." The subject is so delicate that if it were spoken literally it might crush and destroy the beautiful relationship it wished to describe. However, with the use of metaphors it is possible to suggest and to be intimate without being crass and crude.

II. Our Relationship to Our Spouse Must Be Protected by Us (Prov. 5:16–17)

Suddenly the metaphor changes from the singular form for the "cistern" and the "well" to the plural form for "springs" and "streams of water" (v. 16). Without a shift in subject, as some scholars, to the contrary, think they see here, these are symbols of waste and the useless spread of the otherwise much-anticipated gift of refreshing water. Now it appears to be thrown away, and the precious water is being left to run out on the streets and in the public squares. What at first appeared as if it might be something in the line of green theology, such as saving water and not letting the water just run down the sides of the streets, is suddenly interrupted in light of the real subject in verse 18. But just how the metaphor works has been the subject of some discussion, even if what it is driving at is clear enough. On the one hand, it could be said like this: if the husband does not use his domestic supply of water, the well will dry up and go to waste; that is, his wife might then be unfaithful because of her husband's neglect, with waste and shame to follow. But another way to put it is slightly different: the "streams of water" and the "springs" represent extramarital pleasures outside the domestic setting. The domestic tranquility of the home has been destroyed and the spouse has gone searching for other paramours, thereby splashing precious wares (read "springs") all over town in the streets and public squares.

In this case, verse 17 repeats the injunction of verse 16: "Let [your pleasures in your marital fidelity] be yours alone, never to be shared with strangers." Thus, the water sources of verses 15–16 and 18 are to be exclusive and never to be shared or dispersed like water in every direction.

III. Our Spouse Must Be Our Delight (Prov. 5:18–20)

It is in verse 18 that the whole allegory becomes clear. A blessing is pronounced over our "fountain," in that we are to "rejoice in the wife of [our] youth." Here is the central affirmation of the passage, for this statement captures the purpose of the entire proverb.

The young man's wife is sensually compared to "a loving doe, a graceful deer" (v. 19). These symbols of agility, grace, form, and beauty are intentional. They are connected with satisfaction with the breasts of one's own wife. In fact, there is a deliberate wordplay on the Hebrew word for "breasts" (Hebrew, *dad*), which sounds like the Hebrew word for "love" (*dod*). Even the Hebrew word for "satisfy" (*rawah*) has the connotation of "drinking to one's fill," a possible allusion to the five water metaphors in verses 15–16 and 18a ("fountain").

The hope of the husband is that he might "ever be captivated [or 'exhilarated'] by her love" (v. 19c). The word "captivated" (Hebrew, *shagah*) in this context is best rendered by "be intoxicated"; hence the man is to be so infatuated with his wife and to love her with such enthusiasm that it would be similar to his being drunk! All three forms of this verb in verses 19–20 and 23 have the same connotation. By its very repetition, it creates a major contrast between marital and extramarital love (vv. 19–20), while simultaneously reinforcing the parallel between an out-of-bounds love and folly (v. 23). Accordingly, a husband may choose to be intoxicated and stagger in the pleasure and comfort that his wife gives (v. 19), or he may choose to embrace the bosom of another woman and thereby stagger into the arms of death itself (v. 23a).

IV. Our Relationship to Our Spouse Is Exposed to the Gaze of God (Prov. 5:21–23)

Added to the reasons already given as to why we must be true to the spouse God gave to us as the "wife of our youth" are two more arguments. First, God sees everything, so there just is not a safe rendezvous place that will escape the divine notice or be beyond the scope of his all-seeing eye (v. 21a). God examines all our ways, pondering and weighing them carefully, so that he might judge us fairly but surely (v. 21b). That is why the rhetorical question of verse 20 is important: "Why be captivated, my son, by an adulteress?" It is God who gives the gift of human sexuality, and therefore he has a right to expect that we would use it according to the "Manufacturer's instructions."

The second reason why one must be faithful to one's spouse is that the husband who chooses promiscuity eventually will find himself so entangled and bound up by the cords of his own sin that there will be no way out of the trap except through discovery and exposure before God and the community. This line of cheating and acting is nothing but the height of folly (v. 23).

So it is that the five metaphors of connubial love are found in the five words for sources of water. These metaphors are placed over against the images of dripping honey and smooth oil (v. 3), which are found in the first part of the chapter. Indeed, all these images are not that frequent in Wisdom literature, but they do depict the complexity and vitality of such a topic as marital fidelity. The five water images reflect the satisfaction of desires and the vitality they offer to support and to strengthen that marriage. Both the resulting joy at having one's thirst quenched and the water's life-giving qualities enhance the metaphor all the more.

Most interpreters view Proverbs 5:15–23 as an allegory. I first discovered this section of the biblical text was an allegory when I read in seminary Milton Terry's masterful classic, *Biblical Hermeneutics*.[10] An allegory, of course, is a metaphor, that is, an unexpressed comparison (which, unlike a simile or parable, does not use the words "like" or "as") that is extended into a story or carries out a theme beyond the bare metaphorical line or lines.

What really supports the view that this passage belongs to the allegory genre is not only verse 18, which suddenly puts into *sensus literalis* what had been said in metaphorical language, but the preceding context of verses 1–14, with its warnings against the waywardness of adultery and the seductiveness of the "strange woman" (v. 3 KJV).

In addition to these clues, it was not uncommon in the ancient Near East to describe a wife with metaphors from nature. For instance, in the Egyptian writing of the "Instruction of Ptah-hotep," the writer declares of the wife, "She is a profitable *field* for her lord." Or in the Amarna Tablets, also from Egypt, we have, "My *field* is likened to a woman without a husband." One Egyptian maiden sings in an Egyptian love song, "I belong to you like a *field*." Add to this the figures of speech in the Song of Solomon where a "vineyard" and a "garden" appear (Song 1:6; 2:15; 4:12–16; 6:2–3; 8:11–12) along with references to the "loving doe" and a "graceful deer," and the picture begins to add up to a beautiful allegory.

Conclusions

Alvin Toffler (1928–), in his famous *Future Shock*,[11] predicted that marriages in the future would allow husbands and wives to discard each other when they had "outgrown" each other. In a throwaway society, it is amazing how close he has come to capturing, over the last fifty years, exactly what would take place in the institution of marriage, except for the sustaining and enabling grace of our Lord in Christian marriages that are working hard to obey their Lord. No less dramatic was Charles A. Reich (1931–) in his *Greening of America*,[12] for he noted that young people today do not want all the entangling relationships that come with marriage; they want to be *free to love*. But rather than a real freedom, this sounded instead like *free exploitation*.

On the contrary, sexual intimacy within the marriage bonds is not an evil or an annoyance to be endured, but it is a gift from our Creator and Redeemer. Moreover, dead marriages are unbiblical marriages, for they do not honor God who gave marriages, nor do they display what a family is supposed to be.

Therefore, couples must fiercely fight for a daily renewal and for real growth in their marriages. These marriages, if they are truly reflective of their source from God, must be ones that exhibit joy, exclusiveness, attentiveness, mystery, beauty, power, and consciousness of the presence of God. If you are married, do not compromise your love or the gift of God's joy and comfort that he intended to give you.

And if you are not yet married and God has not given to you the gift of singleness, choose carefully one who already is a believer and one with whom you can share the totality of your life. Choose someone who believes in, and has a family history of, monogamy and a strong sense of God's direction to join his or her life with yours.

Bibliography

Heimbach, Daniel R. *True Sexual Morality: Recovering Biblical Standards for a Culture in Crisis.* Wheaton: Crossway, 2004.

Kaiser, Walter C., Jr. "True Marital Love in Proverbs 5:15–23 and the Interpretation of Song of Songs," in *The Way of Wisdom: Essays in Honor of Bruce K. Waltke*, 106–16. Grand Rapids: Zondervan, 2000.

Kruger, Paul A. "Promiscuity or Marriage Fidelity? A Note on Prov. 5:15–18." *Journal of Northwest Semitic Languages* 13 (1987): 61–68.

Stafford, Tim. *The Sexual Christian.* Wheaton: Victor, 1989.

Steele, Paul E., and Charles C. Ryrie. *Meant to Last: A Christian View of Marriage, Divorce and Remarriage.* Wheaton: Victor, 1986.

Wenham, David. "Marriage and Singleness in Paul and Today." *Themelios* 13, no. 2 (January–February 1988): 39–41.

Discussion Questions

1. If God gives the gift of marriage, should it be looked upon as an entangling encumbrance for young people today?
2. Does God really care whether we keep our marriage vows or not? If there are no children, where is the damage if both parties divorce after they have "fallen out of love with each other"?
3. How can extramarital affairs so bind us up that eventually we, as well as those around us, are destroyed?

6

Cohabitation and Fornication

1 Thessalonians 4:1–8

Living Together Unmarried

Many in these modern times tend to substitute for marriage the experience of living together as couples—perhaps even with no thought of ever getting married in some instances. What used to be called "living in sin" or "shacking up together" is now euphemistically called "living together," "partnering," or "cohabitation." But a loving God wants us to know that he did not make us to live like this, nor did he give the gift of sex to have us end up disappointed, for "living together" is not what it might seem to be at first glance.

There is little doubt that this type of lifestyle is on the increase. Between 1960 and 1970, a half million couples chose to live together without the advantages of marriage. By 1990 that half million had increased to close to three million couples, which in turn grew to almost five million in 2000.[1] These figures show no letting up as we go into the twenty-first century; instead, cohabitation continues to grow in popularity.

The issue we are facing here is one where two unrelated individuals of the opposite sex decide to share a common living arrangement with a sexually intimate relationship devoid of any approval or sanction from the church or from the state. It is as if the country suddenly decided to change its mores and ethics about young people living together in a sexual relationship without any of the responsibilities or accountabilities that usually go along with marriage. What used to be called a sin is now just taken for granted. This social upheaval, as with so many others in our day, can generally be traced back to the social revolution that began somewhere around 1960. As society and the church often decided to look the other way, giving neither condemnation nor moral guidance, couples began to be encouraged to cohabit by the advent of "the pill," the sexual revolution, the absence of any major stigma to illegitimate births, the possibility of mothers joining the workforce, and many young people descending on society as victims themselves of no-fault divorce families.

All too frequently the wisdom of the street-smart was "try it before you buy it." The analogy was one of taking a car for a test-drive before you decided to buy it, which made sense for cars, since they were not living beings made in the image of God. But people are not made out of steel and plastic in the way cars are. And, as it turned out, this type of logic usually proved to be positive only for the test-driver; the other partner tended to be treated as if he or she were just part of the equipment, that is, the car that was being test-driven. When the test-driver rejected the car, the car was not left with any psychological aftereffects, but the same could not be said of people who had suffered a much more injurious type of rejection.

The High Risks of "Living Together"

The mischief of the matter is that research has consistently confirmed that couples who begin by cohabiting usually have almost a 50 percent greater chance of getting divorced once they marry.[2] Some have wished to deny this correlation, stressing instead that the figures are flawed since these same types of people are the more unconventional persons anyway, without many of the mores and morals of society. Nevertheless, even when this factor is weighed into the studies, the seriousness of prematurely experiencing the joys of marriage, especially in premarital sexual relations, still comes with the same warning that there is a higher probability of divorce in that relationship.

Scripture, of course, takes an altogether different view, for God demands holiness from his creatures and their cultures. Therefore, when a man joins a woman sexually, he is in that same act thereby taking her to be his wife. Moses taught that if marriage was not intended, there was to be no intercourse. Where intercourse did take place, the two had already become "one flesh" (Gen. 2:24; Exod. 22:16). Likewise, at the Jerusalem Council, the Gentiles were warned, among other things, to abstain from "sexual immorality" (Acts 15:20). The Greek word in the New Testament for sexual immorality is *porneia*, which is where we get our English root for the word *pornography*. This Greek word covered all forms of illicit sexual intercourse. Those who practice "sexual immorality," without any repentance or desire to change and stop the habit, will not inherit the kingdom of God, warned Paul (1 Cor. 6:9), for "the body is not meant for sexual immorality" (6:13). So we must "flee from sexual immorality" (6:18). The same teaching is found in Galatians 5:19; Ephesians 5:3; and Colossians 3:5. The reason our Lord gave such a stern warning against abusing the privilege of sex before marriage is that it causes serious damage to God's purposes for marriage.

When sex is experienced outside of marriage, the purpose of oneness, mutuality, exclusive loyalty, and intimacy is crushed and abused (Gen. 2:18, 24; Eph. 5:21–32). Walter Trobisch underscored this principle in his book *I Loved a Girl*. He commented:

> When I as a pastor am called in to counsel in a marriage crisis, I can almost always trace the origin of the problems to the kind of life which the husband and wife lived before they were married. The young man who has not learned self-control before marriage will not have it during marriage. . . . In a sense, you deprive your future wife of something, even if you do not yet know her, and you endanger your future happiness together.[3]

Premarital sexual experiences raise the stakes exceedingly high for later unfaithfulness in marriage and increase the risk for divorce.

It is true, of course, that in many societies couples marry right after puberty; thus the issue of self-control in that form does not arise as frequently. In Western society, however, young persons tend to delay marriage for some ten or more years after puberty, exactly when they potentially experience some of their highest physical sexual desires. Put that fact together with the fact that the culture tends to treat premarital sex in a very casual way, and it is a situation that calls for the best we can offer as a people of God by way of biblical teaching, counsel, and accountability groups as a preventative measure and as a restorative form of action.

The Anything-Goes Philosophy

Believers just cannot agree with the advice of some newspaper columnists who flippantly counsel, "So long as no one is harmed, anything goes between two consenting adults, assuming also that both are agreeable!" Such advice overlooks the Maker of the couple: Our Lord himself does not agree. It also assumes "no harm will come" of the relationship. But therein lies the hidden agenda. Usually women are willing to accept premarital sex in the hope that the man may eventually marry them (shown to be what 80 percent of the women thought), while the same study showed that only 12 percent of the men entered this relationship with the same expectation.[4]

Marriage is God's plan for an intimate companionship throughout all of one's life (Gen. 2:18). Within that relationship is the call for the procreation and nurturing of children. God's gift also includes his provision for the proper use of our sexual desires (1 Cor. 7:2).

In the same way, when a man joins himself to a prostitute, he becomes physically one with her. Our bodies are "not meant for sexual immorality, but for the Lord. . . . Do you not know that he who unites himself with a prostitute is one with her in body?" (1 Cor. 6:13, 16). God, however, designed oneness between a man and woman to happen only in marriage (Gen. 2:24; Eph. 5:31).

Knowing How to Please God Leading Up to Marriage

The best teaching and preaching text I know of on the topic of fornication and cohabitation is 1 Thessalonians 4:1–8. Let us examine this text as God's strategy for our wholesome living in a world that has gone sex-mad and often lost its conscience before God.

Text: 1 Thessalonians 4:1–8
Title: "Knowing How to Please God Leading Up to Marriage"
Focal Point: verse 3, "It is God's will that you should be sanctified: that you should avoid sexual immorality."
Homiletical Keyword: Ways
Interrogative: What are the ways that we must please God in the area of our sexual purity?

Outline:
    Introduction (4:1–2)
    I. We must avoid all fornication (4:3)
    II. We must know how to conduct a Christian courtship (4:4–5)
    III. We must refuse to cheat a brother or sister in Christ (4:6–8)
        A. Because God will vindicate the wronged party
        B. Because God has called us to holiness
        C. Because the Holy Spirit is offended

The apostle Paul had just concluded a stirring section in this letter to the church at Thessalonica, in Macedonia, about the Lord's second return and our preparation for that event(1 Thess. 1–3). William Lecky (1838–1903) described a rather dismal picture of sexual license during the days of the Roman Empire in the cities of Greece, Macedonia, Asia Minor, Rome, and Egypt. He wrote:

> [These cities] had become centres of the wildest corruption. . . . There has probably never been a period when vice was more extravagant or uncontrolled [than when it was under the Caesars].[5]

But we are surprised when Paul turns to the first order of practical application of this truth in 1 Thessalonians 4:1–8, for his first priority in light of the Lord's immanent return is to talk about sexual purity among red-blooded Thessalonian boys. It was taken for granted, by many, that married couples must of course avoid adultery—but what about young boys who were as yet unmarried? Well, boys will be boys—and for many that was enough said!

But not from God's point of view. There is a whole lot more that needs to be said. And Paul straightforwardly, yet gently, guides all who profess Christ as Savior on what the will of the Lord is for all believers in situations just like these, especially for those who are as yet unmarried.

Paul begins this section with "finally, brothers," which often means that we are approaching the end of most discourses. But that is not true in this instance; in fact, he is just coming to the really important things that must be said in light of so sensational an event as the second coming of our Lord.

But the matter he now raises is one that is doubly important. Therefore he pleads: "Now we ask you and urge you" (v. 1d). This double entreaty calls us sharply to come to attention and warns us that what is now going to be said is something of enormous significance in light of who we are in Christ Jesus. And it is just as important to note that this double entreaty is given on the authority of "the Lord Jesus" himself (vv. 1d, 2). Paul does not put himself, as none of us should either, in a position of superiority or as the source for this injunction; yet neither does he assume a position of timidity and hesitancy. It is our Lord who is our boss and who, by his work as our Creator and by his death on the cross for our sins and for our redemption, has also earned the right to say how we should act. We are indeed most beholden to him for who he is and what he has done for us.

Notice too that what Paul has to say here is aimed at Christian "brothers." Even though the admonition does fit those outside of the believing family just as well, this is a family matter, for those whom Paul treats as equals. Apparently, some in the church were living a loose and free lifestyle that was not fitting for their profession. That same state of affairs exists for many today, who name Christ's name, but whose lifestyle suggests a wholly different allegiance to the norms of our pagan culture. So brothers and sisters: listen up!

Now we come to the point of his earnest entreaty: it is how we must live in order to please God (v. 1b). The old metaphor for our new word "lifestyle" was our "walk," a Hebraism that addressed how people were to live. Christians were so serious about walking and living as the Lord directed them that their religion was at first called "the Way" (Acts 9:2; 19:23). They were followers of "the Way." So we ought to be living in that same "way" as well.

The point, however, is that the whole object of our lives is to be nothing less than the goal of pleasing the Lord. And Paul is quick to add that in many ways the believers were doing just that. The apostle

Paul never remanded and rebuked without at the same time encouraging the audience he was, in part, scolding. Thus, he noted "as in fact you are living" (v. 1c). We too must combine reproof and exhortation with praise and encouragement. There were some positive things that could and must be said for these believers even though some things were really out of whack!

So why was Paul so concerned for a change in this area? He said it was because he wanted them to increase and see multiplication in their lives more and more (v. 1e). It is difficult, if not impossible, to be a genuine fruit-bearing Christian if we are involved in practices such as those that were taking place in this church at that time and possibly in our own time as well. These sins had to be confessed. They were putting a handicap on the ministry, and the body was not producing or seeing any major impact on their culture, as it should have been witnessing. For those who were involved in what we will see was premarital sex, this was not an optional matter in which they could, or they could not, do as they pleased. The Lord Jesus required much more of them; it was altogether necessary for their well-being and for that of the body of believers to which they were joined that they live as Christ directed.

I. We Must Avoid All Fornication (1 Thess. 4:3)

As already noted, the Greek word *porneia* referred to all forms of illicit sexual intercourse. The Gentile pagan world would generally agree that adultery and incest were wrong, but from their viewpoint, what was so wrong, they might murmur, with premarital sex between two unmarried heterosexuals? But Paul, speaking for our Lord Jesus, warned them to have no part of such sexual acts between unmarried persons. The word "avoid" is better rendered "abstain." It is a very strong verb that is also reinforced by a strong preposition (Greek, *ek*, "from") that demands a clean break ("a clean cut"), with total abstinence from all sex until marriage.

Rather than being a recommendation, it is described right from the get-go as "God's will." Too many moan about not knowing what the will of the Lord for their lives is. Well, here is a good place to start. This was not an unreasonable demand, for continence and refraining from illicit sexual intercourse are just another demonstration of the same power of God that brought new life to us in the first place.

II. We Must Know How to Conduct a Christian Courtship (1 Thess. 4:4–5)

Verse 4 is the most difficult verse in the whole passage, but it is extremely determinative of the sense of the whole passage. The key clause is rendered in the NIV as "that each of you should learn to control his own body," whereas the RSV favors: "to take a wife for himself." The NASB renders it: "how to possess his own vessel," while the NJB translates it as: "to know how to use the body that belongs to him," with this footnote, "either a man's own body or that of his wife." So which is it: to gain control over his own body or to take a wife for himself?

The early Greek commentators took the passage to refer to one's "vessel," meaning how we use our own bodies.[6] It is less likely, said others, to call one's wife a "vessel" in a passage inculcating so high a view of marriage, for in that case the wife would be treated simply as a vessel for gratifying her husband's sexual desires. But that objection need not follow either.

A better view is found in the early commentators such as Theodore of Mopsuestia, Augustine, Aquinas, Zwingli, Alford, and others. They correctly noted that the same noun and verb used here is also used in the Greek translation of the Old Testament, called the Septuagint, and in Xenophon, where it meant "to get married."

It is also important to note the position or order of the Greek words: "the his own vessel." Placing the words "his own" between "the" and "vessel" emphasizes the fact that it is speaking to the young man himself going about the process of dating or preparing for marriage.

The Greek verb *ktaomai*, "to acquire," is a verb whose Hebrew equivalent was used in the Septuagint to mean "acquiring a wife." Thus, we would render this clause "that every one of you know how to get himself his own vessel [wife] in sanctification and honor." While there has been no small debate over the meaning of the Greek *skeuos*, "vessel," it is only used in one other place of one's wife, in 1 Peter 3:7, the "weaker vessel."

Paul then urged his listeners to act in a wholly different way as they went about dating and preparing for marriage. It was to be done with "sanctification and honor." He wanted Thessalonian men to display holiness in the way they courted their future wives: it was to be done with "honor"; that is, they were to have some good manners about themselves, going about it with dignity and showing the best courtesies. Both the spiritual aspect and the cultural aspect were connected with one preposition ("in"; Greek *en*), showing how the sacred and the secular were inextricably linked in the mind of God.

III. We Must Refuse to Cheat a Brother or Sister in Christ (1 Thess. 4:6–8)

Paul is concerned that "no one should wrong his brother or take advantage of him [or her]." The word "brother" pointed to a fellow believer, whether male or female. The "matter" (v. 6) under discussion was the same as stated in verse 3, "sexual immorality." If one had sexual relations with another who later married a different Christian partner, then the new partner would have been cheated and disadvantaged by the fact that his marriage partner had already been joined as "one flesh" to another partner prior to their marriage. Even though this also was forgivable under the gracious hand of our Lord, nevertheless it would leave scars as consequences that would need to be worked out and healed. Three reasons are given why this was so serious a matter.

A. *Because God will vindicate the wronged party.* The sin committed before the couple was married wronged the third party, who eventually married that man or woman after one of them had had an affair with another. It was also a sin against God. One could not say, as they tried to do in Proverbs 24:12, that he or she didn't know it was wrong. Ignorance of God's law once again was no excuse for disobeying the law.

God would act as the attorney on the case, nonetheless. He would be the "avenger" (Greek, *ekdikos*), which in the Greek papyri was the regular term for a legal representative, an advocate, or an adjudicator.

B. *Because God has called us to holiness.* Instead of our being satisfied with a life of uncleanness, the call of God was for us to be separate and different from the culture around us. The call of God takes priority over every other claim on our lives. Holiness to the Lord had to be the very air we breathe. We must subordinate all of our natural instincts and impulses as mortals over to the Living God who alone marks the correct path for us to tread.

C. *Because the Holy Spirit is offended.* To reject this instruction
was not something to be taken lightly, for it was a direct rejection of God himself. If one or both of the parties engaging in
premarital sex were believers, and therefore had the Holy Spirit
living within them, then the sexual encounter was no longer
a matter of two consenting adults; it involved the Holy Spirit,
who did not consent. This outraged not only mere mortals
but also the Living God, who at the very moment "keeps on
giving" (Greek present-tense participial form yielding a sense
of ongoing action) to us the Holy Spirit.

Conclusions

1. So serious a matter is this that Paul placed a double entreaty
   at the start of this instruction: we urge and we exhort; we beg
   and we plead by the Lord Jesus that you change your lifestyle
   by the grace and forgiveness of God.
2. Without lording it over his audience, Paul addresses this message
   to those he calls "brothers." The message has special relevancy
   to members of the family of God who are caught in the web
   of this sin.
3. Halting premarital live-in situations is not an optional piece of
   good advice; it is a command from our Savior, who is also our
   Lord and Boss.
4. Stop stunting the growth of grace in your life by continuing in
   known sin such as sexual immorality. Confess what needs to
   be confessed and then ask God for his help. To avoid fornication, let each man have his own wife (1 Cor. 7:2). If God gives
   the gift of celibacy, know that there is also a gift and call to be
   single as well as to be married (1 Cor. 7:7). Do not, however,
   take these gifts and powers for granted. Intimate relationships
   are to be entered into by God's grace and shared with the other
   partner after marriage.

Bibliography

Grenz, Stanley J. "The Purpose of Sex: Toward a Theological Understanding of Human Sexuality." *Crux* 26, no. 2 (1990): 27–34.

————. *Sexual Ethics: A Biblical Perspective*. Dallas: Word, 1990.

Lebacqz, Karen. "Appropriate Vulnerability: A Sexual Ethic for Singles." *The Christian Century*, May 6, 1987, 435–38.

Penner, Clifford, and Joyce Penner. *The Gift of Sex: A Christian Guide to Sexual Fulfillment*. New York: Pilgrim, 1981.

Smedes, Lewis B. *Sex for Christians: The Limits and Liberties of Sexual Living*. Rev. ed. Grand Rapids: Eerdmans, 1994.

Stafford, Tim. *The Sexual Christian*. Wheaton: Victor, 1989.

Wenham, David. "Marriage and Singleness in Paul and Today." *Themelios* 13, no. 2 (January–February 1988): 39–41.

White, John. *Eros Redeemed: Breaking the Stranglehold of Sexual Sin*. Downers Grove, IL: InterVarsity, 1993.

Wilson, Earl D. *Sexual Sanity*. Downers Grove, IL: InterVarsity, 1984.

Winner, Lauren F. *Real Sex: The Naked Truth about Chastity*. Grand Rapids: Brazos, 2005.

Discussion Questions

1. How does one hold to any kind of sexual sanity in a culture that is so full of sexual innuendo in television, reading, and magazines?
2. What are some of the best ways to keep oneself sexually pure while marriage must be delayed in many cases until college and graduate school are completed?
3. How strongly do you regard the biblical case for sexual purity prior to marriage?

7

DIVORCE

Malachi 2:10–16

Today's Divorce Rate

It has been frequently alleged that one out of every two marriages ends up in the divorce courts. It is true that the real numbers are all too frightening and full of tragedy, but the claim that divorce rates are at the 50 percent level is not true. Those who quote that figure are actually comparing two fairly reliable statistics: the annual number of marriage licenses issued and the annual number of divorce decrees issued. But comparing these two numbers as a representation of the total picture is like comparing apples and oranges, for the total number of marriages obviously exceeds the number of those who got married in any given year.

It is true that there are approximately two million marriage licenses issued each year with about one million divorce decrees handed out in that same year. But of those who obtained divorce decrees, twice as many were also married in that same year.

Another way to put it would be to take the "total adult population that is currently or has never been married (72 percent), and to compare that to the number of people who are currently divorced (9 percent), [which] calculation produces a 13 percent current divorce rate."[1]

If the 50 percent myth is exposed as being false, then so is the myth that somewhere near half or more of the marriages in the United States are ending up in the divorce courts. There are over 50 million well-established marriages in this land that are holding together, thank you!

Nevertheless, divorce rates have dramatically increased since the 1960s. It is not just Christians who are alarmed over this growing epidemic. Take for example the confession of a non-Christian clinical psychologist who set out to write a book to help couples facing this transition in their lives. She began her book with this shocker:

> I have to start with a confession: This isn't the book I set out to write. I planned to write something consistent with my previous professional experience—helping people with decision making. . . . For example, I started this project believing that people who suffer over an extended period in unhappy marriages ought to get out. . . . I thought that striking down taboos about divorce was another part of the ongoing enlightenment of the women's, civil rights, and human potential movements of the last twenty-five years. . . . To my utter befuddlement, the extensive research I conducted for this book brought me to one inescapable and irrefutable conclusion: I had been wrong.[2]

There was a day in which divorce was almost unheard of, especially in the church. But that day has long since gone, for the rise in the number of divorces took off from four hundred thousand in 1962 to 1.2 million (a tripling of the number) in 1981. While the older generations stayed true to their marriage vows, those who married in the sixties and seventies divorced at close to the 50 percent level.[3]

The children of these marriages seem to be hit the hardest. Currently, approximately one million children are affected by divorce each year. This presents another major contrast between what happened in the generations before the 1960s and what has happened since, for children of parents who divorced in that previous era were not as widely represented, but today children from divorced parents represent a sizable number of children growing up without one or the other parent in the home.

Scripture and Divorce

Scripture is exceedingly clear from its very beginning that marriage was meant to be a permanent relationship for all the days the couple lived on this earth. The key text is Genesis 2:24–25. As Adam and Eve are brought together as husband and wife, they are bound in a "one-flesh" relationship.

Some misinterpret Deuteronomy 24:1–4 to say that Moses gave in and finally permitted divorce because of the hardness of the hearts of the people. This is incorrect. Moses did not endorse divorce; he set up guidelines to protect the summarily dismissed wife. It was all too common in the ancient Near East for the husband to pontificate in private: "I divorce you, I divorce you, I divorce you!"—and that was it. The wife was out—unless the husband changed his mind the next day or reversed his decision after having had other affairs. What chance would a woman have for knowing what her real status was: was she married or in a state of perpetual divorce? This would allow the serially divorcing husband to claim he was not married (at that moment) for whatever reason he wished to present to other women. Moses put an end to that. "Mister," he said in effect, "put that decree of divorce in writing and stick to it." He was to write a certificate of divorce (Hebrew, *keritut*, literally a "bill of cutting off"). Even though the vocabulary for "divorce" is found in both Testaments, one must not automatically assume that there always were two opposing views on the permanence of marriage in the Old Testament, as there were in Jesus's day.

It is also unfortunate that the KJV, the English Revised Version (RV), and the American Standard Version (ASV) adopted a translation of Deuteronomy 24:1–4 that has added to the confusion. On their rendering, divorce was not just controlled by requiring the husband to put it in writing; it was commanded when some "uncleanness," described in the protasis (the clause expressing the condition in a conditional sentence) of these verses, occurred. However, rather than demanding "then he shall write a certificate of divorcement" in 24:1, and beginning the apodosis (the clause expressing the consequence in a conditional sentence) in verse 1, most commentators agree that verses 1–3 form the protasis ("if a man . . ."), with the apodosis coming only in verse 4 ("Then her first husband . . . is not allowed to marry her again"). The conditional "if," which begins verse 1, continues through verse 3 and without the jussive force of the KJV, RV, and ASV.

Thus, we conclude with R. Campbell, "If Deut. 24:1–4 is properly rendered, it cannot be understood as initiating the practice of divorce. No Old Testament oracle or law institute[d] divorce; Hebrew law simply tolerated the practice."[4] It is true that the practice of divorce appears fairly frequently in the Old Testament (Lev. 21:7, 14; 22:13; Num. 30:9; Deut. 22:19, 29; Isa. 50:1; Jer. 3:1, 8; Ezek. 44:22), but this is much different from establishing divorce as a right or as divinely approved. Divorce is nowhere commanded or even encouraged in either Testament.

Jesus commented on this same Deuteronomy 24:1–4 text and said this so-called "concession" was given because of their hardness of heart (Matt. 19:3–9). Notice, then, that this law from Moses did not command one to divorce. What it did command was that a husband who divorced his wife and married another was not to go back to the first wife.

The Gospel of Matthew gives Jesus's fullest and clearest statement on divorce. Matthew 5:31–32 reports that Jesus said: "I tell you that anyone who divorces his wife, except for marital unfaithfulness [Greek, *porneias*], causes her to become an adulteress, and anyone who marries the divorced woman commits adultery [Greek, *moichatai*]." Again, in Matthew 19:9 Jesus said: "I tell you that anyone who divorces his wife, except for marital unfaithfulness, and marries another woman commits adultery."

Jesus taught, therefore, that marriage was for life. In saying so, he challenged the two rival schools of Jewish interpretation: the stricter school of Shammai, which said "something indecent" (Hebrew, *'ervat dabar*) meant some sexual impurity short of adultery, and the more liberal Hillel school, which interpreted "something indecent" to mean anything that displeased the husband. Jesus used this as an opportunity to set the record straight on what it was that Moses taught. Moses tried to make the husband declare in writing what he was intending when he divorced his wife. Jesus would not be trapped into taking sides in one or the other school of Jewish interpretation.

Scholars have tended to debate the meaning and applicability of the exception clause in Matthew 5 and 19. They wonder why Mark (10:1–12) and Luke (16:18) did not include this clause as well. Actually, Jesus did say the same thing in all three Gospels: there was to be no divorce. Matthew records that the Pharisees wouldn't let it go at that but pressed him even further. The Pharisees wanted to drive a wedge between Moses and Jesus, or at least between the two Jewish schools of interpretation, but Jesus would not allow that either, so he added the exception clause in the Matthew record of this encounter. Some will then accuse Jesus of contradicting his no-divorce principle. But it is not unheard of in Scripture to set the standards in one or more passages and then to give the exception in another. Thus, the standard is "Thou shalt not kill," but exceptions are found for killing animals, killing to protect one's family in a night house-invasion, or killing in a time of war.

The Pauline Privilege

One more exception is given in what is sometimes called "the Pauline privilege." In 1 Corinthians 7:15, one may, without being required, give a divorce on the grounds of permanent desertion. The abandoned person is not "bound" (Greek, *dedoulotai*). They may get a divorce and are permitted to remarry.

Some interpreters have argued for the indissolubility of marriage and therefore would allow divorce on these exceptional cases mentioned in Scripture, but with no privilege of remarriage. This argument insists that the grammar requires that divorce be permitted, but the exception clause does not go with the next clause in Matthew 19:9 (". . . except for marital unfaithfulness, and marries another woman . . ."). If this clause does not go with the next clause as well, then a person could divorce a spouse who is persistently unfaithful, but remarriage would never be possible. But this interpretation is held only by a few grammarians, while most scholars say the exception goes with both divorce and remarriage. Incidentally, both the Hillel and Shammai schools of Jewish interpretation assumed the right of remarriage, so this point Jesus did not contest or correct.

One last matter: Some have charged that Jesus's use of the word for "divorce" (Greek, *apoluo*) in Matthew 19:8 and 9 does not have that sense of "divorce." However, *apoluo* has now turned up in a Greek document of remarriage from Palestine meaning exactly "to divorce."[5]

Malachi 2:10–16

One of the most important, and yet most difficult, texts on divorce is found in Malachi 2:10–16. In this text, we have one of our Lord's most succinct statements on his attitude toward divorce. The significance of this pericope may be seen in the fact that it treats the topic of individual family life from the standpoint of its ties to the life of the nation, from the realm of its spiritual development, and as a covenant made in the presence of God. This passage met head-on with the outbreak of ethical problems it sought to rebuke: disloyalty to the spiritual unity of the national family (2:10), disloyalty to the family of faith (2:11–12), and disloyalty to the marriage partner to whom each had pledged covenantal loyalty before God (2:13–16). The evidences of these disloyalties could be seen in (1) their spiritual harlotry, (2) their mixed marriages with unbelieving partners, (3) their adulteries, and (4) their divorces!

What makes this text so difficult is the state of the present Hebrew text. Almost every commentator takes his or her turn in bemoaning the difficulties found in Malachi 2:10–16. For example, Joyce G. Baldwin complained:

> Here the text becomes difficult, having suffered perhaps at the hand of scribes who took exception to its teaching. . . . It is impossible to make sense of the Hebrew as it stands and therefore each translation, including the early versions, contains an element of interpretation.[6]

Likewise, R. C. Dentan in utter frustration declared, "In Hebrew this [v. 15] is one of the most obscure verses in the entire O.T. Almost every word raises a question."[7] We will examine these issues as they appear in the text.

The Structure and Argument of Malachi 2:10–16

Most of Malachi is in the form of the prophetic dispute. Up to this point the disputants have been the priests against God. Now, however, the scope is enlarged to embrace all the people. Given the fact that the spiritual attainment of the leaders was low, it could not be expected that the spiritual level of the people would be any higher.

The pericope opens with a double question that also amounts to a double promise (much as the proverbial nature of the two-fold assertion in Mal. 1:6 functioned): (1) all Israel has one Father (God); and (2) God created the nation, thus they all should be one happy family. But the sad truth is that (3) they are all profaning the covenant that God made with their fathers (v. 10).

Before the people can dispute this charge, another one is leveled in verses 11–12. Israel has been openly indulging in marrying women who worshiped foreign gods. This action flies right in the face of the divine warnings against *religiously* mixed marriages, as happened in Exodus 34:12–16; Numbers 25:1–3; Deuteronomy 7:3–4; and 1 Kings 11:1–33.

But there are further accusations: "Another thing you do" (v. 13a). "You flood the Lord's altar with tears. You weep and wail because he no longer pays attention to your offerings or accepts them with pleasure from your hands" (v. 13b).

When the people ask, "Why?" (v. 14), God mentions the covenant that was in force between "you and the wife of your youth," to which he also acted as a third-party witness! He also reminds the couple that he made them "one," which in a marriage context refers no doubt to the "one flesh" of Genesis 2:24. Therefore, let us examine the text of Malachi 2:10–16 more closely for our teaching or preaching ministry.

Refusing to Break Faith

Text: Malachi 2:10–16[8]

Title: "Refusing to Break Faith"

Focal Point: verse 16a, c, " 'I hate divorce,' says the LORD God of Israel. . . . So guard yourself in your spirit, and do not break faith."

Homiletical Keyword: Situations

Interrogative: What are the situations where we too might break faith?

Outline:
  I. When we break faith with one another (2:10)
 II. When we break faith by marrying unbelievers (2:11–12)
III. When we break faith with our marriage partner (2:13–16)

I. When We Break Faith with One Another (Mal. 2:10)

Notice that the expression to "break faith with" appears five times, in verses 10, 11, 14, 15, and 16. It is the Hebrew verb, *bagad*, "to be faithless," "to deal deceitfully," "treacherous," or "to betray." The specific connotation of all five references is to marital impropriety. The idiom may reflect the associated noun *beged*, meaning "garment"; if so, could this be similar to what we in our day would call a "cover-up" job?

There is a fourfold use of the word "one" as well (twice each in vv. 10 and 15). The identity of the "one" in verse 10 is not "Abraham your father," as in Isaiah 51:2, or a reference to Jacob, as Jerome and Calvin thought, from whom the twelve-tribe nation descended. Instead, the "one" in verse 10 is God, the "One" who created Israel (Isa. 43:1). The implication, then, was that those who had the same Creator would be one family. However, they turned around and dealt treacherously with each other by breaking faith with God and with their own family members.

Therefore a call is issued for a whole new loyalty and love for the whole people of God. Israel, however, missed their call and instead profaned the covenant God had made with their fathers (v. 10c). So crass will this nation become that they will say to a tree, "You are my father" (Jer. 2:27). All fraternal ties will be neglected and faith with one another will be broken as idolatry replaces a love for the Lord their God alone.

Wounding the whole body in either Testament was never a slight offense. In 1 Corinthians 3:16–17 (NRSV) the text inquires: "Do you [all] not know that you [all] are God's temple and that God's Spirit dwells in you [all]? If anyone destroys God's temple, God will destroy that person. For God's temple is holy, and you [all] are that temple." This is a stern warning about disrupting and upsetting the whole people of God. It invites a similar divine judgment on our lives, just as we poured that kind of destruction on the people of God by allowing our sin to destroy all God's people.

God had set Israel apart from the other nations when he made a covenant with their fathers, but now Israel was desecrating that covenant and dealing wickedly by marrying heathen women and by divorcing their Israelite wives.

II. When We Break Faith by Marrying Unbelievers (Mal. 2:11–12)

The general charge of verse 10 is now given specificity in the indictment about mixed religious marriages. It was not an issue of cross-cultural or mixed racial marriages, but an issue of marriages that forgot about not being yoked to unbelievers. The expression "daughter of a foreign god" (v. 11) pointed to one who was dependent on a deity other than Yahweh. Ezra 9:2–6; 10:18–19; and Nehemiah 10:30; 13:23–27 demonstrate that men were heedlessly marrying women with pagan deity allegiances, which was strictly forbidden by Scripture (Exod. 34:11–16; Deut. 7:3; 1 Kings 11:1–2).

Israel was called to be holy to the Lord, but now she carelessly abandoned all such exclusive dedications to the Lord and took on a syncretistic outlook and stance. As a result of such violation of God's covenant, God himself would wipe out the families "root and branch." This last idiom is almost impossible to translate, but its general intent is fairly clear: the transgressor's family would be involved in the "cut[ting] off" of that family from Israel.

It may well be that the finger was pointing to the Levites, for the last clause in verse 12 would imply it was the Levites, since they were the ones who were given the role of presenting the offerings to the Lord (Mal. 1:7; 3:3).

III. When We Break Faith with Our Marriage Partner (Mal. 2:13–16)

Not only were the people guilty of breaking faith with one another and of marrying unbelievers but they were divorcing their present Israelite wives as well. Long before these violators became aware of the seriousness of their sins, they realized that something was wrong. The Lord had refused to recognize or receive their sacrificial gifts and prayers to him. In an attempt to placate God's anger, the guilty offenders redoubled their efforts to regain God's favor (v. 13d).

But there was an impediment: the Lord's altar was flooded with tears. Where did all the tears come from? Most likely, they came from the heartbreak of the divorced wives, which poured forth such a mist that it clouded the altar of the violator's sacrifices so that the gifts and prayers were completely blocked from God's purview. The women's tears were used figuratively to depict the seriousness of the women's outcry to God. It could be true, on the other hand, that the tears came from the men themselves, whose increased intensity at the altar of God gave forth all the clouds of mist because they realized God was angry with them and nothing was getting through to heaven.

The point, however, was clear in verse 14: Why does God not pay attention or accept our offerings any longer? And for that question there was a ready and definitive answer: "Because you have broken faith with [the wife of your youth]." She was uniquely "your partner, the wife of your marriage covenant" (v. 14). The Lord himself had acted as a witness to this covenant (v. 14b), so why did the men feel it was only a contract between the husband and the wife? Marriage is viewed as a covenant between God and the two partners, as can be seen in this text, in Proverbs 2:16–17 ("the adulteress . . . [and] the wayward wife . . . who has left the partner of her youth and ignored the covenant she made before God"), and in Ezekiel 16:8 ("I gave you my solemn oath and entered into a covenant with you, declares the Sovereign LORD, and you became mine"). Therefore the nuptial contract could not be lightly regarded or easily broken as in other social contracts when one of the two parties got tired and wanted out of it; this was a covenant and not a contract, and it had God as one of the three parties.

In order to show all the more graphically the aggravation that the offense of divorce worked, Malachi used three phrases: "wife of your youth," "your partner/companion," and the "wife of your covenant." The tender memories and associations these phrases should have raised was captured by T. V. Moore:

> She whom you thus wronged was the companion of those earlier and brighter days, when in the bloom of her young beauty she left her father's house and shared your early struggles, and rejoiced in your later success; who walked arm in arm with you along the pilgrimage of life, cheering you in its trials by her gentle ministry; and now, when the bloom of her youth has faded and the friends of her youth have gone, when father and mother whom she left for you are in the grave, then you cruelly cast her off as a worn-out, worthless thing, and insult her holiest affections by putting an idolater and a heathen in her place.[9]

Solomon had enjoined couples to act differently in that profound allegory on marital fidelity and conjugal faithfulness in Proverbs 5:15–23; they were to "rejoice in the wife of [their] youth." Even the word "partner/companion" may echo the "one flesh" of Genesis 2:24. It implies a harmony and a desire to work together to achieve life's greatest goals while sharing all the pain, hardships, and joys.

The final two verses in 15 and 16 are especially difficult to interpret. Some incorrectly render the "one" as a reference to Abraham and make it nominative. If so, then it would say, "Did not one [viz., Abraham] do so?" that is, take a pagan Egyptian woman named Hagar as his wife? But this rendering is open to a number of objections. Abraham is never referred to elsewhere as the "one," nor could his conduct of "putting away" Hagar be considered the case being discussed here, for the wives being divorced were covenant wives and not foreign wives as Hagar was. Moreover, Abraham did not divorce Sarah when he took Hagar as his wife, but Hagar was brought into the picture on the advice of Sarah herself!

The subject, then, would be God, and the "one" would be the object, equal to the "one flesh" mentioned in Genesis 2:24. It is also best to understand this clause as an interrogative, which often is not explicitly so marked in Hebrew (nor does it need to, to be regarded as an interrogative), as is the case here. The thought then would run this way: Why did God make Adam and Eve only "one flesh" when he certainly had the power, ability, and authority (the "residue of the Spirit") to make many wives for Adam or many husbands for Eve; why just one? The clause that follows acknowledges that the "residue/remainder of the Spirit was his" (v. 15b, my translation); that is, God had the power and authority to do what was necessary and right. The answer is clear enough: "Because he was seeking godly offspring" (v. 15c). Apparently that would not be possible in a polygamous (i.e., many wives) or a polyandrous (i.e., many husbands) world. So watch out, for we must guard ourselves in our spirit and not break faith with our Lord or those we have covenanted with in marriage.

Verse 16 is the most difficult verse of all of them to translate. The best way to regard the Hebrew is to notice it has the pointing (or vowels) that would suggest it is a verbal adjective used as a participle, "the one hating." It also seems fairly certain that the personal pronoun "I" (Hebrew, 'ani) has dropped out because of the similarity to the ending on the participle sona'. Thus we have one of the strongest divine assertions on divorce: God declares, "I hate divorce." Here, however, divorce is described as "a man's covering himself with violence as well as with his garment." This expression seems obtuse until we recall the ancient custom in Ruth 3:9, where Ruth asked Boaz to take her as his wife by spreading his garment/robe over her. Similar concepts are couched in biblical texts such as Ezekiel 16:8 and the Hebrew of Deuteronomy 23:1 (literally, "he shall not uncover the covering of his father"; English, Deut. 22:30, second half of the verse).

Divorce is not the answer to the testing and trials found in marriage. The Lord who designed marriage specifically stated that he hated all divorce. Therefore if we are to stay with the "Manufacturer's instructions," and if we are to honor the covenant we made with God and the wife of our youth, we had better work instead on trying to smooth the bumps in the road rather than thinking that divorce will get rid of all of them. Divorce has seldom turned out to be the cure-all answer most thought it would be when they ended their marriage. Instead of the troubles evaporating, often they seem to follow the divorcees into the next marriage or the separated state of one's singleness.

Conclusions

1. No one said that marriage would always be easy and that there would never be any difficulties. All too many people reason that when trouble comes, one can simply get a divorce, but where does that leave us? What problems often remain and follow us even if we are divorced and remarried?

2. Breaking faith with one another often leads to breaking faith with our marriage covenant, with our marriage partner, and with God, all of which are condemned outright by God. What are the implications of this? How serious is courting that kind of divine censure?

3. God hates divorce as a form of a "cover-up" job that often merely perpetuates violence on another person made in the image of God. If we have engendered the wrath of God in this matter, he must be sought out, and in his grace a request must be made to the offended partner and to our Lord as we seek forgiveness. This probably will not remove all the ill consequences of the divorce for the children, the dropped spouse, or ourself, but at least we can know God's forgiveness and go on record as advising others not to follow our course of action. Name some of the consequences and the recommendations we could share with a friend going through this type of issue.

Bibliography

Braun, Michael. *Second Class Christians? A New Approach to the Dilemma of Divorced People in the Church.* Downers Grove, IL: InterVarsity, 1989.

Duty, Guy. *Divorce and Remarriage*. Minneapolis: Bethany, 1967.

House, H. Wayne. *Divorce and Remarriage: Four Christian Views*. Downers Grove, IL: InterVarsity, 1990.

Murray, John. *Divorce*. 1953. Reprint, Philadelphia: Presbyterian and Reformed, 1961.

Richards, Larry. *Remarriage: A Healing Gift from God*. Waco: Word, 1981.

Wenham, Gordon J. "Gospel Definitions of Adultery and Women's Rights." *Expository Times* 95 (1984): 330–32.

Wiebe, Philip H. "Jesus' Divorce Exception." *Journal of the Evangelical Theological Society* 32 (1989): 327–33.

Discussion Questions

1. Is it always best to go immediately for a divorce when a married person has engaged in a sexually intimate act with someone besides his or her marriage partner?
2. Should Christian leaders and clergy persons be denied restoration to the ministerial office once they have committed a sexual sin and been forgiven and restored?
3. Can a person who was divorced before they were converted, but who is now remarried, be admitted to church leadership or to the ministry?
4. What things should believing couples do to maintain a strong marriage?

8

ABORTION AND
STEM CELL RESEARCH

Psalm 139:13–18; Exodus 21:22–25

E ven though abortion is one of the most controversial and divisive topics in our day, it still is the most frequently performed surgery on adults in America. It is claimed that one in every three babies conceived in this country is deliberately aborted.[1]

Abortion in History

Of course abortion is not a recent phenomenon, for the practice or the rejection of the practice has had a long history in the ancient world. The Sumerians, Babylonians, Assyrians, and Hittites all considered abortion a serious crime. Following this tradition, the famous Hippocratic Oath that medical doctors affirmed, up until recently, at the time of their graduation from medical school, contained this sentence: "I will not give a woman a pessary[2] to produce an abortion." Another example of such a strong stand in antiquity against abortion comes from the twelfth-century BC Middle-Assyrian Law Code. Without mincing any words, the Assyrians of old said:

> If a woman has had a miscarriage by her own act, when they have prosecuted and convicted her, they shall impale her on stakes without burying her. If she died in having the miscarriage [i.e., the abortion], [then] they shall impale her on stakes without burying her.[3]

It was the Greek culture, however, that condoned the practice of abortion. Plato had argued that ill-conceived embryos should not be brought to birth, and Aristotle thought deformed children should be left to die by exposure. Paul Cartledge summarized the so-called enlightened view of the Greek city-state Sparta in the fifth century BC in this manner:

> The Spartans . . . were preoccupied with the reproduction of their citizen population, but sheer numbers alone were not enough. Quality mattered. Thus newborn infants were submitted to a ritual inspection and test conducted by the "elders of the tribesman," as Plutarch puts it. They were dunked in a bath of presumably undiluted wine, to see how they reacted. If they failed the test, the consequences were fatal. They were taken to a place called cryptically "the deposits," and hurled to their certain death into a ravine. So too were those infants unluckily born with some serious and already obvious deformity or disability.[4]

Over against such early practices the Jewish culture rejected abortion. The Jewish historian Josephus, writing toward the end of the first Christian century, declared: "The Law has commanded to raise all children and prohibited women from aborting or destroying seed; a woman who does so shall be judged a murderess of children, for she has caused a soul to be lost and the family of man to be diminished."[5] Likewise, the *Didache* (also known as "The Teaching of the Twelve Apostles"), which was often called the "early church manual," gave these terse prohibitions, which included an injunction against abortion: "You shall not murder; you shall not commit adultery; you shall not corrupt children; you shall not be sexually immoral; you shall not steal; you shall not practice magic; you shall not engage in sorcery; you shall not abort a child or commit infanticide."[6]

The church father Clement of Alexandria was just as clear in his comments. He advised:

Our whole life can proceed according to God's perfect plan only if we gain dominion over our desires, practicing continence from the beginning instead of destroying through perverse and pernicious arts human offspring, who are given birth by Divine Providence. Those who use abortifacient medicines to hide their fornication cause not only the outright murder of the fetus, but of the whole human race as well.[7]

The Discovery of the Human Ovum

With the discovery of the human ovum in the 1820s, modern laws against abortion began to appear in the US. These laws remained in effect until 1967, when several states began to relax them. By 1970, eighteen states had passed laws that allowed for abortion under some exceptional circumstances. On January 22, 1973, the Supreme Court of the United States of America handed down its *Roe v. Wade* decision, which was even more permissive than any of the abortion laws that had been passed by the states up to that time.

The evangelical community was at first taken by surprise, since there had hardly been any teaching on this issue from Scripture, as with many other ethical issues. Many evangelical pastors at first even publicly welcomed this action by the Supreme Court. However, slowly the implications of what had taken place began to dawn on the consciences of believers, and a belated, but strong, backlash began to gradually appear.

New concepts and discussions emerged on this issue, including the idea of "personhood" (not mentioned in the Bible), "quality of life," and the "right to privacy" (also not mentioned in the Bible or the Constitution of the US). In the meantime, huge numbers of destroyed, unwanted fetuses and unwanted infants kept raising the issues of abortion and infanticide as never before.

The Discovery of Embryonic Stem Cells

As if this were not enough to handle, in November of 1998, scientists at the University of Wisconsin were able to successfully isolate and culture human embryonic stem cells. The name "stem cells" is derived from their similarity to the stem of a plant that gives rise to branches, bark, and other parts of the plant. In the human body there are 210 different kinds of tissue that can give rise to a similar pattern of stem cells. As the human embryo develops into a blastocyst, the stem cells can be removed from the blastocyst,[8] cultured, and grown into self-replicating cells. The moral problem, however, is that the embryo is destroyed after the stem cells are removed, having come either from (1) *in vitro* fertilization to produce the embryos; (2) frozen embryos that have been left over from an *in vitro* fertilization; (3) embryos gathered from human cloning; or the more ethically preferable source, (4) umbilical cords left after the birth of a baby.

The objection to most human embryonic stem cell research is the same objection made to abortion, for the fact is that in three of the four human embryonic sources mentioned above, the embryo must be destroyed. Even more troubling is the fact that so far those using this source for stem cells have not been able to direct the donated cells in the donor's body. For example, a notable case comes from China where a patient suffering from Parkinson's disease had an embryonic stem cell implanted only to result in an aggressive tumor that eventually killed him.[9]

The objections made to three of the four sources described here do not apply to human adult stem cell research, where the adult recipient is also the donor of the stem cells. Especially successful has been the use of adult bone marrow stem cells, which can migrate through the body to the circulatory system to repair damage and produce cells of the needed tissue type. Human adult stem cell research has experienced many promising advances, yet it carries with it none of the moral questions that surround human embryonic stem cell research.

Persons Are Made in the Image of God

When we turn, as all believers must, to the Scriptures for answers to these problems, many are too quick to gleefully announce that Scripture does not directly face the issue of abortion (and thus human embryonic stem cell research). But such a statement must be qualified immediately, for this could hardly mean that God is indifferent to the issue. Surely the Bible does not *directly* take a stand against the use of cocaine, genocide, suicide, or euthanasia, but few would argue that all or any of these cases are morally neutral from a biblical standpoint! If there were no other references than those in Genesis (and there are), still that handful of texts portrays humanity as God's image-bearers, distinct from all the rest of the created order. The key Hebrew terms in connection with humans bearing the image of God are *tselem*, "image," "likeness," and *demut*, "form," "shape," "likeness" (Gen. 1:26, 27; 5:1; 9:6). To speak of human life is to speak of a distinct divine likeness. Scripture does not wait, as in the developmental models of life, to find the image of God only in the rational and self-conscious person after that person is born; instead, the image of God is invested apart from any such considerations (such as birth or even any good deeds) whenever and wherever there is life. The psalmist portrays humanity as distinguished from all the rest of creation by this image of God. Whether humans are a "little lower than God" (Ps. 8:5 NRSV) or a "little lower than heavenly beings," such as the angels (LXX of Ps. 8:5; Heb. 2:7, 9), the point is still the same: among the whole created order, humankind is unique and has been set over the rest of earth's creatures on divine orders and authority.

Children are not viewed in the Bible as an annoyance; they are "gifts" and a "heritage from the Lord" (Ps. 127:3). Childlessness is not a preferred state, but one in which the person looks to God to open the womb in his providence, for God is also sovereign over our conception (Gen. 29:31, 33; 30:22; 1 Sam. 1:19–20).

The Majestic Omnipotence of Our God in the Formation of Our Bodies

There are two teaching texts that help us to see the value and the sanctity of life. They are Psalm 139:13–18 and Exodus 21:22–25. Let us consider Psalm 139:13–18 first.

Text: Psalm 139:13–18

Title: "The Majestic Omnipotence of Our God in the Formation of Our Bodies"

Focal Point: verses 17–18, "How precious to me are your thoughts, O God! How vast is the sum of them! Were I to count them, they would outnumber the grains of sand. When I awake, I am still with you."

Homiletical Keyword: Characteristics

Interrogative: What are the characteristics of God's omnipotence in the shaping and formation of my body before I was born?

Outline:

    I. God created my inmost being (139:13a)
    II. God shaped me in my mother's womb (139:13b–14)
    III. God saw my embryo and loved me (139:15–16a)
    IV. God ordained all of my days before I had experienced day one
       (139:16b–d)
      Conclusion (139:17–18)

Psalm 139 is one of the greatest psalms in the Psalter on the attributes of God. Verses 1–6 trace God's "omniscience," for he knows all about you and me in detail. Verses 7–12 focus on God's "omnipresence," for there is no place that any one of us can escape from his notice or his help. But it is in the section we have selected here for our consideration in verses 13–18 that our Lord exhibits his "omnipotence." Of course, none of these words (omniscience, omnipresence, or omnipotence) are words found in the biblical text as such; however, they do capture sentiments that are located in the Scriptures.

I. God Created My Inmost Being (Ps. 139:13a)

The Hebrew verb for "created" is from the root *qanah*. There are six places in the Old Testament (Ps. 139:13; Gen. 14:19, 22; Deut. 32:6; Ps. 74:2; Prov. 8:22) where this verb appears to mean "create." Originally this word was a metaphor for procreation, but then it came to signify God's divine activity in creation. The fact is that mortals are known and seen by God even from the very origins of their being.

As Solomon taught in Ecclesiastes 11:5, "As you do not know the path of the wind, or how the body is formed in a mother's womb, so you cannot understand the work of God, the Maker of all things." And so it is true again in Psalm 139:13a—the work of such an extraordinary Lord goes beyond anything any of us could imagine or even begin to wrap our minds around. That is why the Hebrew text begins verse 13 emphatically, as it did verse 2 of this psalm, with: "It is *you* [Lord]."

II. God Shaped Me in My Mother's Womb (Ps. 139:13b–14)

The Creator's work is graphically depicted as one of "weaving, plaiting, interweaving" our bones, sinews, veins, and the like (v. 13b).

With intensely personal language, the psalmist reverts to using "I" and "my." The creature must praise God a thousand times over for the divine work that is so "fearfully" and "wonderfully" carried out beyond the watchful eyes of all except God himself. More than any of the rest of the created order, men and women are the supreme creations. While all of God's works are "wonderful," there is something about the formation of a human body that is breathtaking and startling beyond anything words can match. If you do not think so, then be shocked all over again as you take into your own arms that newborn baby just after he or she emerges from the womb. You count the fingers and the toes and marvel at the fascinating detail that has been secretly unfolding for nine months in the darkness of the mother's womb. How did all of this come together so beautifully and so marvelously! The only thing we know "full well" is that "[God's] works are wonderful" (v. 14b).

III. God Saw My Embryo and Loved Me (Ps. 139:15–16a)

Verse 15 begins with "My frame," which refers primarily to our skeletal form and our bones and includes the sum total of all the elements of our being. But none of these aspects of our emerging form eluded the notice, care, and direction of our Creator.

Our mother's womb is denoted here as "the secret place" (Hebrew, *seter*), as if it were in "the depths of the earth" (Hebrew, *betakhtiyot 'arets*). The writer uses the figure of speech of "the lowest parts of the earth" or its "interior" to signal the secret laboratory of our earthly origins. The figure is natural, of course, for the first Adam was formed from the dust of the earth. As Franz Delitzsch put it,

> According to the view of Scripture, the mode of Adam's creation is repeated in the formation of every man, Job xxxiii. 6, cf. 4. The earth was the mother's womb of Adam, and the mother's womb out of which the child Adam comes forth is the earth out of which it is taken.[10]

Even more dramatically, the text claims that it was none other than God's "eyes [that] saw my unformed body" (v. 16a). The Hebrew word for "unformed body" is *golmi*, meaning "my embryo." This Hebrew word is used since the embryo is in the shape of an egg, which suggestion comes from the Hebrew root for the word "embryo," meaning "to roll, to wrap together," just as the Latin word *glomus* means a "ball." Clearly the work and care of our Lord went all the way back to our being originally formed in the womb. God himself did not think that the embryo was "just so much tissue," and not a living being; on the contrary, his love and affection were placed on us even as we were being stitched together in our mother's womb.

IV. God Ordained All of My Days before I Had Experienced Day One (Ps. 139:16b–d)

As if my whole formation in my mother's womb under the careful tutelage and direction of the great Creator of the entire universe were not enough, God had already registered all the days of my life in his book before I had an opportunity to live even the first one of those days. What an omniscient and detail-oriented Lord over all creation!

The book that is mentioned here is referred to in Psalm 69:28, which again shows God's provision for and knowledge of each of us. Surely that shows there is a real purpose for every individual.

Conclusion

All of these thoughts are just too wonderful and too amazing for the psalmist (vv. 17–18). Besides being so magnificent, they are just too numerous and too exalted for mortals to fathom. In fact, one might just as well try to number all the grains of sand on the seashores as to try to add up the accumulation of all the works of God in the formation of our bodies.

Treating the Fetus as a Person

But there is also a second passage that can help us in the abortion and embryonic stem cell research question; it is Exodus 21:22–25. This text also raises one of the most central questions in the abortion debate: when is the fetus considered to be a human being made in the image of God?

Text: Exodus 21:22–25
Title: "Treating the Fetus as a Person"
Focal Point: verse 23, "But if there is serious injury, you are to take life for life."
Homiletical Keyword: Concerns
Interrogative: What are the concerns we must have if we are to recognize fetuses as real persons?

Outline:
    I. What if an injury causes a baby to be born prematurely? (21:22)
    II. What if the premature baby dies as a result of the injury? (21:23–25)

I. What If an Injury Causes a Baby to Be Born Prematurely? (Exod. 21:22)

The "Book of the Covenant" (Exod. 24:7) introduced several case laws as part of the civil law that God gave to Moses. In the section dealing with personal injuries (Exod. 21:12–36), a possible scenario is introduced where two men are fighting with each other. Suddenly in the midst of that fight, a pregnant woman, perhaps the wife of one of the fighters, intervenes in the fight only to take an accidental blow herself. As a result, she goes into labor and "her child comes out" (the Hebrew literally says just that, *weyatse'u yeladeha*). However the text quickly adds, "but there is no harm" (literal translation of the Hebrew, *welo' yihyeh 'ason*); it is not a capital offense since the "child" (Hebrew, *yeled*) survived.

Some modern translations have presented verse 22 as a reference to a "miscarriage" (e.g., the Revised Standard Version, New American Bible, New Jerusalem Bible, New English Bible), but that would not be a fair translation since this text does not use the regular Hebrew word for "miscarriage." That noun does appear, usually as *meshakkelet, shakul, shikkel*, or its related forms, in Genesis 31:38; Exodus 23:26; 2 Kings 2:19, 21; Job 21:10; Hosea 9:14; and Malachi 3:11. Clearly there was no damage or harm done either to the mother or to the fetus/child.

The only compensation allowed, though, as sanctioned and approved by the judges, is the husband's request for a fine because of the scare that this premature birth has brought to that household.

II. What If the Premature Baby Dies as a Result of the Injury? (Exod. 21:23–25)

The alternative situation is also contemplated, in which real harm does come. Without spelling out to whom the "harm" or "serious injury" comes, whether to the baby or to the mother, the text makes a blanket rule that will cover both. In that case it is a capital offense and the *lex talionis*, the "law of retribution," takes over. This law, of course, was not meant for personal vendettas or for individuals, but it was a guide for the "judges" (Exod. 21:22; 23:8, 9) to administer.

The *lex talionis* was stated in terms of a stereotypical formula that in our day would go something like this: "like punishment for like crime" or "make the punishment fit the crime." But it was clear that if the baby or the mother died as a result of their injuries in this fight, it came under the range of laws that dealt with capital offenses. A real life of a real person had been lost!

Conclusions

God has offered a huge amount of respect and care for the embryo right from its very origins up to the day of death. None of our days before our birth, or after, are inconsequential to our God. On the contrary, he is concerned to see each person made in his image fulfill the purposes for which he or she was made.

That is why, as significant as embryonic stem cell research is, it must find other ways to accomplish the same ends, as it has found so far in adult stem cell research or in the use of umbilical cords from live births of babies. Life is too valuable to waste for any reason whatsoever.

Bibliography

Congdon, Robert N. "Exodus 21:22–25 and the Abortion Debate." *Bibliotheca Sacra* 146 (1989): 132–47.

Cottrell, Jack W. "Abortion and the Mosaic Law." *Christianity Today*, March 16, 1973, 602–5.

Feinberg, John S., and Paul D. Feinberg. *Ethics for a Brave New World*. Wheaton: Crossway, 1993.

Fowler, Paul B. *Abortion: Toward an Evangelical Consensus*. Portland: Multnomah, 1987.

Gorman, Michael J. *Abortion in the Early Church: Christian, Jewish, and Pagan Attitudes in the Greco-Roman World*. Downers Grove, IL: InterVarsity, 1982.

Hoffmeier, James K., ed. *Abortion: A Christian Understanding and Response*. Grand Rapids: Baker Academic, 1987.

Thomson, James A., et al. "Embryonic Stem Cell Lines Derived from Human Blastocysts." *Science* (November 6, 1998): 1145–47.

Tooley, Michael. *Abortion and Infanticide*. New York: Oxford University Press, 1983.

Discussion Questions

1. What is a young woman to do if she is the victim of a rape or incest from which she becomes pregnant?
2. What basis would you give from either Scripture or the Constitution of the United States for the "right of a mother over her own body" or "the right to privacy"?
3. If as a result of amniocentesis it is discovered that the pregnant woman you are counseling has a baby that is suffering from anencephaly (the fetus has no upper brain or skull) or from spina bifida (a condition in which the spinal cord is not covered by skin), what would you advise this Christian mother to do in light of the principles of Scripture reviewed in this chapter?

9

HOMOSEXUALITY

Romans 1:24–27

An Explosive Contemporary Issue

The most explosive contemporary ethical issue in our day is probably the subject of homosexuality. Both in Western society and in mainline denominational churches the tensions are at an all-time high. Thus, the Anglican Bishops meeting at the Lambeth (London) Conference in 1998, by a vote of 526 to 70, declared homosexuality to be incompatible with Scripture. This was followed by another document in the summer of 2002 entitled "Let the Reader Understand . . . ," at the request of the Bishop of New York, wherein nine theologians countered this Lambeth decision with thirteen principles of interpretation of Scripture, without ever once exegeting any of the biblical texts on the subject.

The Modern Gay Movement

The first person to use the word "homosexual" seems to have been a Swiss doctor named K. M. Benkert, who coined it in 1869. The

ancient world knew the practice of homosexuality, of course, but it
really became an item of modern interest and concern when on June
28, 1969, the police raided a gay bar in Stonewall, New York. The
customers, now outside, retaliated as the police barricaded themselves
inside the bar for protection. One other historical note is important,
for in 1974 the American Psychological Association was pressured
by the homosexual lobby to remove "homosexuality" from its list
of "pathological conditions," and no longer regard it as a deviant
perversion of normal sexual relations in its categories of psychological disorders.

Homosexuality, or as it is popularly known, the "gay rights movement," became publicly debated and promoted following 1969. Prior
to that date, in 1966, the British Council of Churches (BCC) Report
rocked the Christian world with these words: "We now realize that
homosexuality and other abnormalities are far commoner than used
to be thought." This certainly was a long way away from the time
of Edward Gibbon's (1734–94) epic work on *The Rise and Fall of
the Roman Empire* in which he, and a wide swath of society since
his time, regarded homosexuality as a sinister threat to the security
of society. Even much before Gibbon's time, a British act passed in
1290 called for a convicted sodomite to be buried alive, which law
Henry VIII relaxed by changing the mode of execution in 1533. Finally in 1861, life imprisonment was substituted for the death penalty
in this type of case. Even up to 1967, an Englishman convicted of
"buggery" could be sentenced to spend the rest of his life in jail.

Today, homosexuality and lesbianism have become a matter of
public policy and morality. Homosexuals march and lobby Congress
for equal rights to those heterosexuals enjoy. They want nothing less
than a total acceptance of the gay lifestyle, free of all harassment,
criticism, legal barriers, and condemnation. Even though they may
only represent 2 percent (or at most 5 percent) of the population according to some popular estimates, their agenda often controls the
actions and their complete acceptance by 98 percent of the people
in this democracy![1]

The Ten Key Teaching Passages against Homosexuality

Traditionally interpreters have found warnings against homosexuality in ten passages: Genesis 19:1–8; Leviticus 18:22; 20:13; Judges

19:16–30; Ezekiel 16:44–50; Romans 1:26–27; 1 Corinthians 6:9–11; 1 Timothy 1:8–10; 2 Peter 2:6–8; and Jude 6–8. Both Testaments are very straightforward in their condemnation of male and female homosexuality.

The foundation of all understanding of human sexuality is found in God's plan, laid out in Genesis 1 and 2. There God limited the sexes to just two genders: male and female, not three, four, or more. He taught that it was not good for a man to be alone (Gen. 2:18), so he "built" Eve as man's counterpart and partner.

The man was instructed to "leave" his father and mother and instead to "cleave" to his wife, so that they would become "one flesh" (Gen. 2:24). Five elements were to be the hallmarks of this understanding of marital love: fidelity, permanence, reconciliation, health and wholeness, and sacrifice.[2]

Fidelity is promised in the marriage vow of "forsaking all others," for the couple promises to limit their sexual behavior and love to each other. Homosexuals explicitly decry any attempt to limit gay sex to monogamy. In their magazine, *The Advocate*, a study done in 1995 of 2,500 gay readers of the magazine found that a mere 2 percent had only one male partner, while 57 percent had more than thirty partners, and 35 percent had more than one hundred partners. Moreover, a married couple promises before God and the assembled church that their marriage will be *permanent*—"until death do us part."

Reconciliation is likewise a huge part of marriage, for after the days of the honeymoon we humbly enter into the mystery of having a person of the opposite gender working with us for our mutual benefit. Opposites attract, but they also find their completion in one another. For homosexuals there is no moral significance in the male/female distinction. Our biological differences mean very little if anything to homosexuals.

Heterosexual marriage also gives *health* and *wholeness* to our partner as we do not expose each other to health risks that are otherwise most prevalent among those living a gay lifestyle. Homosexual partners expose each other to serious health hazards, for as Peter Moore carefully instructed, "The lining of the rectum is not tough and capable of penetration like the lining of the vagina." Leaving AIDS out of the discussion for the moment, Moore called our attention to the fact that "75% of homosexual men have a history of one or more sexually transmitted disease[s], and in any given year 40% of them are sick. Despite the great talk of 'safe sex' the use of condoms is not totally safe."[3]

Finally, true marital love is *sacrificial*, for couples willingly take on the long-term goal of rearing children as a normal expectation of marriage. Procreation is not the only reason for sex, nor is it always possible in each marriage for a number of reasons, but sex was not normally meant to be separated from procreation or from the sacrifices that it demands in terms of time, money, sometimes careers, health, and a number of could-have-beens in an otherwise selfish world. Judaism and Christianity brought erotic love, marriage, and procreation together. Homosexuals do not see sex as being sacrificial in any shape or form; instead, it is self-satisfying and self-centered.

The Challenge to Genesis 19:1–4. The book that opened the way for a new interpretation of Scripture was Derrick Sherwin Bailey's 1955 work entitled *Homosexuality and the Western Christian Tradition.*[4] Bailey challenged the statement in Genesis 19:5 where the men of Sodom wanted to get to "know" ("have sex with them," NIV) the strangers (angels) who had come to Lot's residence in Sodom. Bailey claimed that there was no reference to homosexuality in the Hebrew word *yada'*, "to know," for the men of that city merely wanted "to become acquainted with" these strangers, not "to have intercourse with" them. Bailey's case, however, does not stand up to the comment on this same incident in Jude 7, nor is he correct in the meaning of the word *yada'* in this type of context.

The Challenge to Judges 19. Bailey handled the Gibeah story in Judges 19 in the same manner. But if in this case it was only a matter of hospitality, why did the owner of the house in that city beg his countrymen not to act in such a "vile" (Judg. 19:23) way and then amazingly offer his daughter instead to satisfy their demands?

The Challenge to Leviticus 18:22 and 20:13. Others try to dismiss the two texts in Leviticus 18:22 and 20:13 by saying that they are part of the Holiness Code, which applies to priests and their ritual purity. Their challenge is that if one is going to demand adherence to these texts on sex, then what about the other demands in the same context that warn against sowing two different kinds of seed together (Lev. 19:19c), wearing clothes with mixed fabrics (Lev. 19:19d), and having marital relations during a wife's menstrual cycle (Lev. 18:19).

But the common principle behind these laws was a concern for what was "natural," that is, for maintaining the orders of creation "after their kind." There also was a moral aspect, for when seeds were mixed the result would be a type of hybridization, which would severely limit the potential for seed from that crop to germinate as strongly as it had the year the crop came in. In like manner, the menstrual cycle symbolically showed that only God, not the husband, had sovereignty over the woman. Accordingly, these texts in Leviticus do not address the priesthood and ritual provisions exclusively. It is just impossible to argue that sex with animals (Lev. 18:23) or illicit sex with one's daughter (18:17) were morally irrelevant for the general public. In fact, what Leviticus 18 was doing was setting the practices of the ungodly nations like Egypt and Canaan in contrast to the moral behavior expected of God's people.

The Challenge to the Pauline Opposition to Homosexuality. Again, opponents to the biblical standard on human sexuality have incorrectly explained that the three New Testament texts (Rom. 1:26–27; 1 Cor. 6:9–11; 1 Tim. 1:8–10) are only calling for temperance and moderation and not for opposition to homosexuality. Paul's list of sins in the Corinthians and Timothy passages warned that "male prostitutes" (Greek, *malakoi,* literally, "soft to touch") and "homosexual offenders" (Greek, *arsenokoitai,* literally, "males in bed") will not inherit the kingdom of God.

Exchanging Natural Relations for Unnatural Ones

But let us look at Paul's words in Romans 1:24–27 for a passage that could well summarize the teaching on homosexuality in the Bible.

Text: Romans 1:24–27
Title: "Exchanging Natural Relations for Unnatural Ones"
Focal Point: verse 26, "[They] exchanged natural relations for unnatural ones."
Homiletical Keyword: Exchanges
Interrogative: What exchanges did mortals make for the truth of God?

Outline:
I. An exchange of sexual purity for impurity (1:24)

II. An exchange of the truth of God for a lie (1:25)
III. An exchange of natural relations for unnatural ones: females (1:26)
IV. An exchange of natural relations for unnatural ones: males (1:27)

I. An Exchange of Sexual Purity for Impurity (Rom. 1:24)

Few New Testament texts, if any, have suffered more open assaults on their teaching than Romans 1:24–27. Central to all the discussion is the meaning of the Greek word *physis* in verses 26–27. Rather than rendering this word as "natural relations," John Boswell, Letha Scanzoni, and Virginia Mollenkott, along with many others, render the term "natural" as in "what is natural for me."[5] In their view, Paul is not condemning homosexuality; rather, he is chastising heterosexuals who are acting as homosexuals ("perverts") in a context of idolatry and lust. Paul does not condemn true homosexuals, who are born as "inverts," for doing what is in their nature, they claim. That is the background against which this whole text needs to be understood in the modern challenge that is coming to the way the Bible is usually interpreted.

The apostasy of the Gentile persons in verses 21–23, which began in the religious and theological areas, culminates in gross idolatry at the end of verse 23. It is because of this religious disaffection that the divine retribution must come on those apostatizing. God's retribution is operative only because there is sin that must be judged.

The retribution that God brings is the giving up (vv. 26, 27) of these same persons to uncleanness. Interestingly enough, sin in the religious realm is punished in the moral sphere. Accordingly, the phrase "in the sinful desires of their hearts" (v. 24) describes the moral condition in which they now found themselves. Thus, while they were given up to "uncleanness," that uncleanness did not come from God's judicial act, but from themselves. In other Pauline passages, the term "uncleanness" is shown to be connected with sexual aberrations (2 Cor. 12:21; Gal. 5:19; Eph. 5:3; Col. 3:5; 1 Thess. 4:7).

These Gentiles were given over, then, to an existing moral condition. Therefore, they "degrade[d] . . . their bodies with one another" (v. 24b). As John Murray summarized the situation:

God's displeasure is expressed in his abandonment of the persons concerned to more intensified and aggravated cultivation of the lusts of their own hearts with the result that they reap for themselves a correspondingly greater toll of retributive vengeance.[6]

II. An Exchange of the Truth of God for a Lie (Rom. 1:25)

The truth of God in this context refers to what God has taught and who God is in the awesomeness of his being and glory. God has made himself and his truth known through his word and in the revelation of himself. Lo and behold, this got inverted, as well as the fact that men and women worshiped and served the creature rather than the Creator who had brought all these created things into being.

The exchange was a silly one, for it took the result of God's work as being greater and worthy of more attention, love, worship, and service than the Maker of it all. In our day, some feel more affinity for saving the whales than they do for saving human babies, or for giving thanks to God for making the whales.

Verse 25 closes with a doxology that comes from a spontaneous outburst for who God is and what he has done. Paul adds his "Amen" to this doxology, for the dullness of mortals and the way they typically get it all wrong is mind-boggling.

III. An Exchange of Natural Relations for Unnatural Ones: Females (Rom. 1:26)

Another reason why God has given Gentiles over to this judicial indictment is because of more "shameful lusts." Now Paul will finally just say what these disgraceful passions are. They are women changing their natural use of their sexuality into what is against nature: women having sexual relations with other women.

It is apparent that what he has in mind here are lesbian forms of sexual perversion. Women, instead of demonstrating their delicate nature, now indulge in homosexual degeneracy. Because it concerns women, Paul will not go into any details as he will in the next verse with the men. But clearly the women have "abandoned natural relations for unnatural ones." Natural use of a woman's sex functions would be to employ their use in a marital state with a man. But the emphasis here, sadly, falls on the "unnatural" character of this vice. Sex as God intended it is now desecrated into lesbian forms of sexual relations with another woman. It is unnatural and must therefore be noted as a form of perversion against what God created sex to be.

IV. An Exchange of Natural Relations for Unnatural Ones: Males (Rom. 1:27)

Now in verse 27, male homosexual vice is described in even more detail. Three expressions are especially critical: (1) "men also abandoned natural relations with women," (2) they were "inflamed with lust for one another," and (3) "men committed indecent acts with other men." All of this was counter to the honorableness of heterosexual unions grounded in the natural order of things established by God.

The key offense in the homosexual act is that it is a direct affront to God as it abandons his divinely appointed design and function for human sexuality. When one abandons God and his instructions, it is clear that one has decided to take God on as an opponent and to challenge his law and his ways as being useless and meaningless. But he who sits in the heavens will hardly take such an affront easily. It will call forth his judicial decree of judgment and punishment.

The intensity of the sexual passion is further captured in the word "inflamed." This is not the same kind of "burning" Paul mentioned in 1 Corinthians 7:9, where the normal sexual desires are seeking the God-intended outlet. This inflammation is a desire that has been perverted and distorted beyond what God had intended for sex. It is a lust that is illegitimate and altogether unnatural.

To put the matter bluntly, Paul finally says that what is wrong here is that "men committed indecent acts with other men." The whole matter is a "shameful thing" (cf. Eph. 5:12), and it is disgusting to even have to talk about it in polite company. Instead of mortals acting like those who have dignity, worth, and value, as creatures made in the altogether unique image of God, they act instead like animals that have no boundaries or morals in this area of their sexuality.

Now as this short passage concludes, it looks back over verses 24–26 and seeks an overview of what this abandonment has brought in the wake of the community's apostasy. It adds this new thought: they have "received in themselves the due penalty for their perversion." Therefore there is a close correspondence between the sin and the

penalty. Leaving the worship of the one and only true God led to these
unnatural vices that distorted normal sexual relations to unnatural and
indecent acts between persons of the same sex. The moral morass of
their new abandonments has raised debauchery to almost unheard-of
levels in society and among persons of the same sex. A blindness has
occurred right at the noonday of God's revelation.

The judgment of 1 Corinthians 6:9–10 is no less severe, for apart from
full repentance and a change from the gay lifestyle, Paul warns,

> Do you not know that the wicked will not inherit the kingdom of God?
> Do not be deceived: Neither the sexually immoral nor idolaters nor
> adulterers nor male prostitutes nor homosexual offenders nor thieves
> nor the greedy nor drunkards nor slanderers nor swindlers will inherit
> the kingdom of God.

Mercifully, Paul adds in verse 11, "And this is what some of you were."
Thanks be to God for his cleansing and forgiveness and the healing
of his death on the cross for all of these rebellions against him for
those who will believe.

Conclusions

1. Even if some of the immediate origins of homosexual attraction
   remain unclear, ultimately these attractions must relate to our
   fallenness and rebellion against God.
2. The New Testament speaks of many who once were participants
   in homosexual practices but who are now identified as those
   who no longer practice homosexuality.
3. Many today assume that science has identified a biological/
   genetic causative factor that makes the homosexual state beyond the control of the person, but this evidence has not been
   found. So far patterns within families and brain differences
   seem to play some part, but at most, even if fully identified,
   they would merely be *contributing causes* rather than the real
   or final causes.
4. The power of the gospel is greater than any inflamed passion
   for another person of the same sex. If the gospel cannot work
   in this area, how can it be trusted to work in our resurrection
   in the final day?

Bibliography

DeYoung, James B. *Homosexuality: Contemporary Claims Examined in Light of the Bible and Other Ancient Literature and Law*. Grand Rapids: Kregel, 2000.

Gagnon, Robert A. *The Bible and Homosexual Practice: Texts and Hermeneutics*. Nashville: Abingdon, 2001.

Grenz, Stanley J. *Sexual Ethics: A Biblical Perspective*. Dallas: Word, 1990.

Jones, Stanton L., and Mark A. Yarhouse. *Homosexuality: The Use of Scientific Research in the Church's Moral Debate*. Downers Grove, IL: InterVarsity, 2000.

Lovelace, Richard F. *Homosexuality: What Should Christians Do About It?* Old Tappan, NJ: Revell, 1984.

Webb, William J. *Slaves, Women & Homosexuals: Exploring the Hermeneutics of Cultural Analysis*. Downers Grove, IL: Inter-Varsity, 2001.

Discussion Questions

1. Is there a danger in substituting lifeless rules, codes, laws, and morals for dynamic, updated ways in which God can be speaking anew to our day vis-à-vis a former day?
2. Is it possible that God has changed his mind since he originally gave the teaching in the Old and New Testaments on homosexuality? Does God ever change his mind?
3. Does our experience shape the way we understand Scripture? If it does, then can not our experiences be self-authenticating and stand outside the hand or judgment of Scripture?
4. If there are things that once were forbidden in the Bible but are now permitted, then part of God's law has only a temporary purpose, such as the civil or ceremonial parts. Can the regulations against homosexuality be treated like some of those laws?

10

CRIME AND CAPITAL PUNISHMENT

Genesis 9:5–6; John 8:1–11

Crime Defined

"Crime occurs when an act is committed, or omitted, in violation of public law deemed necessary for the protection and general welfare of persons governed by such law."[1] Accordingly, such antisocial acts as rape, treason, murder, or burglary each require punishments set by society. The desire is not for revenge primarily but to obtain justice for as many persons as possible. The hope is to ameliorate these acts of injustice as much as possible in this life through the courts established by human governments.

The Cost of Crime

In 1994 crime in America could almost be counted with the ticking of the clock: one murder every twenty-two seconds, one rape every five minutes, one robbery every forty-nine seconds, with a cost that is almost too staggering to comprehend. Americans put out an amazing $674 billion each year for the costs of crime, including $78 billion for the criminal justice system, $64 billion for private protection, $202 billion in loss of life and work, $120 billion in crimes aimed at businesses, $60 billion in stolen goods, $40 billion from drug abuse, and $110 billion from drunk driving.[2]

The general public and Christians today have learned to live with crime and to lock up doors, windows, and cars, and to install alarms on houses, cars, and everything else, while also often living in gated communities. Despite reports every once in a while that the crime rate is declining, the fact is that since 1960 the crime rate nationally has steadily risen some 300 percent with the largest increase coming in the category of violent crimes, some 550 percent. To our shame, the United States has the worst violent crime rate of any other industrialized country.[3]

The Reasons for the Increase in Crime

Much of the blame for the increase in the crime rate is to be found in these facts: (1) the median age of criminals is getting younger and younger each year, (2) the use of drugs among early teens increases the potential for crime, and (3) the introduction of the gun culture (not to mention the proliferation of automatic weapons) has brought with it wars between gangs over turfs and drugs.

Some would want to view crime as an irrational act. This may be true of some crimes of passion or of drug-related crimes, but most crimes are calculated decisions often based on the probability of being arrested as weighed against the possible profit that could come from the crime. Some alarming statistics say that three out of four convicted criminals are not incarcerated and that only one in ten serious crimes results in imprisonment.[4] In another study carried out by Morgan Reynolds of Texas A&M University, 98 percent of all burglaries never result in a jail sentence, only 2 percent serve time, and the average time served is only thirteen months![5]

Add to all of these statistics the fact that currently the recidivism rate (repeated relapse into crime) in the United States is 70 to 80 percent, and the task becomes enormous for society and the church. However, in the few instances where programs such as ones sponsored by Chuck Colson's Prison Fellowship are operating, the rate of recidivism drops into the single digits! Here is a most worthy place for the church to show the power of the gospel and how it can impact and change society by the power of Christ and his word.[6]

Along with such programs of criminal reform and rehabilitation is the task of crime prevention, especially among the youngest element of society—often the ones who are facing hopelessness and extreme poverty, or teens who are looking to gang leaders for strong male role models, which are frequently absent in their fatherless homes. Where the number of illegitimate births is increasing, where single moms are pressed beyond economic reasonableness to keep the family together by working long hours while still trying to guide the family—this is exactly where the programs of the church must be aimed if any impact is to be made on the issue of crime prevention.

The Bible calls for both justice and compassion to be carried out for both the victim and the perpetrator of the crime. While the gospel stresses that there is always forgiveness that is available for all sin and crime, that does not do away with the fact that evil carries with it civil consequences that must also be dealt with.

Incarceration is costly—according to the last figures I have, about $25,000 per year per prisoner. Yet it is even more costly to turn the offender loose, for according to some estimates the costs zoom up to seventeen times more than incarceration.[7]

Capital Punishment and First-Degree Murder

Even though the Old Testament records a number of instances in which God commanded the use of capital punishment, all but one of the sixteen to twenty of those Old Testament examples could be commuted by a "ransom." But, as Numbers 35:31 taught, this was not true in the case of a premeditated murder, where the perpetrator deliberately thought a plan out in advance and was "lying in wait" (KJV terminology) for the victim. Many Jewish and conservative interpreters note the extraordinary wording of Numbers 35:31, which states: "Do not accept a ransom [or 'substitute'] for the life of a murderer, who deserves to die. He must surely be put to death."

Out of the twenty crimes that demanded a capital punishment, only in the case of the murderer was no substitution or alternative ransom to be offered or accepted; that person who snuffed out the life of another person made in the image of God was to be offered back to God by the governing authorities. Otherwise the guilt for failing to do so was accepted by all of the surrounding society and the blood, as it were, of the victim got tracked into the house of God and into the halls of the government of the city that refused to give back to God the life of the perpetrator of that offense. The community that was reluctant to carry out God's mandate for the death penalty in the case of premeditated murder now had to bear that penalty itself.

However, even though the designation of a capital offense indicated the seriousness of the crime (such as in the case of a kidnapping), all capital offenses except first-degree murder could be ransomed (the Hebrew root of the word "ransom" means "to deliver or to ransom by a substitute"), and the substitute could atone for the guilty act perpetrated, if it were accepted by society and the judges.

It is not uncommon to hear in the Christian church that capital punishment does not apply to us today, for Jesus did away with the death penalty in the Sermon on the Mount (Matt. 5:43–48). But a careful study of the Sermon on the Mount will reveal that Jesus was warning against the desire for *personal vengeance*; he was not limiting the power or the responsibility of government, which he made explicit in Romans 13:1–7.

Others complain that the government is involved in murder when it carries out the death penalty, for the sixth commandment strictly forbids what the state does when it sentences a person to death for committing a murder: "You shall not murder" (Exod. 20:13). As a matter of fact, Hebrew possesses seven words for "to kill." The word used in the sixth commandment, *ratsah*, occurs only forty-seven times in the Old Testament, with the weight of evidence limiting it to premeditated murder or, in some instances, to the avenger of the blood of some guilty of manslaughter.[8] This word (*ratsah*) was never used for killing an enemy in battle or for killing an animal for sacrifice. The government, then, is within its divinely authorized rights when it demands the death penalty in cases in which it is proven beyond a reasonable doubt that the murder was committed by premeditation. Exodus 21:12–36 demanded that the government was to punish such murderers as the presence of the "sword" in Romans 13:4 implied as well.

But it is time that we turn to the Scriptures to examine a teaching passage in connection with the use of capital punishment in the case of first-degree murder.

Murder Victims Are Not Junk

Text: Genesis 9:5–6

Title: "Murder Victims Are Not Junk"

Focal Point: verse 6, "For in the image of God has God made man."

Homiletical Keyword: Demands

Interrogative: What are the demands God makes on society when someone is murdered with malice and forethought?

Outline:
  I. God demands an accounting from society (9:5)
  II. God demands the guilty to be punished (9:6a)
  III. God demands that the value of life match his gift of the image of God (9:6b)

A growing abhorrence for capital punishment has occurred over the last few decades. As long ago as 1764, however, Cesare Beccaria, who had a great impact on penal reform, wrote, "Is it not absurd, that the laws, which detest and punish homicide, should, in order to prevent murder, publicly commit murder themselves?"[9] But this objection fails to notice that the same Bible that ordered capital punishment ordered government to carry it out, as noted above.

I. God Demands an Accounting from Society (Gen. 9:5)

The simplicity of this divine mandate must be noticed, for God hereby turns over to mortals what he had reserved to himself. This was a mandate for men to punish their fellow men for the crime of (first-degree) murder. This mandate, of course, was not initially motivated by the Mosaic law, for it had preceded it in time by many centuries. Moreover, if one wishes to transfer verse 6 to the Mosaic law, then he must be prepared to transfer verses 4 and 5 as well, which deal with the matter of eating meat instead of a strictly vegetarian diet.

This mandate is objected to by some who point to God's prior treatment of Cain after he murdered his brother. Did not God give to Cain, as it were, a second chance, without demanding that he die for his heinous act? Genesis 4:13–16 reads:

Cain said to the LORD, "My punishment is greater than I can bear. Today you are driving me from the land, and I will be hidden from your presence; I will be a restless wanderer on the earth, and whoever finds me will kill me." But the LORD said to him, "Not so; if anyone kills Cain, he will suffer vengeance seven times over." Then the LORD put a mark on Cain so that no one who found him would kill him. So Cain went out from the LORD's presence and lived in the land of Nod, east of Eden.

Of whom was Cain afraid? It was God! Why? Because he feared God would execute the death penalty against him, or that other men would do the same if they found him. But why, then, in apparent contradiction to other later Scripture, is it that a God who does not change moves to protect Cain from being killed?

God's purpose, however, was not to protect Cain, for his protection was only a by-product of his more overarching purpose, which was to protect the family. God would have had to call the family to act in the roles of witnesses against a family member, then to serve as judges, as well as a jury to condemn Cain, and finally to serve as executioners of a family member. Every one of these moves would be destructive of the family law order God was eager to preserve. Therefore, it was not Cain that God wanted to protect, but his own family law order.[10] Since there were no others to serve in these roles as yet, God did not want the family to destroy, or turn on, itself in these roles.

However, that situation changes after Noah's flood. God will now expect mortals to give an accounting for the life violently ended by any of their fellow humans. This is not an accounting that is to be rendered to the victim's family to help their grieving, or to society in general in order to do things such as retard the growth of murder, but it is an accounting that is made directly to God. That is what makes this mandate so unusual and of such importance.

II. God Demands the Guilty to Be Punished (Gen. 9:6a)

The necessity of capital punishment is summarized in the Hebrew verb *yishapak*, "it shall be shed." Is this merely a suggestion, "It may be shed," or is it a command, "It must be shed"? Is this a descriptive word or a prescriptive command? Since verse 5 said that God "will demand an accounting for the life of [one's] fellow man," this cannot be a suggestion, with mere permission attached to it. It is an order from on high.

The one requiring this action is God himself, but the ones who carry it out must be other mortals: "Whoever sheds the blood of man, by man shall his blood be shed." The task would be difficult, but the order was the most divine executive order ever given to mortals about a most serious infraction against another mortal.

III. God Demands That the Value of Life Match His Gift of the Image of God (Gen. 9:6b)

The reason for such an extraordinary mandate from God is immediately attached to this legislation: "[Because] in the image of God has God made man" (v. 6b). The meaning does not point just to the perpetrator as being made in the image of God, so that he or she should not be put to death; rather, the victim was the one made in the image of God and of inestimable value and significance. People made in God's image are not just trash or junk.

In giving this causal reason, the value of mortals was raised above that of the animal world or all other forms of life. Murder, then, amounted to the shooting, mugging, or slaughtering of God himself in effigy. Murder is so serious because it is a crime against the majesty of the divine image in each individual. No matter how disgraced or debauched a person may appear, they are not to be equated with disposable litter or seen simply as disheveled wretches of humanity; they are still made in the image of God and carry enormous intrinsic potential and importance.

Therefore, mortals must represent their Maker in the exercise of authority and in the administration of justice. When citizens fail to carry out this mandate of God, they bring on their own heads and communities the judgment that should have fallen on the head of the murderer.

Conclusions

The state, then, is mandated by God to punish the murderer. This does not contradict or deny the teaching that God gave his Son to die for the sins of the world, including those of the murderer (John 12:47). In his theological forgiveness, our Lord vicariously bears the debt and thus offers forgiveness to all. But to be forgiven is not also to obviate the civic consequences that flowed from the act of snatching away someone else's life prematurely. Therefore, a murderer may subsequently truly repent and receive God's forgiveness, but so drastic was this crime that the effects are permanent in the life of the victim. To keep life from becoming cheaper each day from one murder to the next, these premeditated murders must be requited according to the mandate of God as announced long before the law was given to Moses.

Some will claim that "progressive revelation" takes away the necessity of insisting on this ancient address to the problem of first-degree murder. If the legal requirements of the civil and ceremonial law have been abolished, then why, according to the same reasoning, has not this injunction that came way ahead of the law also been abolished? Furthermore, do we not have in the New Testament the demand for mercy and forgiveness that would supersede any Old Testament requirement for justice? Didn't the death of Christ pay for all our sins making any further expiation altogether pointless and an evidence of a lack of faith?

To be sure, "progressive revelation" is the gradual unfolding of the truth of God over the history of divine disclosure. Thus, God proportioned and measured out his revelation in the eras of his making things known to us. All of that is true, but it is also true that a principle must be found in the text that shows that what God had originally said is now superseded in the progress of revelation. Alas, none can be found. Nor is this command merely attached either to the theocracy, which comes later, or to the Mosaic law, which also comes later. Add to this the fact that the New Testament gave to human government the power of capital punishment in Romans 13:4 and that the apostle Paul recognized that there were crimes worthy of death. Paul, in his defense before Festus said, "If I have committed a crime or done anything deserving death, I do not seek to escape the death penalty" (Acts 25:11 NAB). This too was a recognition of the biblical teaching on capital punishment.

A Special Case of the Woman Caught in Adultery

Frequently John 8:1–11, though not dealing with a case of murder, is cited widely as a case where Jesus set the Mosaic law aside.[11] The scribes and the Pharisees came to Jesus saying they had caught a certain woman "in the act of adultery."[12] How they knew where to get a woman of this type of trade at the "dawn" of the day (8:2) is an interesting question. Nevertheless, it was an extremely clever trap they set for Jesus, from their point of view, for he had to either go against the law (and not enforce the sanction of the law, a form of antinomianism) or call for stoning the woman, which apparently was not being practiced in that day, thus making Jesus unpopular with the masses. It was a win-win situation for these teachers of the law and Pharisees.

It is most important to notice where Jesus was when they accosted him: he was in the temple (v. 2). The woman's accusers declared to Jesus, "Teacher, this woman was caught in the act of adultery" (v. 3). They went on, "In the Law Moses commanded us to stone such a woman. Now what do you say?" (v. 5). John's Gospel says in verse 6, "They were using this question as a trap, in order to have a basis for accusing [Jesus]."

Amazingly, our Lord did not give an immediate rejoinder, but, instead, he bent down in the temple precinct and started to write with his finger on the ground. There are numerous people who seem to know exactly what it was that Jesus wrote (most of whom differ from each other), but the text never once hints what Jesus might have written. As they continued to pummel him with questions, he straightened up and merely said, "If any one of you is without sin, let him be the first to throw a stone at her" (v. 7b). Again, he resumed his writing on the ground.

Slowly, but surely, the accusers began to slip away, the older ones first, until only Jesus and the woman were left. Why this sudden faintheartedness, especially when they had worked so hard and so decisively to trap Jesus? Was it what Jesus said, what he wrote, or what he signaled by his writing in the earth of the temple, that made them all decide suddenly that they had a more important engagement at that very moment than to stick around and see justice done toward this woman? Suddenly religious zeal languished. But why so sudden and why at that precise moment?

The fact that Jesus stooped down in the temple and wrote on the ground must have triggered in their minds and hearts the passage with the only ordeal in the Old Testament. In Numbers 5:16–24, a husband who suspected his wife of adultery would bring her to the tabernacle before the Lord. The priest would take an earthen vessel filled with holy water and add some dust from the floor of the tabernacle. (Was this what Jesus was reenacting here once again?) Then with the water in his hand, he would charge the woman with an oath and ask her to drink the bitter water as an ordeal. If she were guilty, her body would swell; if she were innocent, nothing happened. The point seemed to be that the guilty party would swell by the psychosomatic impact that guilt would have on their body. According to traditional belief, this test could also be required of the husband if a woman suspected her husband of being guilty of the same crime he accused his wife of committing.

In this scenario, the teachers of the law and the Pharisees were acting in the place of the jealous husband. Apparently, when they saw Jesus stooping down and continuing to write or scratch in the dirt of the temple, their trained minds reverted back to Numbers 5, and they decided they had better get out of there before things became too hot for them.

Jesus did ask, "Woman, where are they? Has no one condemned you?"

She responded, "No one, sir."

"Then neither do I condemn you," Jesus declared. "Go now and leave your life of sin" (vv. 10–11).

Jesus recognized that this woman had sinned. That is why she was to go and sin no more. The point was that the *legal* case against her had collapsed when the accusers decided suddenly to abandon the cause they had constructed so carefully for trapping Jesus. It seems they themselves could not have passed the test, so it was better to let the thing drop and look for another occasion when they could form a different plot against Jesus.

Jesus offered the woman religious forgiveness, but there was no civil or juridical forgiveness possible since the legal case against her collapsed. Should her husband have gotten wind of this and returned with the forgiven wife and some witnesses, the legal case could still have been engaged, even though she was spiritually forgiven. However, it also seems that Jesus refused to be made a judge in legal matters, as in another case where there was a contested estate in Luke 12:13–14. Civil condemnation is for crimes done against the civil law. Civil forgiveness can only occur when a condemned person pays the penalty for his or her crime.

But one must not conclude from this story, assuming it is authentic in the stories of Jesus (as I do), that Jesus relaxed the law in favor of mercy or kindness. That would be a misuse of this narrative.

Bibliography

Bailey, Lloyd R. *Capital Punishment: What the Bible Says.* Nashville: Abingdon, 1987.

Baker, William H. *On Capital Punishment.* Chicago: Moody, 1985.

Davis, John Jefferson. *Evangelical Ethics: Issues Facing the Church Today.* Phillipsburg, NJ: Presbyterian and Reformed, 1985, especially pp. 193–207.

Geisler, Norman L. *Christian Ethics: Options and Issues.* Grand Rapids: Baker Academic, 1989, especially pp. 193–213.

Henry, Carl F. H. "Does Genesis 9 Justify Capital Punishment? Yes." In *The Genesis Debate*, edited by Ronald F. Youngblood, 230–50. Grand Rapids: Baker Academic, 1990.

House, H. Wayne, and John Howard Yoder. *The Death Penalty Debate.* Dallas: Word, 1991.

Lewis, Clive Staples. "The Humanitarian Theory of Punishment," in *God in the Dock*, 287–94. Grand Rapids: Eerdmans, 1970.

———. "On Punishment: A Reply to Criticism." In *God in the Dock*, 295–300. Grand Rapids: Eerdmans, 1970.

Murray, John. *Principles of Conduct.* Grand Rapids: Eerdmans, 1957, especially pp. 107–22.

Reid, Malcolm A. "Does Genesis 9 Justify Capital Punishment? No." In *The Genesis Debate*, edited by Ronald F. Youngblood, 230–50. Grand Rapids: Baker Academic, 1990.

Van Ness, Daniel. *Crime and Its Victims.* Downers Grove, IL: InterVarsity, 1986.

Discussion Questions

1. What responsibility does the church have in assisting programs of crime prevention that reach beyond the bounds of its immediate membership?
2. How can the church be more actively engaged in seeing the numbers for crime recidivism reduced? How can believers show concern and compassion for those who are incarcerated?

3. Does the story of the woman taken in adultery show that the Old Testament law has been replaced by mercy and forgiveness?
4. Within the whole debate about capital punishment, how significant is the argument from the image of God in humanity?

11

SUICIDE, INFANTICIDE, AND EUTHANASIA

Job 14:1–6

The ethics of life and dying have been pushed to the forefront in recent years by a number of media-promulgated cases. But even more vexing for laypersons, pastors, and physicians is the issue of when "to pull the plug," or what is a proper definition of "death" and when does it occur. Advances in technology have made some of these questions increasingly difficult to answer.

Definitions

Suicide was a word coined by Walter Charleton in 1651. His claim was that "to vindicate one's self from extreme and otherwise inevitable calamity by *sui-cide* [his hyphenation], is not a crime." This hyphenated word is not one Latin word; rather, it links two Latin words: *sui*, which is "self," and *cide*, "to kill."

Earlier, John Donne, in his infamous *Biathanatos*[1] (a garbling of the Greek "to die violently") had proposed "self-homicide" as a milder and more neutral term, but Charleton's "suicide" carried the day. In German, *Selbstmord*, "self murder," is the usual term, but *Suizid*, "suicide," is the more technical and clinically preferred term. However, suicide is no longer the antiseptically neutral term Charleton meant it to be. Taking one's own life is a violation of the sixth commandment given by God.

Suicide, in fact, involves the intentional taking of one's own life as an ultimate end in and of itself, or as a means to another end, such as putting a final stop to enormous pain, either through acting (such as by taking a pill) or refraining from acting (such as refusing to eat). There are cases, however, where one does intentionally take one's own life, but only in order to avoid a greater tragedy. For example, if a truck driver spots at the last minute children playing on a bridge who will certainly be killed unless he takes defensive action, and then purposefully drives off the cliff to avoid hitting the children, his death indeed was intentional, but it does not seem fair to put it in the same category as committing suicide. Such an action, in this case, would seem to be more of a sacrifice in order that the children might live.

The term *euthanasia*, like suicide, is also made up of two parts: in this case, the Greek prefix *eu*, meaning "good" or "easy," and *thanatos*, meaning "death." However, from a Christian standpoint, what is promoted under this term is neither "good" nor "easy."

The History of the Discussion on Euthanasia, Infanticide, and Suicide

These debates over euthanasia, infanticide, and suicide are not of recent vintage. The Greeks, for instance, carried on an ongoing debate over these topics. For example, the Pythagoreans opposed euthanasia, but the Stoics urged its use, especially in cases of incurable diseases. It was not uncommon for unwanted or deformed children in ancient Greece to be abandoned; in fact, in the case of the city-state of Sparta, it was required by law that they be abandoned, or worse.

In Plato's *Republic*, the philosopher recommended that, in the ideal state, children with defective limbs should be buried in some obscure place. Likewise, Aristotle wanted "nothing imperfect or maimed" to be brought up in the ideal state. Moreover, the state should regulate the number of children each married couple could have. Similar regulations were enacted in Rome, which legislated that any children beyond the permitted number were to be aborted. Rome's Twelve Tablets forbade anyone to rear deformed children. Even in pre-industrial Japan, infanticide was rather common and was referred to as *mabiki*, which means "thinning," as one would do with rice seedlings in the rice paddies.[2] In a related destruction of life in India, a Hindu custom called *suttee* requires that a widow submit to cremation on the funeral pyre of her husband.

In orthodox Judaism, on the other hand, is what is called *Kiddush Ha-shem*, "Sanctification of the Name," based on Leviticus 22:31–32. A Jewish person was to do everything in his or her power, including taking his or her own life, to glorify the name of God. Accordingly, 960 men, women, and children took their lives at Masada to prevent the Romans from taking them alive in AD 70. Again, in the *Talmud*, *Gittin* 57b, four hundred boys and girls were carried off for "immoral purposes" by the enemy, but to avoid the planned immorality by these pagans, the children threw themselves into the sea and drowned.

St. Augustine taught that suicide was worse than murder, for it too violated the sixth commandment. His syllogism was: You shall not kill a person; I am a person; therefore, I must not kill myself. Likewise Thomas Aquinas (1225–74) taught a triple indictment on those who took their lives: It was a failure of one's duty to one's self; it was a failure of one's duty to the community; and it was a failure of one's duty to God.

Christian principles on the value of mortals made in the image of God did much to stop the spread of these ideas of self-destruction. Also the Hippocratic Oath played its part as physicians regularly used to pledge: "I will neither give a deadly drug to anyone if asked for it, nor will I make a suggestion to that effect."

Nevertheless, by 1935 the Euthanasia Society of England began to promote the idea of a "good death" for patients facing incurable diseases. A similar society appeared in America a few years later. Derek Humphry was especially active in forming the "Hemlock Society" to promote euthanasia in the US, as explained in his best-selling book

Final Exit: The Practicalities of Self-Deliverance and Assisted Suicide for the Dying. In 1975 he assisted his wife's death, as detailed in *Let Me Die Before I Wake*.

Another person in the US who has exercised an enormous amount of influence and assisted a fairly large number of people with his patented suicide machine (called "The Mercitron") is Dr. Jack Kevorkian. His book is called *Prescription-Medicine: The Goodness of Planned Death*. The doctor would meet people for dinner, and then they would drive to his Volkswagen van where his machine awaited them for their final end. Kevorkian, who is now out of jail, ran for elected office in the state of Michigan in 2008. His method of helping people commit suicide is well-documented. He would place an intravenous tube into the patient's arm into which he dripped a saline solution until the patient pushed a button that sent a drug into their system causing unconsciousness, followed by a lethal drug that killed them.

On June 26, 1997, the Supreme Court of the United States of America voted against euthanasia and struck down laws in those states that held that physician-assisted suicide was constitutional.

There are six cases of suicide in the Bible. The first was by Abimelech, the son of Gideon, who called for his armor-bearer to run him through with his sword so that people would not say he had been killed by a woman, who had just dropped an upper millstone on his head and cracked his skull (Judg. 9:50–56). His armor-bearer obeyed Abimelech's command, and so he died.

The second instance is of King Saul, who was wounded in battle with the Philistines. He too ordered his armor-bearer to put him out of his misery, but when the armor-bearer refused to do so, Saul fell on his own sword and took his own life (1 Sam. 31:1–6).

The third case of suicide is that of the judge Samson, who as a final act of vengeance for the loss of his eyesight at the hands of the Philistines pulled down the two central supports for the two-story building in which the Philistines were celebrating his capture and imprisonment. He literally pulled the house down on himself and some three thousand Philistines (Judg. 16:23–31).

A fourth instance of suicide is the case of Ahithophel, David's very wise and gifted counselor. When David was driven from the city by his son Absalom's conspiracy, Ahithophel sided with Absalom and not King David. David, however, sent another advisor, Hushai, back to the city to counter the wise advice of Ahithophel. In the end the dramatic and exciting, but bad, advice of Hushai was accepted by Absalom's renegade government. When Ahithophel realized the impact of what all this meant, he went home and "put his house in order" and hanged himself (2 Sam. 17:23).

In the fifth instance, King Zimri, who holds the record for the shortest reign in Israel (seven days), was surrounded at Tirzah by the usurper Omri. Seeing there was no way out, Zimri went into the citadel of the royal palace and set it on fire around himself. He too died of his own doing (1 Kings 16:15–19).

Jesus's disciple Judas is the sixth case in Scripture. After he betrayed the Lord and realized what he had done, he took the thirty pieces of silver he had been paid by the Jewish authorities and threw them on the temple floor, then he went out and hanged himself (Matt. 27:3–10; Acts 1:1–19).

Forms of Euthanasia

Four categories of euthanasia are usually distinguished in ethical and medical discussions of the issue. They are:

1. *Voluntary, passive euthanasia.* This form assumes that medical personnel will merely let nature take its course. This must be at the patient's request. The physician will not do anything to hasten the patient's death, but will only provide care, comfort, and counsel to the patient.
2. *Voluntary, active euthanasia.* In this case, the patient requests that the physician hasten his or her death by some active means, such as giving a lethal injection. It is a matter of debate if non-medical personnel, such as a spouse, friend, or relative, should be permitted to help bring about the person's death as well.
3. *Involuntary, passive euthanasia.* In this situation, the patient has not indicated a willingness to die and is unable to do so. Therefore, the medical personnel do not take extraordinary measures to save the patient, but they often will remove naso-gastric tubes, antibiotics, and life-support systems such as a respirator.
4. *Involuntary, active euthanasia.* In this case, the physician does something to hasten death, regardless of the patient's wishes. The reasons may be economic, humanitarian, or even genetic.

Only the first form listed above, "voluntary, passive euthanasia," (and possibly the third form) is not euthanasia in the modern sense of our word. In the judgment of the medical staff, attempts to cure the disease are now pointless, so all of the medical attention is turned toward making the patient as comfortable as possible. The other forms are types of taking life that Scripture prohibits.

Physician-assisted suicide is one of the hot topics in the United States these days. If some of the state legislators get their way, then many physicians will be turned from being healers into being killers. The experience in Holland should have been enough of a warning to the US, but it does not seem to be heeded at the present given the drift of sentiment at this time. The original guidelines for Dutch doctors (to be used only with terminal illness and with a persistent voluntary request from the patient) have been expanded by Dutch doctors such that 25 percent of the physicians admit to ending a patient's life without the patient's consent and 60 percent do not report such cases (as required by law).[3]

The Biblical Perspective on Taking Life

There can be little doubt that the guiding principle in Scripture, presented in Exodus 20:13, roundly condemns the taking of one's own life or that of another person. This would include all forms of infanticide, suicide in its usual meaning, and all active forms of euthanasia. The only exceptions in Scripture are self-defense, capital punishment, and just war causes.

The so-called right to die argument runs right in the face of the doctrine of divine providence and the doctrine of God's sovereignty over all things in this life and world, including our own lives. Even though we may lack at the present time a clinical diagnosis and description for when death occurs, theologically it would seem that death occurs when the spirit leaves the body (Eccles. 12:7; James 2:26). That, of course, is not the sort of sign the medical profession can use. Therefore, it would seem advisable in the meantime to say that a patient should be cared for as long as brain activity and crucial vital signs are present.

The preacher in Ecclesiastes teaches that "there is a time for everything, and a season for every activity under heaven: a time to be born and a time to die" (Eccles. 3:1–2). Everything, the preacher urges, comes as a gift from God's hand, with God making "everything beautiful in its time" (Eccles. 3:11). It is to the Lord himself that we must look for the meaning of the boundaries of life and death, for he remains in charge of both the entrance to and the exit from life, plus everything in between.

God Alone Sets the Number of Our Days

For a teaching passage, I suggest we go to Job 14:1–6.

> Text: Job 14:1–6
> Title: "God Alone Sets the Number of Our Days"
> Focal Point: verse 5, "Man's days are determined; you have decreed the number of his months and have set limits he cannot exceed."
> Homiletical Keyword: Questions
> Interrogative: What are the questions we have with regard to God being in charge of all of our days?
>
> Outline:
>   I. Are there limitations on our days already? (14:1–2)
> II. Has God placed us under his incessant vigilance? (14:3–4)
> III. Is the length of our days already determined by God himself? (14:5)
> IV. Would God ever turn his vigilance away from us until it is our time to die? (14:6)

I. Are There Limitations on Our Days Already? (Job 14:1–2)

Life, taken in its most general sweep, is one of relatively short duration and yet one that is filled with trouble. While this word is painted with a broad brush, and applied to "man" generically (Hebrew, 'adam, connoting probably one who comes from the "ground," 'adamah), it surely signals real mortals who like ourselves are fairly limited and weak by nature.

There are three short phrases that emphasize to some extent these limitations: "born of woman," "of few days," and "full of trouble." This should help us to recognize our frailty, though some want to have it point to our ritual impurity. But there does not seem to be any need for that focus, for it reads too much into the reference to our being born of a woman, thereby suggesting, without any textual support, that all discharges connected with a birth make a mother ritually unclean (unless one would argue that it anticipates verse 4).

The reference to our being "of few days" seems to be a direct reversal of the otherwise standard terms such as a person dying "full of years" or "having enjoyed long life" (Gen. 25:8; 1 Chron. 29:28). But not always were all of those days without any ailments or suffering; some were filled with trouble.

Our comparatively short lifespan is illustrated with two analogies: the flower and the shadow (v. 2). The figure of the dying flower or grass is not unknown in Scripture, for it can be found in James 1:10; Psalm 37:2; 90:5–6; 103:15; and Isaiah 40:6–7. When spring comes in the Holy Land, the flowers bloom in all their glory in places that one would have thought just a short time before was little more than a desert. But then, disappointingly, the blooms suddenly languish and all the plants disappear.

But the brevity of life is also illustrated by comparing life to a "shadow." One of Job's "friends," Bildad, along with David, as well as Solomon in Ecclesiastes, compared life to a "shadow" (Job 8:9; 1 Chron. 29:15; Ps. 102:11; 144:4; Eccles. 6:12). Yet despite the realities of the swift passage of time, contemporary mortals do everything they can to retard the evidence and reality of the fast passing of time. We exercise, we use ointments, we take plenty of vitamins; yet we still witness the declining of our strength and the wrinkling of our bodies.

II. Has God Placed Us under His Incessant Vigilance? (Job 14:3–4)

But all of this slippage in time and strength only raises two more questions: (1) Is it fair of God, then, to keep such a frail, troubled, and ailment-ridden creature as we are under such constant inspection? (2) And can he extricate purity out of impurity? (v. 4). God's might and power are so beyond anything mortals could even begin to think about that there is no comparison. That being true, why then does God still seek to bring us into judgment with himself?

Job seems to be asking these questions in response to the probing challenge of Bildad in Job 8:12–13. Bildad argued that God cuts down only the wicked right in the prime of their lives. But Job will have none of that, for he believes it is incorrectly applied to him and his life. Surely righteous persons accused unjustly have the right of redress directly to God and to win their call for justice (v. 3).

Verse 4 is much harder, for it cannot mean that even God cannot make a person clean who is unclean. Job's point seems to be that surely God does not expect persons to be flawless. So, how is the problem of "bring[ing] what is pure from the impure" to be solved? The next verse will clear it up.

III. Is the Length of Our Days Already Determined by God Himself? (Job 14:5)

Of course, verse 5 is exactly the point. That is what makes those who usurp the right to take life and put it into their own hands a matter of great concern to God. In this tricolon, "days," "months," and "limits" are parallel to each other, just as are "determined," "decreed," and "set." God is sovereign over the span of each human life. Instead of such a word causing us to despair, it should give us hope and comfort that we need not be on the lookout for that ending day or for any other day, for each will come as a gift from God as set in the eternal council of heaven.

IV. Would God Ever Turn His Vigilance Away from Us until It Is Our Time to Die? (Job 14:6)

For the moment, Job wants God to look away from him and leave him alone. Job feels like a hired hand, one who can't wait until it is time to go home so he can get some rest. This constant gaze of God has put too much stress on him.

But that is only for the moment, for Job will suddenly exalt in another analogy. In verse 7 he recalls how when you cut down some trees, suddenly out from the sawed-off stump often comes a shoot of life that is still resident within the old stump. And that is exactly the analogy for mortals as well, as verse 14 teaches. Yes, "If a man dies, will he live again? All the days of my hard service I will wait for my *renewal* to come." The Hebrew word for "renewal," *khalipah*, is the same Hebrew root used of the "shoot/new life" in verse 7 (*yakhalip*). Mortals who live with this hope in the Messiah will sprout again to new vigorous life just as it happens in some trees (v. 7).

Conclusions

Life, therefore, is a gift from God and is under his constant guidance. Grace and strength sufficient for each day are granted from on high. Those who end life at their own hands assume that they are equal to God and that they can do with life as they please because of all sorts of ratiocinations that are given, but that will not hold up to examination in the final day.

Since God is the giver of all life, he is the one who can also take it at his appointed time. Stealing infants' lives or stealing our own lives is a crime against God. Yes, forgiveness is possible, even for murder, but the pain and the consequences that follow in many instances are all so unnecessary. Let us anchor our concepts of life in the Living God and not in ourselves.

Bibliography

Anderson, Norman. *Issues of Life and Death: Abortion, Birth Control, Genetic Engineering and Euthanasia.* Downers Grove, IL: InterVarsity, 1976.

Baucom, John Q. *Fatal Choice: The Teenage Suicide Crisis.* Chicago: Moody, 1986.

Davis, John Jefferson. "Infanticide and Euthanasia." In *Evangelical Ethics: Issues Facing the Church Today*, 158–92. Phillipsburg, NJ: Presbyterian and Reformed, 1985.

Koop, C. Everett, and Timothy Johnson. *Let's Talk: An Honest Conversation on Critical Issues: Abortion, AIDS, Euthanasia, and Health Care.* Grand Rapids: Zondervan, 1992.

Schemmer, Kenneth E. *Between Life and Death: The Life Support Dilemma.* Wheaton: Victor, 1988.

Discussion Questions

1. What is wrong with arguing that we all have a "right to life" on our own terms? If my life is not my own, then whose is it and how do I know?

2. If someone is suffering intensely, is helping that person die as quickly as possible the loving and compassionate thing to do? Who wants to see people suffer in a protracted way?
3. If I take my own life for selfish reasons, does that mean I cannot go to heaven or be buried in a Christian cemetery?
4. Why would any Christian want to keep alive children with severe deformities, spina bifida, or severe Down Syndrome? Would not the loving thing be to let them die rather than face a life of pain and hardship?

12

GENETIC ENGINEERING AND ARTIFICIAL REPRODUCTION

Genesis 1:26–30; 2:15–25

The Age of Aquarius (remember the song of the 1960s?) seems to have passed and we now seem to be in the Age of Genetics. So rapid and so impressive are the advances in the field of genetics that the output of its work is doubling every few years. Genetic technology has offered contemporary citizens of planet earth a whole new array of applications; many of them promise good in their effects, but as usual there are a number that also carry with them bad or at the very least questionable advances from an ethical standpoint.

A professor of molecular biology at Princeton University, Lee Silver, commented: "For better and worse, a new age is upon us—an age in which we as humans will gain the ability to change the nature of our species."[1]

Scientists are referring to this advance in science as a "revolution"[2] and as "the most awesome and powerful skill acquired by man since the splitting of the atom."[3] No matter what metaphor is used, there can be little doubt that the "threshold" on which science stands at the moment is extremely large and one that could seriously alter the way human physical endowments are experienced.

The power of genetic engineering promises to completely redesign existing organisms, including men and women, in ways never dreamed possible before. The changes envisioned here are those that occur at the microscopic level and that go way beyond the ordinary processes of reproduction. For example, for the first time in history, it is now possible to make multiple copies of any living organism by cloning it from existing organisms. The Human Genome Project (HGP),[4] under the direction of the evangelical Dr. Francis Collins, has identified every gene in the human body for the first time. This HGP is a three billion dollar project stretching out over fifteen years, which tells us that one full set of DNA (the genome) contains three billion bits of information.[5] The genes it has identified are composed of deoxyribonucleic acid (DNA), which directs our development from conception to adulthood. It also means that techniques may soon be available to treat and cure many genetic diseases, with the possibility of cloning most animals and human beings.

Treating Genetic Diseases

It has only been in recent years that we have learned how genes work. It was also a mystery how inheritance worked until we began to understand a little more from the work of an Augustinian monk named Gregor Mendel, who studied pea plants in his monastery's garden and posited units of inheritance in these plants. However, we had to wait until 1953, when James Watson and Francis Crick recognized the physical structure of these inherited units as DNA. It took the coordinated efforts of private research, industry, and a massive infusion of funding from the United States Department of Energy and the National Institutes of Health to finally chart the sequence of chemicals that form the human genetic code.

In April 2000 Marina Cavazzana-Calvo and Alain Fischer announced in *Science* magazine that their team had saved the lives of two babies afflicted with SCID-XI (severe combined immunodeficiency-XI). In other words, the bone marrow of the babies lacked part of the genetic instructions needed for a working immune system. The physicians were able to insert the needed genetic material, now that the Human Genome Project had identified the genes that should have been on the chromosome pairs. These implanted genes in turn multiplied and replaced the defective genes and the two babies, at last count, were doing well.[6] Amazing indeed!

Genetic diseases can arise from a number of causes. It is less complicated when there is just a single gene involved. But in some single-gene diseases, that gene is dominant and therefore masks a second normal gene on the other strand of the chromosome pair. An example of this type is Huntington's chorea (which is fatal, striking later in life, and leads to physical and mental deterioration). Other diseases result from chromosome abnormalities, where there is an additional chromosome, or a deletion, a rearrangement, or translocation of the gene sequence.[7]

The Ethics of Genetic Engineering in Counseling

It is now possible for a couple to get genetic counseling before they decide to have children. In this way it can be predicted whether the couple will have a child with a genetic disease. As family histories and blood samples are checked (for chromosome counts and for recessive traits), it is possible to make some predictions not previously possible.

There are now available, as well, new technologies to detect defects while the child is still in the womb. By now most are aware of the technique known as "ultrasound," which is a type of sonar that depicts the size, shape, and sex of the fetus. The ethical issue here (in case the couple is dissatisfied with the fetus's sex or other traits), however, is that the mother is already pregnant and a child is being formed within her. Therefore, it is not so much a matter of treating a bunch of tissue, but one of caring for another human being.

Another tool is called "laproscopy," where a flexible fiber-optic rod is inserted by the physician into a small incision in the mother's abdomen to assess whether the pregnancy is proceeding normally.

Similarly, an "amniocentesis" involves the insertion of a four-inch needle into a woman's anesthetized abdomen to withdraw an ounce of amniotic fluid. This fluid will allow the physician to discover the sex and the genetic makeup of the fetus. There is some discussion about making this procedure a standard test with the possible future state-mandated requirement that all diseased fetuses be aborted by order of the state.[8] This would raise enormous questions of conscience and ethics for believers. However, in some cases the results of this test would also allow for medical intervention while the child was still in the womb for the curing of some of these defects.

Another area of genetic counseling deals with infertility. For male infertility, "artificial insemination" is available. For female infertility, women (who are impregnated by donor sperm, either from the husband or someone else) act as "surrogate mothers," thereby allowing the couple to adopt the child.

In vitro (meaning "in glass") fertilization is another means of treating female infertility. This method has conception take place outside the womb, and then after selection of one embryo from a petri dish, the fertilized egg is inserted into the womb of the mother. Some do this to determine the sex of the baby in advance, but this too raises ethical questions since there usually follows the destruction of those fertilized eggs that do not meet the specifications that the couple was seeking. This method is called "preimplantation genetic diagnosis" (PGD). Embryos with desirable traits are therefore implanted, while those with undesirable traits, as specified by the parents, are destroyed.

Artificial Reproduction

A London doctor named John Hunter seems to have been the first to use an alternative means of reproduction in 1785. In our day, there are two types of artificial insemination: one using the husband's sperm (AIH: artificial insemination by the husband) and the other using the sperm of a donor (AID: artificial insemination by a donor).[9]

Male infertility surprisingly appears today in the United States in one of ten males. In fact, one of every six couples of childbearing age faces the problem of infertility. There may be a host of reasons why this is so. In men it may be traced to things like pesticides, chemicals in the food, and high levels of stress, but for women it may also be the sustained presence of low-level gynecological infections that damage the reproductive system if left untreated.

Recombinant DNA Technology: Gene Splicing

In the 1970s a new genetic technique appeared, known as recombinant DNA research (rDNA). The technique introduced was one that allowed scientists to cut pieces of DNA (called plasmids) into small segments that could in turn be inserted into host DNA. These new creatures were called DNA chimeras (in mythology the chimera is a creature with the head of a lion, the body of a goat, and the tail of a serpent). Using this recombinant DNA technology, scientists were able to produce a whole new set of genetic circumstances.

At first the unknown results of this rDNA frightened many scientists so much that they called for a moratorium on this technology until it could be assessed further. But at present the technology is proceeding since it can produce insulin, interferon, and a human growth hormone. Its greatest application seems to be in the field of immunology. It is also being used in the field of agriculture to improve the genetic structure of plant species and for industrial and environmental needs such as in the manufacture of drugs, plastics, industrial chemicals, vitamins, and cheese production. It has also produced microorganisms that dissolve oil spills and reduce frost on plants.

The Supreme Court has ruled that genetically engineered organisms and genetic processes can be patented. At last count over twelve thousand such patents had been granted since 1981 by the US Patent and Trademark Office.[10] But this raises a key ethical question: Can life ever be patented? If life is a creation of God and not one effected by humans, why would the Patent Office grant patents for what God made originally?

Scientists are very sanguine that with rDNA they now have the tools they need to drive the assumed evolutionary spiral to new heights. So how should a believer respond to this new technology? Surely it is a major gain that should be approved, especially when rDNA is able to repair defective sequences and improve the quality of the lives of people prone to genetic diseases. Even though genetic disease is the result of the fall in Genesis 3, it is not God's fault that these diseases are present. Thus to use rDNA for such purposes is not to fight against God's will, for we are merely tracing God's work on how to restore what God had originally made complete.

Human Cloning

The debate over whether scientists can or cannot clone a mammal is over, for in 1997 scientists in Scotland cloned an adult sheep named "Dolly." They took normal mammary cells from an adult ewe and starved them so that the cells reached a dormant state, which allowed all the cells to reach their potential of being played on all their tracks (normally, a cell that is not dormant or "quiescent" will only play one track).

In order to produce "Dolly," however, researchers took 277 cell fusions, which produced only 29 embryos that survived longer than six days, and only one lamb was born as a result. If these same ratios were to be used on a human, then the enormous loss of human embryos would be mind-boggling, if not unconscionable. Other theological questions follow in rapid order: Would a clone have a soul? If a believer was cloned, which one (the donor or the clone) would go to heaven, especially if the donor of the clone died first? In the traducian view of the soul (where it is passed through the seed of the parents), each cloned human would have a soul and thus would be somewhat like an identical twin. All of this calls for a reinvestigation of how humankind was created and what it was that went into their creation.

God Has Invested Mortals with Immortal Value and Significance

The crowning work of God's creation came on the sixth "day," the creation of a man, Adam. Whereas God had previously said, "Let there be," the Lord now speaks directly and immediately of the creation of man as one that is very personal: "Let us make man." This act presented no more difficulty than any of the other acts of creation, but there was a supreme dignity and excellence about it. Whether the "us" directly referred to the Trinity, or only made provision for it, cannot be determined from this small amount of text.

Text: Genesis 1:26–30; 2:15–25

Title: "God Has Invested Mortals with Immortal Value and Significance"

Focal Point: 1:27, "So God created man in his own image, in the image of God he created him; male and female he created them."

Homiletical Keyword: Ways

Interrogative: What are the ways that God has invested mortals with immortal value and significance?

Outline:
I. We are made in the image of God (1:26–27)

II. We are entrusted with the rule over creation (1:28–30)
III. We are granted the joy of work (2:15–17)
IV. We are given a companion to alleviate our loneliness (2:18–25)

I. We Are Made in the Image of God (Gen. 1:26–27)

Men and women are made in God's "own image" and "likeness." It does not appear that there is much difference between the two words *image* and *likeness*. Thus, the concept of the "image of God" implies a likeness to him in moral attributes, as the words of Paul imply in Colossians 3:10 ("put on the new self, which is being renewed in knowledge in the image of its Creator"). The same thought seems to come from Ephesians 4:24 ("put on the new self, created to be like God in true righteousness and holiness").

This image, of course, does not signify a physical representation of corporeality, for God indeed is a spirit. Therefore the term must figuratively describe human life as it represents God's spiritual nature. Humans have more than just a physical body; they have ethical and moral sensitivities, a conscience, spiritual life, and the ability to love and communicate.

It was Gerhard von Rad who made the analogy that just as kings set up statues of themselves on the borders of their land to symbolize their sovereignty, so God has established his representatives, namely, men and women, in his land to demonstrate his sovereignty.[11] Men and women have the responsibility of producing life similar to themselves by virtue of their being in the image of God.

The fact that we are in the image of God must not be confused with new age thinking where some believe that they become God. So important is this image of God that even after the fall of the man and the woman in the Garden of Eden, the image is not erased but continues seminally in each mortal (Gen. 5:1; 9:6). The only true man to fully and completely express the original purpose of the image is no one less than Christ, the second Adam.

II. We Are Entrusted with the Rule over Creation (Gen. 1:28–30)

As part of the image of God, mortals were to be "dominion-havers." Humanity was appointed by their Creator to have a relationship over the animals and the created realm strikingly similar to that which God himself sustains toward humanity. The use of the plural pronoun in verse 26 ("let them rule") shows that both the man and the woman, that is, the whole collected race, were to exercise this dominion over the created order. It could well be that Adam's control over the animal order was even more extensive before the fall than it now is after the fall as a consequence of his and Eve's transgressions. Nevertheless, even though we do not as yet see all things under humanity's dominion, we do see Jesus Christ, who is the express image of the Father, who will ultimately reestablish that dominion once again (Heb. 2:8–9).

God not only set humanity over the animals, but he also told them to "rule over the fish of the sea and the birds of the air and over every living creature that moves on the ground" (v. 28). In doing so, God "blessed them," which has reference to the multiplication of the seed and the productivity of all creation, including mortals themselves.

This blessing and charge to have dominion is to be understood as a call for men and women to wisely steward the work of agriculture, the mining of minerals, the leveling of mountains, and the filling up of the valleys so as to make it useful for humanity's well-being.

III. We Are Granted the Joy of Work (Gen. 2:15–17)

In Genesis 2:15 the writer of this Scripture, probably Moses, resumes the thread of the narrative he has broken off in verse 7 of chapter 2. That interim was filled with the story of the Garden of Eden. God now "took the man and put him in the Garden of Eden" (v. 15). This was not a physical lifting up of him, but it was a way of saying that God induced Adam through the use of Adam's free will to go and "to work" that garden and "take care of it." This involved the labor of cultivating the ground, planting it, and caring for the vegetation. Work was not an arduous effort in man's innocence in the pre-fallen garden, for work was still a joy. Before the fall, man was not to pass the time in indolent relaxation with no work, for due to his very constitution, exercise and work were essential for him. The labor of tilling the ground with times of sowing and planting was not a part of the curse or a result of the transgression of mortals. What really brought anguish and bitterness to all of humanity's labors was the exhaustion and loss of energy due to caring for the fields and the planet after the fall.

But the care for the earth was placed in the hands of mortals as those who had to give an account to God. Adam was to "guard" the garden and to "preserve" it.

[handwritten: Deut 17:12-14 follow his law → reproduce law]

IV. We Are Given a Companion to Alleviate Our Loneliness (Gen. 2:18–25)

It was God's estimate that "it is not good for the man to be alone" (2:18). His separation, and his existence in a solitary state, was found to be outside the good plan of God. In other words, mortals were made to be social beings; that is how they would enjoy their highest happiness. The Creator therefore proposed that the best way to end Adam's dreary solitude was for God himself to "build" a companion who would be a counterpart to him.

Eve, here in verse 18, is called a "helper" (Hebrew, 'ezer), but the first letter of this word may be an original *ghayin*, in which it has fallen together with the later Hebrew 'ayin. If so, there is a Ugaritic word (a Canaanite tongue that shares about 60 percent of its words with Hebrew) spelled *ghezer*, which means a "power" or "authority" "corresponding to him." In that case, Eve is a full partner with Adam.

When God brought Eve to Adam, Adam was so elated that he just about came out of his skin. He had seen all the rest of God's creation, but none of them were his type. With this woman, it was different. He gasped: "This is now bone of my bones and flesh of my flesh; she shall be called 'woman,' for she was taken out of man" (v. 23). He was one happy man!

The way God made the woman is that he caused a "deep sleep" to come over Adam, which the Greek Septuagint version renders adequately as a "trance," similar to what often came over the prophets. God took one of Adam's ribs and used that as the base to form the woman. Said the theologian George Bush: "That omnipotence which bids the embryo grow up into the full proportion and stature of a man, can with equal ease expand the smallest atom of nature into the perfect symmetry of the human frame."[12]

The expression "bone of my bones and flesh of my flesh" points both to the woman's origin from the man and to her closeness as a marriage partner. They both were to be "one flesh" and in a nuptial state designed to be one of utmost tenderness and endearment.[13]

Conclusions

The Genesis narrative unfolds a carefully planned work of God that places the man and the woman, and their descendants, in the same relation to the earth as he, God, is in relation to both of them. They are original patents of God and not of any US department. Their task was to manage all that was on earth and to do it as stewards that must report to God.

All genetic engineering must come under the same set of guidelines, for mortals were free to imitate the hand of God in what he had already built within the gene code itself.

But they must also "guard" it and "keep" it as trustees enabled by God, not as usurpers who would challenge the Creator and assume his place and authority.

Bibliography

Anderson, Kerby. *Christian Ethics in Plain Language.* Nashville: Thomas Nelson, 2005, especially pp. 64–83.

———. *Genetic Engineering.* Grand Rapids: Zondervan, 1982.

Bird, Lewis P. "Universal Principles of Biomedical Ethics and Their Applicability to Gene-Splicing." *Perspectives on Science and Christian Faith* 41 (June 1989): 76–86.

Feinberg, John S., and Paul D. Feinberg. *Ethics for a Brave New World.* Wheaton, IL: Crossway, 1993.

Grenz, Stanley J. "Technology and Pregnancy Enhancement." In *Sexual Ethics: A Biblical Perspective*, 142–55. Dallas: Word, 1990.

Peterson, James C. *Genetic Turning Points: The Ethics of Human Genetic Intervention.* Grand Rapids: Eerdmans, 2001.

Discussion Questions

1. Should a couple bank their sperm and eggs for use later in life, so that the wife can have an opportunity to get her career started and in order to guard against the possibility that the husband may come down with cancer that will require chemotherapy and possible sterility?

2. In what ways does genetic engineering bring some of the same problems that are undesirable in abortion or in embryonic stem cell research?
3. What ethical problems can you foresee with aspects of rDNA (recombinant DNA) research and applications?

Humans made in the image
of God (God's image)
1) Soul from God
2) Collosians 3:10 - put Jesus
   in the driver's seat
3) spiritual compass?
4) soul?

13

ALCOHOLISM AND DRUGS

Proverbs 23:29–35

Of all drugs, alcohol is the most commonly used and abused by both teenagers and adults. Some nationwide surveys put the level of at least some experimentation with alcohol by our young people at a staggering 90 percent mark. The nation's high school seniors come in at about 65 percent with some 40 percent of them, in one recent survey, indicating heavy drinking episodes within the previous two weeks of the survey sampling.[1]

There is no question that alcoholism is often viewed as both a sickness and a sin. From the standpoint of the Bible, however, drunkenness is a sin in Deuteronomy 21:20–21; 1 Corinthians 6:9–10; and Galatians 5:19–21.[2] Those who have been caught in its addictive powers have already witnessed some of the terrific costs that it brings as part of its consequences.

The Problems Alcoholism Creates

Alcoholism is the third largest health problem in the United States (coming right after heart disease and cancer). At one point in American history, a large number of citizens saw the evil that alcohol could bring; thus in 1919 the eighteenth amendment to the United States Constitution was passed. For fourteen years the manufacture and sale of alcoholic beverages was prohibited, until the repeal of the amendment in 1933. Since that time, we have seen a gradual erosion of the strong conviction that brought such legislation into fruition from the general public.

Today, the use of alcohol as a beverage has continued to spell ruin and death to thousands per year. For example, in those born to alcoholic mothers, the risk of problems is exceedingly high, as over forty thousand babies born with Fetal Alcohol Syndrome demonstrate each year. Children of alcoholics exhibit a number of common traits that spell possible difficulties for them in the future. Some of these include difficulty following a project from beginning to the end, severe judgment of themselves with little or no mercy, and difficulty forming intimate relationships with others.

Alcoholism is responsible for some twenty-five thousand traffic fatalities each year. Alcohol is involved in two-thirds of the murders each year and one-third of all suicides annually. Added on top of all this is the way alcohol contributes to family disruptions, spousal abuse, child abuse, family neglect, loss of wages, divorce cases, and the high cost of medical insurance.

Some place the average age of the first taste of alcohol at twelve or thirteen years old. Some 93 percent of all teenagers in the United States have experimented with alcohol by the end of their senior year in high school, says the National Institute on Drug Abuse, and close to two-thirds of that same group have tried illicit drugs in that same period of time.[3] The statistics for churched young people are not as encouraging as one would hope, running usually not more than 10 percent behind those who were in the same age brackets but who were unchurched.

Problems with Other Drugs

Add to the alcohol problem the abuse of other drugs, such as mari-juana, heroine, cocaine, and PCP, and the picture is not a bright one for the future. The annual medical cost for drug abuse in our country easily tops one hundred billion dollars.[4]

For example, marijuana comes from the hemp plant (*Cannabis sativa*) and is grown around the world. As an intoxicant, it is usually smoked and supplies a feeling of euphoria that lasts for two to four hours. Some of its short-term effects include reduction in memory, learning abilities, judgment skills, and complex motor skills, often leading to industrial accidents, absenteeism, and lung and pulmonary damage. Since the 1970s, over ten thousand scientific studies have shown repeatedly adverse consequences of marijuana usage, yet the pressure builds constantly for the decriminalization of its usage in many states today.[5] Moreover, Carlton Turner, former director of the National Institute on Drug Abuse and head of the Marijuana Research Project at the University of Mississippi, concludes: "There is no other drug used or abused by man that has the staying power and broad cellular actions on the body that cannabis [marijuana] does."[6]

Cocaine is no less serious a drug, with its use being both addictive and destructive. It comes from the leaves of coca plants. At first it was chewed by natives, then later used in beverages such as Coca-Cola, and now is used as a stimulant and an ego-builder by smoking or snorting it through the nose.

When cocaine is mixed with baking soda and water, then heated, the sound it makes in the heating gives it its name of "crack." This form of cocaine is even more dangerous and addicting than regular cocaine.

Other hallucinogenic drugs include LSD and PCP. Add to these the synthetic drugs manufactured clandestinely, such as "ecstasy," and the problems mount even more dramatically.

The Church's Response to Drug Abuse

It is clear by now that government programs alone are not enjoying a great deal of success in fighting drug abuse. The cry for the decriminalization of drugs is loud and growing in the US—and at times from some in the church as well. The theory is that if drugs were legalized, then the cost of drugs would go down and the supply would almost die for lack of a criminal profit from them. But history has not been kind to these types of theories, for when cocaine went from being extremely expensive and hard to locate, to being less expensive and more plentiful as "crack," drug-related crimes did not decline but increased. This argument suffers from the same faults as the argument for environmental determinism: that is, change the environment and everyone will shape up. Place one good solid Yakima Valley apple in a bushel of rotten apples and the other apples will see how different a really good one is and thereby drop their rottenness. But rottenness does not work that way, and neither does drug addiction or evil.

The church must shift away from claiming that we are only responsible for what goes on inside our walls and our fellowship. This view does not face up to the growing, unrecognized problem even within our own congregations, among our youth groups and bored middle-agers and senior citizens. Instead, pastors must rally church members and staff to recognize that substance abuse is not only a spiritual problem, it is also a medical and psychological issue. That means staff and congregants must know the causes, effects, and treatments for those who are already addicted and be prepared to launch helps that go right after the problems directly.

The church must be active in a program of abuse prevention for all in its body as well as for the community. This means getting the best available material as part of our teaching, along with the best resource material for our church, school, and community libraries. We must go to those who have been redeemed and rescued from each of these kinds of addictions and ask them to spearhead a program of help, instruction, and compassion for all who are in trouble in our communities.

Support groups for those in the bonds of these habits must be provided within the church or community, built around programs such as Alcoholics Anonymous. We must "bear one another's burdens" as Christians and as fellow human beings. It will be the way we earn an entrance into ministering to the spiritual needs of our community as well.

But this struggle, as with any other, is simultaneously a struggle for the soul of a young person, a senior, a community, and a nation. That struggle must be fortified with good soul food, which authoritatively can only come from Scripture itself. Since men and women do not live by bread (instruction, programs, or the like) alone, but by every word that comes from the mouth of God (Deut. 8:3), there must be solid biblical teaching. Therefore, we now turn to a teaching passage that can help supply that need.

Taking a Stand against Alcoholism and Drug Abuse

Text: Proverbs 23:29–35
Title: "Taking a Stand against Alcoholism and Drug Abuse"
Focal Point: verse 32, "In the end [wine] bites like a snake and poisons like a viper."
Homiletical Keyword: Steps
Interrogative: What are the steps in taking a stand against alcoholism and drug abuse?

Outline:
    I. We must face the real questions (23:29)
   II. We must accept the only real answer (23:30)
  III. We must heed God's command (23:31)
  IV. We must avoid the real consequences (23:32–35)

I. We Must Face the Real Questions (Prov. 23:29)

Proverbs 23:29–35 is juxtaposed with the lure of the foreign or unfaithful woman in Proverbs 23:26–28. The charming vixen is placed over against the charming product of the vine.[7] The seductiveness of the wine is pictured in verse 31 as it "presents itself as red" and as it "makes itself go down" (my translation).

The literary form used in the passage goes from the riddle posed in verse 29 to an answer in verse 30, a command in verse 31, and a series of consequences in verses 32–35. That is how the passage is laid out for us.

A riddle is expressed in a six-fold repetition of the Hebrew *lemi*, "who has?" The initial *l* denotes possession and *mi* represents "who?" For each of the six questions, this repeated anaphora (the "carrying back" of the idea to a set of words that have already occurred in the text) appears. In this way the intensity and significance of the questions are thereby heightened, and the questions are all the more demanding in their need to be answered. The drunkard's problems are laid out one after another in these six interrogatives that almost have a rhetorical force. So what are the questions?

"Who has woe? Who has sorrow?" The two seem to go together, for the onomatopoeic sound of the two words for "woe" (Hebrew, 'oy) and "sorrow" (Hebrew, 'aboy) form what is known as the figure of speech called "farrago" (i.e., a mixture or a hodgepodge that sounds alike). So, where is there anxiety, and where does anyone face grief?

But the questions continue to fire away like the beat of a drum: what about strife and what about complaints? Surely drunkenness has raised a multitude of outcries against the drunkard, not to mention the trouble it has inflicted in the home, in the community, in the church, and on others.

It gets even more serious. Where did you get those bruises from? Were you involved in drunken brawls that you cannot even explain or remember? And what about those bloodshot eyes? Some would render the "bloodshot" also as "flashing" eyes, which would indicate eyes that were set on a pugnacious course of action. A drunken fight is often a sure twin to heavy drinking, especially if the slightest argument breaks out over the dumbest of topics. All of these questions are enough to embarrass, if not move, one to a whole new course of action. The addictions have run to a point of no return for the good or for the health of those around me.

II. We Must Accept the Only Real Answer (Prov. 23:30)

In a poetic form of synthetic parallelism, the wisdom teacher knows what the answer to the barrage of questions is. The problem comes from "lingering" too long over wine (v. 30). The Hebrew root used here ('akhar) is the intransitive Piel form of this verb meaning to "hesitate," or to "delay." The writer will return to this same root in verse 32 with the phrase "in the end."

But at least the problem has been identified: the imbiber has resisted leaving the presence of wine, and thus he or she is well on the way to becoming drunk. One escalates one's exposure to trouble by lingering long over drinking wine.

The parallel expression confirms this diagnosis. It is in the "hanging" around the stuff that the problem is exacerbated. The NIV uses the translation of "sample," which seems to suggest a small amount was imbibed, but that gives the wrong sense to the passage. The idea, instead, is one of constantly coming and searching, if not deeply probing, the jugs of wine (v. 30b).

Rather than this serving as a case for moderation only, this text warns about a pattern or habit of indulging constantly, without any boundaries being established. Moreover, some cannot even go as far as tasting, for it immediately forms in some people's chemistry an addiction with very little prompting.

III. We Must Heed God's Command (Prov. 23:31)

The text advises swift and certain action. Cut the habit at its very inception. Nip the temptation in the bud, for if it is not possible to use alcohol wisely, then do not use it at all. That is not an impossible position to take. For some, addiction begins with the first drink. It is important to know how you yourself tend to react in situations like this and what your own tendencies are in these matters.

By all means, resist its enticements from the very start. Don't be taken in by any of wine's charms. Do not let its color, its sparkle, its taste, or even the joy of swishing it around in a goblet entice you. Sometimes, what goes down easily may be the very thing in the end that binds you so that you become a prisoner to it.

IV. We Must Avoid the Real Consequences (Prov. 23:32-35)

Once again the word for "end" (Hebrew, 'akharit) appears in verse 32. In the end, lingering over one's wine results in it biting like a snake and poisoning like a viper. These two similes strike a lethal picture to say the least. The sting is deadly in a very real sense.

There are other consequences as well. Both the eyes and the mind are adversely affected. The "strange sights" (v. 33) are perhaps the result of the delirium tremens (also known as the "d.t.'s"). At the very least the drunken stupor causes nightmarish effects. Add to this the work of one's imagination in this state, and reality is perverted and one becomes easily deluded. The word for "strange sights" could also possibly be rendered as "incredible or disgusting sights."[8] The picture is not a pretty one for individuals made in the image of God!

The consequences continue to pile up for the drunkard as the hallucinations increase. Now one's mouth starts to speak perverse things. The drunkard feels as if he is sleeping up on top of the rigging out on the high seas. He claims that someone has hit him, but he may only be inflicting the calamity on himself as his imagination is now as out of control as his footing underneath him, which is handicapping the movement of his legs. Mentally he feels spent; physically he is nauseated. Where will all of this end?

Curiously enough, when he awakens from his drunken hangover, this witless drunk has learned nothing from his experience. Instead, he wants nothing more than another drink. He acts as if he has been anesthetized and is totally unaware of what harm he is serving to himself and to others. His only craving is not to be released from his new master, drink; instead, he craves the same thing that has just made a fool out of him and sent his faculties spinning out of control. This is strange and most sad indeed!

Conclusions

1. Scripture does not teach total abstinence as a divine requirement, but it does vigorously condemn drunkenness and speaks against the overindulgence in alcohol as a beverage. Proverbs 20:1 (NRSV) says, "Wine is a mocker, strong drink a brawler; and whoever is led astray by it is not wise." Even rulers are warned against wine and strong drink in Proverbs 31:4–5 (NASB), "lest they drink and forget what is decreed, and pervert the rights of all the afflicted."
2. The Bible labels drunkenness as a sin in Deuteronomy 21:20–21; 1 Corinthians 6:9–10; and Galatians 5:19–21. Therefore, one must repent and ask for God's forgiveness and power to rid his or her soul from the thirst that has thrown him or her into this form of slavery.
3. Severe church discipline is recommended in 1 Corinthians 5:11 for the drunkard who refuses all help and has no desire to change.
4. What is said of the abuse of alcohol can also be said of the misuse of drugs with just as strong a warning, for it too has many, if not all, of the same effects and consequences. God has called his followers to live holy lives, not drunken, wasted lives.

Bibliography

Addington, Gordon L. *The Christian and Social Drinking*. Minneapolis: Free Church Publications, 1984. See his ninety-four bibliographic items on pp. 44–50.

Anderson, Kerby. *Christian Ethics in Plain Language*. Nashville: Thomas Nelson, 2005, especially pp. 153–65.

Pulliam, Russ. "Alcoholism: Sin or Sickness?" *Christianity Today*, September 1981, 22–24.

"Substance Abuse: The Nation's Number One Health Problem." Princeton, NJ: Institute for Health Policy; Brandeis University for the Robert Wood Johnson Foundation, October 1993.

Discussion Questions

1. Is the policy of "Just Say 'No' to Drugs" a sustainable and workable policy? Consider the drastic decline in HIV and AIDS infection in Kenya in the last ten years (where rates had been as high as 50 percent of the population infected) in the context of an abstinence program today with only 10 percent of the population infected.

2. How seriously should the church become involved in battling against drug and alcohol addictions in the community? Will not such social action steal from the church's mission to spread the gospel to every creature?

3. What is the best prevention program for ourselves, the community, and the church?

*writing from
1) mainstream
Evangelical
Church*

14

CIVIL DISOBEDIENCE

Acts 4:1–22

*✗ Did not
mention
Martin Luther
King*

All believing Christians carry a dual citizenship: they are citizens of heaven and citizens of one nation-state or another here on earth. It would be wrong, however, to deny this dual citizenship and to declare that we are only true citizens of heaven, thereby separating ourselves from every form of involvement in the earthly state as best as we possibly could. On the contrary, the more one acts in accord with his or her heavenly citizenship, the better citizen he or she will be on this earth. Nowhere does the Bible teach isolationism from all forms of the nation-state. Therefore, to take just one or two examples of noninvolvement, a decision not to vote in any local or national elections or not to participate in any civic forms of government would be contrary to our calling as Christians and our calling as citizens in a local setting.

Submission to Governmental Authorities Is Not Optional

Scripture is clear that every believer must also submit to the governing authorities, for the apostle Paul taught in Romans 13:1–5 that God established every human state authority. To rebel against that authority was not to be considered a trifling matter, but it was counted as a rebellion against God himself, since God was the one who instituted all governing authorities. That is what the apostle Peter taught as well in 1 Peter 2:13–14. We are to submit ourselves to every authority "for the Lord's sake," "whether to the king, as the supreme authority, or to governors, who are sent by him to punish those who do wrong and to commend those who do right." The apostles gave these injunctions while Christians were living under two of the most despotic rulers most people had ever seen up to that time in history, in the persons of the Roman emperors Caligula and Nero. If ever there were two madmen, these two surely would have qualified. Moreover, under their reigns Christians were treated with a hatred and scorn seldom reserved for even the most violent of society's disrupters. It seems almost beyond belief that such Roman emperors and the system of government they fostered was "ordained by God."

That same type of advice had been given to the Judean captives when King Nebuchadnezzar carried them off to Babylon. The prophet Jeremiah told the captives to "seek the welfare of the city where I have sent you into exile, and pray to the LORD on its behalf, for in its welfare you will find your welfare" (Jer. 29:7 NRSV). Once again the principle is clear, but we are not directly advised in explicit terms of any biblical exceptions or circumstances where that principle would not hold true.

Accordingly, the commands to obey civil authorities are very clear and straightforward. But, when, if ever, *may* a Christian resist? And when *must* he or she resist that divinely instituted authority? Under what sort of circumstances should a Christian ever consider that it is possible, or it is his or her duty, to disobey the government?

While Scripture gives us some basic guidelines on how believers are to understand and respond to governments, it does not offer an exhaustive treatment of the issue. This may provide us with some latitude, for not all Christians have the same views on various political issues and parties. But this latitude does not mean that we are without any kind of guidance or that each may respond as he or she feels appropriate. That would lead to anarchy, which Scripture never condones. So what are the parameters or guidelines, if any, that are found in Scripture?

Biblical Examples of Civil Disobedience

Surprisingly, there are some examples of individuals who resisted their governments, with what appears to be divine approval. For example, the Egyptian midwives Shiphrah and Puah (Exod. 1:15–21) had a higher regard for the lives of the Israelite male babies and for the God of the whole universe than they had for the pharaoh of Egypt. Therefore they refused to obey Pharaoh's injunction to kill all male Israelite babies while the mothers were still on their birth stools.

Likewise, Rahab the harlot, in Jericho, feared the Lord God of the Hebrews more than she feared the king of Jericho; therefore, she hid the Jewish spies that came to her establishment (Josh. 2:1–14). This does not mean that some approval in either of these situations was an approval of all that the midwives or Rahab did or said, for both parties lied. God, however, singled out the fact that they feared and believed him more than they feared and believed the local government; that is why both the midwives and Rahab were blessed. But approval in one or more areas of a person's life is not an approval in all areas of their life; we must distinguish between what the Bible reports and what the Bible teaches. Again, when during Daniel's day, Shadrach, Meshach, and Abednego just plain refused to bow down on command to Nebuchadnezzar's golden image (Dan. 3), God gave them deliverance from on high. Likewise, God rescued Daniel from the evil trap set up by the satraps of King Darius: his edict was that no one could pray to God for the next thirty days, as was the known daily habit of Daniel, upon the threat of being thrown into the lions' den. But God delivered Daniel from both these evil men and the lions. Whether to obey this edict of the king or to obey God was not an option for Daniel; he obeyed God and continued to pray every day despite the evil and sinister motivations of the satraps who wanted to trap him into opposing the king's edict.

Advocates of Civil Disobedience

Americans have experienced quite a long history of examples of civil disobedience. It began with the American Revolution, in which many are still questioning whether there was a proper biblical basis for resistance against Britain. This same type of civil disobedience continued up to the Civil War over the slavery issue and moved into the twentieth century with the Civil Rights Movement, the protests against the Vietnam War, the protests against nuclear arms, the gay rights movement, and the environmental movement. All of these examples, some possibly defensible, and some more questionable, are part and parcel of the two centuries of American history.

Kerby Anderson rightly points to Henry David Thoreau (1817–62) as the most influential writer in the modern discussion of civil disobedience in his often-referred-to essay entitled "On the Duty of Civil Disobedience."[1] Thoreau wrote this essay after spending a night in a Concord, Massachusetts, jail in July 1846 for refusing to pay his poll tax. He refused to pay it on the grounds that the government supported slavery. Fortunately for him, someone paid the tax on his behalf that night, and he was released from jail. However, had he been a student of Romans 13:7, he would have known that there is no moral or ethical obligation to the one who pays taxes, at least no more than there is for any other person who performs services for us (see the discussion on this point in chap. 15 and the exegesis of Rom. 13). The popularity of Thoreau's essay, however, may be judged by the fact that Mahatma Gandhi always carried a copy with him in his several imprisonments and also had the essay printed in India and widely distributed. Thoreau's point was that obedience to one's conscience was more important, and more to be adhered to, than obedience to the government. However, this would imply that one's conscience was formed and shaped by the moral law of God. The problem with Thoreau, of course, is this: Who is going to make that decision about when it is time to oppose one's government and on what grounds? Will it be on biblical grounds? Thoreau left it up to the individual and to one's innate sense of goodness! But that is a recipe for disaster and anarchy, since no absolute standard of right and wrong or objective standard of reference is set forth in Thoreau's writings.

Samuel Rutherford (1600–1661) was another contributor to this discussion. In rejecting the seventeenth-century "divine right of kings," he instead posited God's law (thus the title, *Lex Rex*). When the government and the king disobeyed the law, then one could appeal to the law itself as being superior to that king and government. Rutherford was part of the Westminster divines, who brought forth the Westminster Confession and Catechisms.

Is Resistance by Force Ever Justified?

Francis Schaeffer did justify armed revolution under some limitations. He argued:

> In *Lex Rex* [author Samuel Rutherford] does not propose armed revolution as an automatic solution. Instead, he sets forth the appropriate response to interference by the state in the liberties of the citizenry. Specifically, he stated that if the state deliberately is committed to destroying its ethical commitment to God, the resistance is appropriate.
>
> In such an instance, *for the private person*, the individual, Rutherford suggested that there are three appropriate levels of resistance: *First*, he must defend himself by protest (in contemporary society this would most often be by legal action); *second*, he must flee if at all possible; and *third*, he may use force, if necessary, to defend himself. One should not employ force if he may save himself by flight; nor should one employ flight if he can save himself and defend himself by protest and the employment of constitutional means of redress.[2]

Since according to Rutherford the civil authority was only a "fiduciary figure," whose office was held in trust for the benefit of the people, the people had a basis for resistance when that trust was violated. No wonder, then, that *Lex Rex* was banned in England and Scotland, for it was viewed as being seditious.

Biblical Basis for Civil Disobedience

Anderson[3] lists five principles to guide an individual when making a decision whether he or she should disobey the authorities that are duly constituted. They are as follows:

1. The law or the command being resisted must be clearly unjust and unbiblical. It would not be an adequate basis to resist just because we disagree with the command or the law. If the case for justice or biblical principle is not clear, then obedience to that law and command should be expected.
2. Every ordinary means of redress must be exhausted before one decides to resist what was ordered by the powers that be. In other words, opposition and resistance to this law should be the avenue of last resort.

3. Nevertheless, those who disobey that mandate of the government should be ready to pay the penalty for breaking the law. Such disobedience should not be easily confused with anarchy, for Scripture would not condone such lawlessness.
4. In the midst of disobeying, the act of civil disobedience is not to be carried out with anger or rebellion but with love and humility, which are the hallmarks of Christians.
5. The most controversial of all the principles is this one: we should only carry out civil disobedience when there is some possibility for success. If there is little or no chance for any success, then what would be the point of putting society through such social disruption and the promotion of what could be interpreted by others as plain lawlessness?

These five principles read very much like some of the principles for a "Just War." There are some nuances, to be sure, but the list is very similar. (See chap. 15 on war.)

Obeying God Rather than Civil Government

One passage of Scripture seems to be a natural for understanding the rights and the wrongs of this topic of civil disobedience: Proverbs 24:3–12. More than any other group, the pro-life advocates of "Operation Rescue" in the abortion debate have pointed to Proverbs 24:11 as their basis for peaceful picketing of abortion clinics, since the words of the proverb say, "rescue those being led away to death; hold back those staggering toward slaughter." A parallel text in James 4:17 reads, "Anyone, then, who knows the good he ought to do and doesn't do it, sins."

The people who are "being led away to death" are those who have been wrongly accused and convicted. They are being unfairly accused and convicted of a crime they did not commit. If that is the principle of justice for society, then those in the womb are also real persons, as are those who are being delivered into this world by mothers; they both qualify for the same protection based on the same divine principle in this biblical text. Scripture calls for believers to stand with the oppressed, for God will not accept any excuses; as Proverbs 24:12 notes, "If you say, 'But we knew nothing about this,' does not he who weighs the heart perceive it? Does not he who guards your life know

it? Will he not repay each person according to what he has done?"
Accordingly, all weak and lame excuses are immediately set aside by
God as pointless. Notice, it is one person who "say[s]," but it is a
plural number who claim that "we knew nothing about this." This
linking the singular protest with the plural mantra of ignorance is
not the result of a defective text but is a sign that "we are trying to
spread the blame, broaden the responsibility and blend into the crowd.
The evaluator of such justifications is the omniscience of God. He
'weighs the hearts' (Prov. 21:2) of all. . . . He will 'render to man according to his work' (Job 34:11; Ps. 62:12; Prov. 12:14; Matt. 16:27;
Rom. 2:6)."[4]

There is probably no greater New Testament passage dealing with
the issue of civil disobedience than that which describes the time when
Peter and John were called before the Sanhedrin for speaking with
and teaching the people in Acts 4:1–22.

Text: Acts 4:1–22

Title: "Obeying God Rather than Civil Government"

Focal point: verse 19, "But Peter and John replied: 'Judge for yourselves
   whether it is right in God's sight to obey you rather than God. For
   we cannot help speaking about what we have seen and heard.'"

Homiletical Keyword: Situations

Interrogative: What are the situations when we may or must disobey the government?

Outline:

   I. When we declare the message of Jesus's resurrection (4:1–4)
  II. When we are hauled before the court to account for acts of
      kindness (4:5–12)
 III. When we are told not to speak or teach in the name of Jesus
      (4:13–22)

I. When We Declare the Message of Jesus's Resurrection (Acts 4:1–4)

Peter and John had been speaking to the people about Jesus, who
had been raised from the dead by the power of God. This, however,
greatly disturbed the priests, the Sadducees, and the captain of the
temple guard in Jerusalem. Since it was late in the evening, these of-

ficials seized Peter and John and had them jailed overnight in prison for such seditious actions against the government and the religious leaders of the community.

The people, nevertheless, responded with belief, and the number of the church grew immediately to about five thousand. This appeared to make matters worse for the two apostles, for the leaders feared this Jesus movement and the fact that the one they had tried to murder was now being declared to be alive.

II. When We Are Hauled before the Court to Account for Acts of Kindness (Acts 4:5–12)

On the next day, when the rulers, elders, and teachers of the law met in Jerusalem, a whole galaxy of officials assembled to consider this case, including Caiaphas, John, Alexander, and other men from the high priest's family. This was to be no small tempest in a teapot, to say the least; it was a major deal!

Peter and John were brought in, and the questioning focused on this issue: "By what power or what name did you do this?" (v. 7b). To be sure, a marvelous work had been done, which few could deny, for it had been done publicly before all the people present in the temple. A crippled man had been healed in the name of Jesus Christ of Nazareth. These officials had known this was the name and that it was on the authority of the name of Jesus of Nazareth that this miracle had taken place. They just wanted to hear it from the lips of Peter and John, so they quizzed them sanctimoniously in the way officialdom tends to do this sort of thing.

It was Peter who responded on behalf of the team. He did so being "filled with the Holy Spirit" (v. 8). Neither was he shy in boldly announcing that it had been done in the name and power of this risen Jesus whom they had crucified, but whom God had raised up from the dead. Talk about a reversal and a rebuttal to end all rebuttals: this surely was the one to top them all!

Moreover, Peter announced before the assembled adjudicators of his and John's case that this same Jesus was the one Psalm 118:22 declared "the stone you builders rejected, which has become the capstone" (v. 11). That is why there is "salvation . . . in no one else, for there is no other name under heaven given to men by which we must be saved" (v. 12). That must have shaken up the powers that be very severely. This Jesus was the "stone" whom they had rejected outright, as predicted by their own sacred Scriptures.

III. When We Are Told Not to Speak or Teach in the Name of Jesus (Acts 4:13–22)

The courage and careful responses of Peter and John amazed the assembled authorities, for they knew both were unschooled and rather ordinary men. The point they did have to reckon with was the fact that "these men had been with Jesus" (v. 13). What is more, the crippled man who had been healed was standing right there alongside Peter and John. In the face of such startling evidence, what could they say or do? "There was nothing they could say" (v. 14).

The Sanhedrin went into executive session and discussed the question of possible actions they could take. It was most difficult, for "everybody living in Jerusalem [knew] they [had] done an outstanding miracle, and [they could] not deny it" (v. 16).

The only course of action left to them was an attempt to "stop this thing from spreading any further among the people." Therefore, they warned Peter and John that they were "to speak no longer to anyone in this name" (v. 17). Their hope was that the whole incident would die down by itself and the populace would stop believing in this Messiah. Surely Peter and John would be so intimidated by their official threats that they would never attempt any more healings and preaching in Jesus's name—or so they thought!

But the principle of civil disobedience is now invoked by Peter and John. For them it was a case of obeying God or obeying mortals. Given that choice, they were going to obey God. Moreover, how could they help doing otherwise after all they had seen and heard (v. 20)?

Conclusions

One must obey the civil authorities so long as they do not require of us anything that contradicts what God has told us in his word or person. If the contest must finally come to a choice between the one or the other, the believer must always choose to obey God. End of story.

Bibliography

Alcorn, Randy. *Is Rescuing Right?* Downers Grove, IL: InterVarsity, 1990.

Childress, James F. *Civil Disobedience and Political Obligation.* New Haven: Yale University Press, 1971.

Geisler, Norman L. "Disobedience to Government Is Sometimes Right." In *Christian Ethics: Options and Issues*, 239–55. Grand Rapids: Baker Academic, 1989.

Mott, Stephen Charles. "Civil Disobedience as Subordination." In *Biblical Ethics and Social Change*, 142–66. New York: Oxford University Press, 1982.

Piper, John. "Rescue Those Being Led Away to Death." *The Standard.* May 1989, 27–32.

Robertson, O. Palmer. "Reflections on New Testament Testimony on Civil Disobedience." *Journal of the Evangelical Theological Society* 33 (September 1990): 331–51.

Ryrie, Charles C. "The Christian and Civil Disobedience." *Bibliotheca Sacra* 127 (April 1970): 153–62.

Schaeffer, Francis A. *A Christian Manifesto.* Rev. ed. Westchester, IL: Crossway, 1981.

Wallis, Jim, ed. *The Rise of Christian Conscience.* San Francisco: Harper and Row, 1987.

Discussion Questions

1. Should you and your fellow Christians take a public stand by picketing in a section of your city or county where "adult bookstores" draw large numbers of teens and married men to watch pornographic movies and the like?
2. Should a church or Christian institution resort to nonviolent, public violation of the law to protest the injustice of a city or county government that refuses to act on a request for a building permit for the church or Christian institution after years of delay and no official response to repeated requests for explanation?
3. Should Christian leaders under an atheistic government that forbids all forms of evangelizing sponsor a public bap-

tism and thereby risk a possibly violent response from that government?

4. If you were asked to smuggle Bibles into a country where it was illegal to own one, would you still try to do so in order to get them into the hands of believers in that country who are desperately hungry for the Word of God?

15

WAR AND PEACE

Romans 13:1–7

Peace is not the absence of war, it is the restoration of justice in relationships.[1]

More people have been killed in wars in the twentieth century (what had been predicted to be the so-called Christian century as we entered the 1900s) than in any other previous century in the history of the world. In World War I, thirty-nine million (thirty million of whom were civilians) died. In World War II another fifty-one million (including thirty-four million civilians) lost their lives. Since 1945, in approximately one hundred and fifty more wars of varying sizes in assorted places, an estimated additional sixteen million people have perished as a result of these scattered wars, such as the one in Korea around 1950 and another in Vietnam in the 1960s and 70s.[2] No one can deny that war inflicts terrible pain and surely is the result of some type of moral failure.

Basically there are three major positions for Christians to choose from on the subject of war and military intervention.

1. *Activism*, which holds that Christians are to support every military effort whenever their country declares war. Since Scripture says in Romans 13:1–7 that we are to submit to the political leaders that are governing us, we assume that these leaders have access to better information than we do; therefore, in this scenario we trust the government's judgment and follow its lead.

2. *Pacifism*, which holds that it is never right to participate in a war as a Christian, since, as disciples of Christ, we must live as he lived—in a nonviolent way. The way of the world is the way of the sword, but the way of the cross is altogether different. The conduct of wars in the Old Testament has no bearing on how we as Christians should act, nor should we resist an evil person (Matt. 5:39), but instead we are to love our enemies (Matt. 5:44).

3. *Selectivism*, which holds that Christians may participate and fight in some wars, when those wars are based on morally defensible causes described in the seven "Just War" guidelines.

The Old Testament Teaching on War

Since the Scriptures are the final source for all ethical questions, it is appropriate that we go to them for guidance in moral matters such as the one before us. It would not be fair to segment off the New Testament from the Old Testament, or to bracket it off from our consideration for this topic, for both portions claim that they are the Word of God, exhibiting one consistent and harmonious unity, unless the text indicates otherwise.

The most obvious comment must be that in the Old Testament God directed the Israelites to do battle with specific nations that had filled up the "cup of [their] iniquity" (in a different, but parallel expression in Gen. 15:16: the "sin of the Amorites has not yet reached its full measure") by divine standards and so had to be punished and removed from the land that God was now giving to Israel. Yahweh himself was also described occasionally as "a man of war" (Exod. 15:3–4).

The Old Testament clearly taught that "whoever sheds the blood of man, by man shall his blood be shed" (Gen. 9:6). Yet Exodus 20:13 also taught, "You shall not murder." When Exodus 20:13 is interpreted in light of Genesis 9:6, it is enough to show that not every death caused by mortals is a violation of the sixth commandment. Presumably this would also affect certain actions in the conduct of war.

A Yahweh War: Deuteronomy 20:1–20

Actually, on a number of occasions the Old Testament instructs Israel not only to wage war but also to capture the land of Canaan, or to go to war in defense of the land. The entire chapter of Deuteronomy 20 is devoted to giving specific instructions about war. Notice, however, that the instructions of Deuteronomy 20 are not the opinions of particular groups or even of certain redactors of the Holy Scriptures; they are God's rules for conducting warfare.

Deuteronomy 20:1–20 is given as one long sermon by Moses in his day. The attempt to late-date this text to the time of the monarchy or later, because of the foreign nations mentioned in Deuteronomy 20, 21, and 23, as T. Raymond Hobbs has claimed,[3] is answered by the similarity between the second millennium suzerainty treaties and the structure of the book of Deuteronomy. Deuteronomy is better placed toward the middle of the second millennium than in the first millennium as Hobbs wants it. Chris Wright also has responded by saying:

> It seems to be as likely that the idealization *preceded* Israel's wars in the land (i.e., as a prior statement of what should have happened, but did not), as that it was a seventh-century *post*-idealization of what should have happened, but everybody knew had not. It is hard to see what possible point the distinctions of vv. 10–18 would have had centuries after the actual settlement of Israel in the land, or indeed what purpose this ch. [Deut. 20] would have served at all in relation to a seventh-century reformation.[4]

While Deuteronomy 21:10–14; 23:9–14; and 24:5 also treat the issue of war in the Old Testament, Deuteronomy 20:1–20 makes up the only large teaching passage in the older covenant. This full chapter is positioned here in the text because it is connected with the teaching in chapter 19 on homicide. Each of these chapters, therefore, is an extension of the sixth commandment, explaining both the legitimacy and illegitimacy of taking human life.

The structure of Deuteronomy 20 is marked syntactically with a number of conditional sentences that begin with a "when" (Hebrew, *ki*), accompanied by a verbal clause in the imperfect in verses 1, 10, and 19. The resulting outline looks like this:

Outline:
  I. The nature of Yahweh wars (vv. 1–9)
      A. A Yahweh war (v. 1)
      B. Preparations for war (vv. 2–4)
      C. Mustering of the troops (vv. 5–8)
      D. Appointment of leaders (v. 9)
  II. The distinctiveness of Yahweh war (vv. 10–18)
      A. Conduct of the war (vv. 10–15)
      B. Principles that govern Yahweh wars (vv. 16–18)
  III. The concern for the environment (vv. 19–20)
      A. Ecological restraint (v. 19)
      B. Mounting a siege (v. 20)

The rules of warfare for Israel differ widely from those of her neighbors, especially in one major respect: Israel was never commanded or allowed to expand her land or territories by conquest of any of the surrounding nations. All imperialistic motives for warfare were to be summarily rejected. The reason was clear: there was no need to prove Israel's greatness in terms of acquisitions, wealth, or military hardware. Her glory was not in her possessions, power, military strength, and technology; her wars were won or lost by the presence and power of the Lord. That is why Israel did not need to trust in her weapons, but only in the Lord. Psalms 33:16–19 and 118:8–9 make that same point:

> No king is saved by the size of his army;
>   no warrior escapes by his great strength.
> A horse is a vain hope for deliverance;
>   despite all its great strength it cannot save.
> But the eyes of the Lord are on those who fear him,
>   on those whose hope is in his unfailing love,
> to deliver them from death
>   and keep them alive in famine.

> It is better to take refuge in the Lord
>   than to trust in man.
> It is better to take refuge in the Lord
>   than to trust in princes.

In light of some of the contemporary uses of the term, it is better to drop the reference to "holy war," for they were never labeled as such in Scripture, and to use the biblical term "Yahweh war(s)." Accordingly, verses 1–4 present the perspective that Israel's wars, fought in obedience to Yahweh's command, would be Yahweh's own wars. That is the basic assumption of chapter 20 in Deuteronomy.

Surprisingly, instead of this chapter exhibiting a militaristic spirit, it actually comes off as being *anti*-militaristic, as it calls for the *reduction* in the size of the army and the release of what were probably their youngest and most fit men. Three exemptions were handed out immediately: (1) those who had just built a new house but had not dedicated it as yet, (2) those who had just planted a new vineyard but had not enjoyed it as yet, and (3) those who were pledged to be married but had not married as yet. All of these were to be released from military service, along with any who were psychologically spooked about going into battle. Part of the reason was that if this war was to be the source of blessing and the gift of the land, the slaying of a man under the circumstances mentioned in the three exemptions would seem to be the source of a curse rather than a blessing and would tend to reflect poorly on the fallen warrior who had not had time to enjoy what he was about to realize.

This chapter goes on to make a distinction between cities that were nearby and those that were at a distance (vv. 15–16). The rationale for slaying all the Canaanite nations was the same as that given in Deuteronomy 7:1–6, 25–26—it was a judgment on their accumulated wickedness (i.e., the filling up of the "cup of iniquity") and the threat of syncretism they posed to Israel (Deut. 20:18). The nature of the text is a *sermon* and not a military briefing. Idolatry must not creep into the land, for Israel was to be wholly dedicated to the Lord.

These rules were as humane as they were ecologically sensitive. Israel was to offer peace to cities at a distance (vv. 10–11). If those cities accepted, they were to be treated gently and left in their own land. Fruit trees were not to be destroyed or cut down to be used in siege works, as the Assyrians did, for example (vv. 19–20). Captive women were to be treated mercifully as well, for if an Israelite married one, he could never sell her or treat her like a slave if she no longer pleased him.

Chris Wright summarizes it well:

When we allow ourselves, then, to see past the slaughter of the Canaanites as a moral stumbling block to the other features of Deuteronomy's rules of war, we can hardly remain unimpressed. Without a Geneva Convention, Deuteronomy advocates humane exemptions from combat; requires prior negotiation; prefers nonviolence; limits the treatment of subject populations; allows for the execution of male combatants only; demands humane and dignified treatment of female captives; and insists on ecological restraint. We may even, as in the case of slavery, detect something that seems to undermine war itself, even if only in whispers.[5]

The Just War Theory

Cicero (106–43 BC) in his *De Officiis* tried to plot out a rationale for war as he spoke of "a righteous ground for going to war" (I, 38). But it was Augustine who enlarged on Cicero's theory in his *Reply to Faustus* (XXII, 74) and in his *Letter* 138 and *Letter* 189.

The "Just War" (*jus ad bellum*, "rule [governing going] to war," i.e., conditions for declaring war)[6] and *jus in bello* ("rule [of conduct] in war," i.e., guidelines to be followed once in war) provided a doctrine that traced its roots back to St. Augustine (354–430), who developed it as an extension of Romans 13:1–7. Not all wars were morally justified, argued Augustine. A seven-point criteria was developed as a framework for evaluating the commencement (five rules of the Just War Theory, *jus ad bellum*) and progress ([*jus in bello*] the last two of those seven rules) of a war. They are as follows:

1. *A Just Cause.* Every form of aggression is to be rejected once and for all. An unprovoked war is no cause for a nation going to war against another nation. One may only participate if there is a just cause or a defensible reason.
2. *A Just Intention.* Nations may not go to war out of revenge or for conquest of another's territory; it must be to secure the peace of all the parties involved.
3. *A Last Resort.* After a nation has made the offer of peace and tried diplomacy and every form of economic pressure, only then may it go to war as a last resort.
4. *Formal Declaration.* There must be a formal declaration of war to initiate hostilities.
5. *Limited Objectives.* Complete destruction of another nation or the like is an improper objective. War must be waged to

make sure that peace is the result and that war is the only way to attain that peace.

6. *Proportionate Means.* The types of weapons and force must be limited to those that are needed to quell the aggression and to secure a just peace.

7. *Noncombatant Immunity.* Military operations must carefully avoid involving those not participating in the conflict. Only governmental forces and their agents may serve as targets for action.

Thomas Aquinas also argued for a just war as he searched the Old Testament for backing. See his *Summa Theologica* I–II, Q 105, Article 3.

Christian pacifists make two main objections against the just war theory: (1) It is never right to go to war, but we should instead turn the other cheek (Matt. 5:39); and (2) Jesus told Peter to put away the sword, since the kingdom of God is not of this world and is not advanced by means of the sword (Matt. 26:52–53). However, Jesus was addressing individuals who were personally being harrassed in these cases and was not laying down principles for the way nations or groups of people at large were to act.

More recently, others have claimed that the just war theory applies only to nations and not to terrorists. But that objection does not appear to be correct, for the concept of just war predates the concept of modern nation-states,[7] where ethnic, social, and religious groups of people were the object(s) of attack.

The key teaching passage, of course, is Romans 13:1–7. It is to that passage that we now turn for ethical teaching on political obedience.

Submission to One's Government Is Required by God

Since Christians have become members of a kingdom that is not of this world, one would think that they would be excused, or perhaps excuse themselves, from all obligations of obedience to the rulers of this age, especially when it comes to serving actively in the military forces, since these human authorities are not usually believers anyhow. However, the teaching of this chapter is addressed to "everyone," including believers.

Moreover, the apostle Paul does not limit this required obedience to just one or two forms of government; he makes no exceptions, whether they be democracies, monarchies, republics, or a mixture of all the above and more. Every form of government has to be obeyed for the sake of obedience to God. What is more, Paul writes this during some of the harshest times of oppression against Christians by the caesars of Rome.

Text: Romans 13:1–7

Title: "Submission to One's Government Is Required by God"

Focal Point: verse 1, "Everyone must submit himself to the governing authorities, for there is no authority except that which God has established."

Homiletical Keyword: Reasons

Interrogative: What are the reasons for submitting to the governing authorities?

Outline:[8]

I. We must all submit to human government (13:1–5)
   A. Because human government comes by God's decree (13:1b)
   B. Because rebellion against government is rebellion against God (13:2a)
   C. Because we will be punished if we resist (13:2b)
   D. Because government is a restraint against evil (13:3a)
   E. Because government promotes our good (13:3b–4a)
   F. Because rulers are empowered to punish disobedience (13:4b)
   G. Because government should be obeyed for our conscience's sake (13:5)
II. We must all pay taxes to our governments (13:6–7)
   A. Part of our submission is in paying taxes (13:6a)
   B. Part of the ruler's job is to collect taxes (13:6b)
   C. Part of our tax paying is a spiritual obligation (13:7)

I. We Must All Submit to Human Government (Rom. 13:1–5)

Because Human Government Comes by God's Decree (v. 1b). First Paul gives us our duty, and then he states why this is true. All governments universally are embraced in this reference to "governing authorities," not just Roman rulers. No matter what means these rulers used to come into power, every one of them, without exception, is where he or she is by the command of God. Jesus himself recognized that the successors of Caesar and Jeroboam were appointed to their leadership positions by God. Even tyrants who think they seized power by their own hands never got to any such power until God gave it to them. Therefore, each ruler is a minister/servant of God (v. 4). So, both the form of civil government and the governors themselves are ordained by God.

The word for "submit" in Greek is *hypotasso*, usually a military term, where soldiers were to be ranked under or subject to the authority of a superior officer. The verb is a passive imperative, meaning the principle is a command, not an option. Thus Christians should be willing to place themselves under all the governing authorities in every land where each is a citizen or resident.

Some, indeed, are wicked rulers, but then God can use such types of rulers to punish nations as well as to work his purposes.[9]

Because Rebellion against Government Is Rebellion against God (v. 2a). Resistance to a government is the same as resistance to God, except in one major area: when government requires of us anything that is contrary to the law of God. When Peter and John were told by the authorities that they must stop preaching, the two apostles replied: "Judge for yourselves whether it is right in God's sight to obey you rather than God" (Acts 4:19). Naturally, Peter and John had to be willing to face the punishments inflicted by the government if they were caught preaching once again.

Because We Will Be Punished If We Resist (v. 2b). In Numbers 16:3, 13, some 250 malcontents gathered together as a protest against Moses and Aaron's administration. The Lord's response to this uncalled-for opposition was to split the earth open to swallow up the discontented and to send fire forth from himself to consume the rebels. Instead of being sobered by this tragedy, the next day the people went back with additional rebellion against their leadership. This time 14,700 died in a plague. More would have followed had not Aaron made atonement for the people (Num. 16:49). It is a serious matter to take on those whom God has appointed to govern if there is not a higher command that comes from God and runs directly counter to what those rulers require.

Because Government Is a Restraint against Evil (v. 3a). This statement is not meant to qualify or to give alternative grounds for our obedience, for those grounds have already been stated in verse 1. Instead, it states the reason why God has appointed civil governments and thereby gives us a further reason for doing what has already been commanded to us. The good or evil spoken of here is not with regard to Christianity but with regard to society in general. Even the worst of governments can be a source of blessing, even if not in every case.

Because Government Promotes Our Good (vv. 3b–4a). It is fair for Christians and all others to look to governments for the protection of life and property as well as the adjudication of justice. Paul took advantage of such characteristics when he appealed to Caesar for justice (Acts 25:11). He also used the resources of government when the crowd was incited by Demetrius, the silversmith, to riot against Paul's preaching. The city clerk pronounced that the court was ready to hear all complaints against Paul, but that mob action would not be tolerated (Acts 19:38–39).

Because Rulers Are Empowered to Punish Disobedience (v. 4b). The sword, which is the weapon of death, is given to government to bring deserved punishment on all who practice evil. This is merely an extension of the institution of capital punishment given by God to the state in Genesis 9:6. True, Peter was warned by the Lord to put away his sword (Matt. 26:52), for if he took life, he was liable for killing, which would lead to his execution by the state. Paul likewise recognized that if he was found guilty as a wrongdoer, he too might be worthy of death (Acts 25:11). The apostle thereby acknowledged that capital punishment was sometimes justified. Therefore, God has given to nations, states, and police forces worldwide the authority to take life if necessary, but all the actions of government are also reviewable by the Supreme Judge, our Lord himself.

Because Government Should Be Obeyed for Our Conscience's Sake (v. 5). Believers must instinctively realize that submission to the rulers of the land must be carried out not out of fear of the ruler's wrath but for the sake of our conscience before God. We need to earn the praise of those who do what is right. When we obey in this way we put to "silence the ignorance of foolish men" (1 Pet. 2:13–15 NASB).

This might be a difficult task for believers in the face of some tyrants, but it is not a hard thing for God, who rules over the rulers. Robert Haldane said: "When God chooses to overturn the empire of tyrants, He is at no loss for instruments. He is not obliged to employ the heirs of glory in such scenes of blood: He [often] uses the wicked to overturn the wicked."[10]

II. We Must All Pay Taxes to Our Governments (Rom. 13:6–7)

Part of Our Submission Is in Paying Taxes (v. 6a). This does not command us to enjoy paying our taxes, but pay them we must! Tax fraud is huge, amounting to almost one hundred billion dollars a year according to Internal Revenue estimates recently. This is indeed a scandal! Neither Jesus nor Paul made any exceptions. The reason why taxes must be paid is in light of all that is done for us as noted in verses that preceded this one. Taxes were owed as debts.

Part of the Ruler's Job Is to Collect Taxes (v. 6b). For the third time in this context, we are reminded that these rulers are God's servants/ministers. It is for "their full time governing" as God's ministers that the taxes are to be paid.

Part of Our Tax Paying Is a Spiritual Obligation (v. 7). Haldane again makes a most important observation:

> Here, also, it ought to be particularly remarked that [Paul] calls taxes and customs "dues" or *debts*. A tax is a debt in the true sense of the word. . . . It is here explicitly taught that taxes stand by the law of God on the same footing as private debts, which every man is therefore under an equal obligation to discharge. . . . Christians have much reason to be thankful that they are thus, by the authority of God, freed from all responsibility respecting the application of every tax, and that this responsibility rests entirely with the government. Were it otherwise, they would be in constant perplexity on the subject, and almost in every case unable to determine whether it was their duty to pay or to withhold payment. They would thus be exposed every moment to be placed in opposition to the rulers, while at all times it would be actually impossible for them to live in a heathen or a Mohammedan country.[11]

This is an important distinction. If our taxes were not similar to payment for services rendered, it would cause direct conflict when we decided to withhold payment. It would be as if a carpenter came to our house and we asked him first how much he charged per hour. When he said about $20.00 an hour, we asked him how he spent his earnings. Did he get drunk and carouse with loose women? After being put off for the moment, the carpenter admitted he did do these things, but that was none of our business. If we retorted and said, "Yes, it is. I as a Christian cannot support those kinds of activities. Since you said 20 percent of your earnings goes to those kinds of activities, I can only give you $16.00 an hour, for I cannot support the sinful things you do."

This scenario, however, is unthinkable. We pay for services rendered and we are under no moral obligation to pay our carpenter in accordance with our values or ethics or his lack of the same. The same is true of taxes owed to any and all governments (including democracies and republics) by its citizens, for they too are owed as debts. Therefore, those who deducted a portion of their taxes in protest against the Vietnam War were in error, for taxes are "dues" or "debts," and they do not come with ethical demands on the taxpayer as to how that money will be spent by the government.

Peace (Hebrew, *shalom*) comes from God, for as Solomon taught, "When a man's ways are pleasing to the LORD, he makes even his enemies live at peace with him" (Prov. 16:7). The great danger the false prophets exhibit is that they cry "Peace, peace," when there is no peace (Jer. 6:14; 8:11, 15; 14:13; 23:17; 28:9; Ezek. 13:10, 16). And the reason the land has no peace is that men and women are not right with God (Mic. 3:5). However, the person(s) who finds wisdom also walks in the paths of *shalom* (Prov. 3:13–17)—"all [wisdom's] paths are peace."

Conclusions

Even though war is a most unpleasant duty that must be engaged in from time to time by a government, the rules of a "just war" must always fully apply. While believers may disagree over whether they should personally serve a government in any just war, the teaching of Romans 13:1–7 and Deuteronomy 20 do not seem to leave that option open. Believers must not hold back or refuse to pay their federal taxes, for taxes are owed as debts and do not involve any more of a moral decision on our part than paying a workman for services rendered on one's home.

Bibliography

Boettner, Loraine. *The Christian Attitude Toward War*. 3rd ed. Phillipsburg, NJ: Presbyterian and Reformed, 1985.

Clouse, Robert G. *War: Four Christian Views*. Downers Grove, IL: InterVarsity, 1981.

Craigie, Peter C. *The Problem of War in the Old Testament*. Grand Rapids: Eerdmans, 1978.

Harris, Douglas J. *The Biblical Concept of Peace: Shalom*. Grand Rapids: Baker Academic, 1970.

Hess, Richard S., and Elmer A. Martens, eds. *War in the Bible and Terrorism in the Twenty-First Century*. Winona Lake, IN: Eisenbrauns, 2008.

Holmes, Arthur F. *War and Christian Ethics*. Grand Rapids: Baker Academic, 1975.

Johnson, James Turner. *Can Modern War Be Just?* New Haven: Yale University Press, 1984.

Knight, George W., III. "Can a Christian Go to War?" *Christianity Today*, November 1975, 4–7.

Sider, Ronald J. *Non-Violence: The Invincible Weapon?* Dallas: Word, 1989.

Sider, Ronald J., and Richard K. Taylor. "Jesus and Violence: Some Critical Objections." In *Nuclear Holocaust and Christian Hope: A Book for Christian Peacemakers*, 106–13 and 138–43. Downers Grove, IL: InterVarsity, 1982.

Swartley, Willard M. *Slavery, Sabbath, War and Women*. Scottdale, PA: Herald, 1983.

Wink, Walter. *Jesus and Non-Violence: A Third Way*. Minneapolis: Fortress, 2003.

Discussion Questions

1. How do we as believers reconcile the teachings of Jesus on war, violence, and treatment of one's enemies with the teachings of the Old Testament?
2. In what ways were the instructions to the Israelites on the conduct of war similar to those of the Geneva Convention, which came centuries later?
3. Why is paying taxes like paying someone for performing a service in our home?
4. How should we act toward Christians who disagree with us, and we with them, over what the "correct" Christian attitude toward war should be?

16

Wealth, Possessions, and Economics

Deuteronomy 8:1–20

Frequency of Wealth Being Mentioned in the Bible

If all wealth and possessions come from God, then why are some cultures so wealthy and others so poor? Has God forgotten some and overly blessed others? Even more challenging, what is the believer's responsibility in a world that has so much poverty and hunger? Does God favor one economic system of production over another? Does he favor, for example, capitalism over socialism, or a governmentally guided market over a free market? Is the health, wealth, and prosperity gospel a true biblical teaching or is it a Western gospel devoid of biblical backing?

Many do not even like to talk about money, for they believe it is a subject that is very personal and one that should not be discussed in public. But our Lord must have thought differently about that charge, for as John MacArthur has taught:

sixteen of Christ's thirty-eight parables speak about how people should handle earthly treasure. In fact, our Lord taught more about such stewardship (one out of every ten verses in the Gospels) than about heaven and hell combined. The entire Bible contains more than two thousand references to wealth and property, twice as many as the total references to faith and prayer. What we do with the *things* God has given to us is very important to Him.[1]

In a similar manner the eighth commandment of the Decalogue states, "You shall not steal," which introduces a whole gamut of related topics, including the accumulation of wealth, one's earning power, one's spending habits, one's inheriting of wealth and property, and the use of all our possessions. No book in the Old Testament deals more with the curse and the blessings of wealth, affluence, and possessions than the book of Deuteronomy. For example, Deuteronomy 8:17–18 teaches:

> You may say to yourself, "My power and the strength of my hands have produced this wealth for me." But remember the LORD your God, for it is he who gives you the ability to produce wealth, and so confirms his covenant, which he swore to your forefathers, as it is today.

The Source of All Wealth

God, then, is the creator and proprietor of everything in heaven and on earth (Ps. 24:1). Indeed, he claims that all "the silver is mine and the gold is mine" (Hag. 2:8). Therefore, it is not that material goods and things in and of themselves are ungodly or strictly of this age. Everything that God made in the created realm he pronounced "good" as he created it (Gen. 1).

But possessions, wealth, and goods also bring with them responsibilities. We are constantly warned in Scripture that ownership of anything in this world is not an absolute good, but only a relative good. We must use all that we are given in a manner fitting of our role as God's stewards, for what we have is to be shared with our Lord and others; it is all on loan from the Lord—to be used for his glory.

Almost thirty years ago John White wrote a book entitled *The Golden Cow*. In it he gave this satirical but sober analysis:

Not a calf, if you please, but a cow. I call her a *golden cow* because her udders are engorged with liquid gold, especially in the West where she grazes in meadows lush with greenbacks. Her priests placate her by slaughtering godly principles upon whose blood she looks with tranquil satisfaction. Anxious rows of worshipers bow down before their buckets. Although the gold squirts endlessly the worshipers are trembling lest the supply of sacrificial victims should one day fail to appease her. . . .

Fundamentalism is my mother. I was nurtured in her warm bosom. She cared for me with love and taught me all she knew. I owe her (humanly speaking) my life, my spiritual food and many of my early joys. She introduced me to the Savior and taught me to feed on the bread of life. Our relationship wasn't all honey and roses, but she was the only mother I had. I clung to her then and find it hard not to lean on her now. If she let me down at times, I'm old enough to realize that no mother is perfect. But to find out that she was a whore, that she let herself be used by mammon, was another matter. And as the wider evangelical movement gradually took her place in my life it was painful to make the same discovery twice.[2]

The Dangers of Trusting in Wealth

By the time the Old Testament prophets began to minister, the idolatry of *nouveau riche* over their wealth was becoming legendary. The prophet Amos, for example, thundered against his people Israel for selling "the righteous for silver, and the needy for a pair of sandals" (Amos 2:6). Moreover, the nation of Israel trampled on the poor and forced them to give gifts of wheat while building stone mansions and planting lush vineyards (Amos 5:11). Meanwhile the spoiled wives of these robber barons were "haughty, walking along with outstretched necks, flirting with their eyes, tripping along with mincing steps, with ornaments jingling on their ankles" (Isa. 3:16), all the while oppressing the poor and crushing the needy and saying to their husbands, "Bring us some drinks!" (Amos 4:1).

All wealth comes with mixed blessings, for some "rich [persons] may be wise in [their] own eyes" (Prov. 28:11), which can lead to a fall (Prov. 18:10–12). The abundance of a rich man's possessions "permits him no sleep" (Eccles. 5:12). In place of wealth, one ought to consider that "a good name is more desirable than great riches" (Prov. 22:1).

Many famous people have borne testimony to the fact that wealth is not all that it is cracked up to be. Some have humorously picked up the phrase "Show me the money!" from the popular 1996 film *Jerry Maguire*. But that has not been a ticket to happiness either. For example, John D. Rockefeller moaned, "I have made millions, but they have brought me no happiness." Cornelius Vanderbilt also despaired that "the care of millions is too great a load. . . . There is no pleasure in it." Likewise John Jacob Astor complained, "[I am] the most miserable man on earth." Even Henry Ford despaired over the loss of any free time, for "[I] was happier doing mechanic's work." Happiness and ease of mind do not come from possessions and wealth in and of themselves.

Even though the "prosperity gospel" of some religious teachers is still going strong in many parts of the world and on television screens in America, its teaching does not match Scripture at all. It cannot be shown from the Bible that God wants his followers to be rich, to have expensive automobiles, and to own expensive homes, yachts, and gorgeous wardrobes. Despite the popularity of this teaching, it celebrates greed and forces a view of God that makes him little more than one who constantly doles out material goods to his people. This false emphasis appears under a number of modern labels, but it detracts from the call of God, which rests on a larger and more scriptural base than this "name it and claim it" sort of jingoism.

How Is Wealth Expanded?

Nevertheless, it is true that God is the source of any and all wealth and possessions that exist in the world around us, for he is the one who supplies two other accompanying factors: he supplies the resources that are used in making wealth, and he grants the efficiency with which wealth is organized. Some argue that wealth's resources are but natural endowments of some humans, such as the giftedness of the people who create wealth, their intellectual know-how that works on wealth, the plants and utilities that form more new products; but on the contrary, even these are given to mortals as trusts from God. No one can declare what E. F. Hutton used to enjoy saying: "I did it myself; I earned it."

Brian Griffiths, a Christian and an international economist, as well as a director of the Bank of England, noted that:

> The creation of wealth takes place when an individual or corporation employs the potential labour and capital resources available and uses these to produce something . . . which has greater value than the resources used.

In this sense wealth creation is the value added during the production process. For it to take place successfully, . . . the end product must have a monetary value greater than that of the resources drawn on; there must be some technical process of production; there must be some person or group of people who take the entrepreneurial initiative in bringing the resources together; and there has to be some entity within which the whole process takes place—a family, a partnership, company or public utility.[3]

Wealth and Economics

Some who advocate the simple lifestyle frequently assume or declare that those who amass wealth do so at the expense of others. In their view, all evidence of wealth is the result of the oppression and the exercise of power in some cruel way or another. But defenders of free-market economies argue that these critics are playing the "zero-sum game," which assumes that when one side wins, the other side loses, as in a baseball game. But the flaw in this type of argument is that it is possible to have both sides win in those kinds of economic exchanges that are "positive-sum."[4] In voluntary exchanges, both parties may end up in better economic shape than when they began.

In the last century, machines and basic ingenuity have dramatically increased productivity. For example, a giant combine can now sweep through hundreds of acres of wheat, corn, oats, or rice, and can produce more than hundreds of farmers who previously used slow methods of plowing with horses and threshing grain in one gathering place with an immovable machine.

If this change has come, then the question now is: How should a society decide to distribute its wealth? One answer is the "Free-Market Approach," wherein there is a minimum of interference from the state or government, and the individuals are on their own to design better ways of doing old tasks. It was Adam Smith (1723–90), a Scottish economist, who made famous the metaphor that there is an invisible hand that guides a society's use of wealth as each person makes his or her own decisions on how to produce something better than has been produced before with a greater profit.[5] This approach is basically individualistic, even though the government watches for fairness and honesty in its practices.

In contrast to the free-market system, others contend for the "Guided-Market Approach," in which the planners guide the economy toward certain desirable goals through the use of taxes, tariffs, subsidies, and monetary policies. Private interests, left to the laissez-faire approach of the free markets, these advocates argue, will never achieve certain social goals such as building a highway system like the Eisenhower Interstate System, or making sure that public values, such as clean air legislation, are enacted against industrial polluters. Some central government controls are needed, claim the Guided-Market economists.

Others argue that some type of middle-road theory is needed between the laissez-faire type of free-market approach and the government control model, for if individualism is left to itself, it will lead to a totalitarian socialism. In fact, one by one, many former capitalistic economies in Europe and North America are abandoning pure capitalism and adopting a mixed sort of capitalism. Free-market purists scoff at these moves and derisively call them "Redistribution Economies" or "Interventionist Economies."

Morality and the Market System

The best conclusion seems to be that it is impossible to ease, reduce, or eliminate poverty by slicing the economic pie into small enough pieces so that everyone in the world gets an equal portion of the pie. There is just not enough pie to go around! But history seems to have demonstrated that the best way to benefit the poor is by increasing the productivity of the market systems.

Up to this point in time, the free-market approach has done more to provide for the masses around the globe than any other market system. Though the market invariably will have competitors, those who best cooperate tend to succeed in the marketplace better than others.

Did not Jesus teach in Luke 16:9 that his people should use their resources as wisely as the unjust steward? And did not our Lord commend the rich farmer in Luke 12:16–21 for being a successful businessman, while he castigated him for his self-centered materialism? So what does Scripture teach on these matters?

Cautions in the Use and Love of Money

There is a strong possibility that some will come to love money more than they love God (Job 31:24–28; Prov. 11:28; 1 Tim. 6:17–18). This in turn could lead some to a false sense of security, which is in itself self-deceiving (Matt. 13:22; Mark 4:19). This could further lead to building our lives on an unstable foundation (Prov. 23:4–5). Some are led to steal from God (Mal. 3:8) and then to steal from others (1 John 3:17).

To focus only on making money is to be bent on making money in every way possible. The appetite becomes almost insatiable, for some never seem to have enough. Often this leads to flaunting it before others and developing a stingy attitude toward the needs of the poor and the work of God.

The cure for these and other ills is found in Scripture, but especially in the great teaching text of Deuteronomy 8:1–20.

Remembering Where Everything and Anything Come From

Text: Deuteronomy 8:1–20

Title: "Remembering Where Everything and Anything Come From"

Focal Point: verse 11, "Be careful that you do not forget the LORD your God."

Homiletical Keyword: Reminders

Interrogative: What are the reminders, lest we forget the Lord in what we have?

Outline:
  I. We do not secure our own well-being by our own strength (8:1–6)
  II. We must not forget God when we are full and have plenty (8:7–11)
  III. We must not forget God, the giver of all we have (8:12–18)
  IV. We must not follow other priorities in place of God (8:19–20)

I. We Do Not Secure Our Own Well-Being by Our Own Strength (Deut. 8:1–6)

Moses cautions us to "be careful to follow every command [the Lord is] giving [them and, by extension, us] today" (v. 1). This reinforces the relevancy of this teaching for our day as well as for that time. The call is to be careful and to follow all that the Lord has commanded us to do.

God did not immediately abandon the rebels of that day, but lovingly pursued these same people "with a pardon in his hand," as John Bunyan would put it in *Grace Abounding* (paragraph #173). It is the reminder of God's former acts of goodness and graciousness that should prepare us for future cares.

Surely our Lord wants us to enjoy life, but life is more than eating and drinking. Life is about feeding the soul, for that is what persons really live on—the Word of God (v. 3). To only eat and drink is merely to exist.

It is also true that God disciplines his sons and daughters, so do not forget to trust him during those dark nights of the soul. This work of disciplining us (v. 5) completes a trilogy of fatherly acts of training that come to God's children: he humbles us (v. 3a), he teaches us (v. 3b), and he disciplines us (v. 5).

But in no way do we secure for ourselves any of the good things that have come to us, for they have come from God.

II. We Must Not Forget God When We Are Full and Have Plenty (Deut. 8:7–11)

Once again, verse 11 warns, "Be careful," for after the people of that day and ours have eaten and are full, there is always the temptation to forget who provided all of this. However, the land that God was giving to his people was indeed a "good land." An Old Egyptian story about a man named Sinuhe describes his impression of the land of Canaan, where he ended up. Sinuhe used many of the same terms used in verses 7–9 to describe that same land of Canaan. In fact, so plentiful are the products of the land into which the Israelites are going that "[they] will lack nothing" (v. 9).

Once they and we have eaten and been satisfied with all the provisions that come from the hand of God, what should be more natural than to give thanks and to "praise the LORD [our] God for the good land he has given [us]" (v. 10).

Unfortunately, it is all too true that receiving so many good gifts and possessions from our God often leads not to praise but to a forgetting of the Lord who provided all of these gifts. Such a rejection

of God involves deliberately putting out of our mind how much we
have received that was not the result of our good works or efforts.
The affluent society just doesn't get it at times. So much from such a
wonderful Lord; yet so little praise and remembrance of all that God
has done for such wealthy nations!

III. We Must Not Forget God, the Giver of All We Have (Deut. 8:12–18)

Many to whom so much is given yield little more than a personal
pride that tends to completely replace God (v. 14). The Giver of the
gifts is quickly forgotten now that we think we are on our own feet,
and the gifts replace the Giver. Self-sufficiency takes over as we begin
to say, "My power and the strength of my hands have produced
this wealth for me" (v. 17). What a tragedy! Widespread prosperity
in that day, and in ours, leads too often to gross ingratitude. And
when we disregard God's kindnesses in bringing us to where we are
in our possessions and wealth, it is not long before we also disobey
his word.

In that sense, the gifts God gives to prosperous nations come as a
test. We will now see if, after we leave and abandon such a gracious
Giver, it will "go well" with us (v. 16). Alas, all too often, rather than
worshiping and thanking God for what we have, we instead worship
the work of our own hands (v. 17). So the question is a very real one:
Is it only when we are without any goods representing affluence,
property, or possessions that we rely on the Lord suddenly in those
desperate circumstances? That too would be tragic.

But look at the gifts Israel had received up to this point: God "led
[them] through the vast and dreadful desert" (v. 15a), he delivered them
from "venomous snakes and scorpions" (v. 15c), "he brought [them]
water out of hard rock" (v. 15d), and he fed them with "manna to eat
in the desert" (v. 16a).

So, people, "Remember the LORD your God, for it is he who gives
you the ability to produce wealth, and so confirms his covenant,
which he swore to your forefathers, as it is today" (v. 18). Since it
is God who creates wealth, to God must be rendered all honor and
praise, not to the system of free enterprise, capitalism, guided market, or any other system or method of managing the accumulation
of wealth.

IV. We Must Not Follow Other Priorities in Place of God (Deut. 8:19–20)

Should Israel, and we, still go after other gods in spite of this warning, abandoning our God will mean disaster (v. 19). Since all of this is still relevant for our day, once again Moses repeats that this warning is coming "today" (v. 19), as he has reminded them in verses 1, 11, 18, and 19. To abandon God is to invite God's destruction of us as a nation and as personal participants in the grace and covenant of God.

Therefore, we cannot worship success, money, power, status, reputation, or acclaim, no matter how much or how little we have. One would think that the nations that were destroyed before us for their turning away from God would have been a warning and a cause for correcting our wayward course.

Conclusions

1. Some say we need to "Remember Pearl Harbor," or "Remember the Maine," or "Remember the Alamo." But far and away from all of these great events in history, we had better "Remember our Lord" and what he has done in our lives.
2. The place where God tests those who have been given much of this world's goods is in the area of their hearts (v. 2).
3. The dangers of wealth are real, but so are the dangers of the so-called wealth, health, and prosperity gospel. Both can lead to a practical atheism that ends up in outright disregard for the Giver of life and all the gifts we own.
4. The most precious possession any people ever had was not life, goods, or their abundance; instead, it was the gift of the Word of God. It is from this word that folks really live. We do not live by our wits, our degrees, our grandchildren, or our acumen. We live by every word that proceeds out of the mouth of God (v. 3).

Bibliography

Alcorn, Randy. *Money, Possessions, and Eternity*. Wheaton: Tyndale, 1989.

Barnett, Jake. *Wealth and Wisdom: A Biblical Perspective on Posses- sions*. Colorado Springs: NavPress, 1987.

Clark, David K., and Robert V. Rakestraw, eds. *Readings in Christian Ethics*. Vol. 2, *Issues and Applications*, 339–80. Grand Rapids: Baker Academic, 1996.

Clouse, Robert G., ed. *Wealth and Poverty: Four Christian Views of Economics*. Downers Grove, IL: InterVarsity, 1984.

Davis, John Jefferson. *Your Wealth in God's World: Does the Bible Support the Free Market?* Phillipsburg, NJ: Presbyterian and Re- formed, 1984.

Griffiths, Brian. *The Creation of Wealth: A Christian Case for Capi- talism*. Downers Grove, IL: InterVarsity, 1984.

———. *Morality and the Market Place: Christian Alternatives to Cap- italism and Socialism*. London: Hodder and Stoughton, 1982.

MacArthur, John. *Whose Money Is It, Anyway? A Biblical Guide to Using God's Wealth*. Nashville: Word, 2000.

Nash, Ronald H. *Poverty and Wealth*. Westchester, IL: Crossway, 1986.

Sider, Ronald J. *Rich Christians in an Age of Hunger*. 3rd ed. Waco: Word, 1990.

Wogaman, J. Philip. *Economics and Ethics*. Philadelphia: Fortress, 1986.

Discussion Questions

1. What is so bad (or good) about money from a biblical point of view?
2. Does Jesus want everyone to be rich, wealthy, and healthy? If so, how do you know? If not, why not, according to the Bible?
3. What are the responsibilities of those who are rich? First toward God? Then toward the poor of the world?
4. Does the Bible prefer one market system over another? What biblical clues can we use to form the preferred economic system we think is best for answering the poverty of the world and for being responsible to God?

17

Animal "Rights" and Factory Farms

Isaiah 11:6–9; 65:25

The story of the Bible begins with God's creation of animals and man. In that narrative, God subordinated the animals to humanity and gave humans the responsibility for them as well. Humanity was to care for the animals just as God cared for all of creation. However, in the same way that God may use all of his creation for his own glory, in all of his holiness and goodness, so humanity may use the animals, yet it must be ready to answer for this responsibility to God.[1]

Even so, animals were not meant for eternal life. God approved of animal sacrifice, not because he approved of any purported suffering and death, but because he disapproved of sin. Since blood was the symbol of life, it was divinely decreed that it should also be the symbol of humanity's atonement. God is as merciful to animals as

211

he is to humanity, but they along with the rest of creation and all humanity share in God's wrath against sin, as seen in the destruction of the world in the flood.

Various texts in Scripture point to God's call for care of his creation. For example, in the teaching of the Decalogue, animals were also given a time of "rest" on the Sabbath (Exod. 20:10). Again, Nathan's story of the rich man who stole the little ewe lamb from a poor man to feed his guests outraged David for the rich man's insensitivity and miserliness (2 Sam. 12:5–6). Add to this the book of Jonah's contribution to this subject. There God's mercy extended to the cattle in the city of Nineveh along with mercy extended to the one hundred twenty thousand youngsters (Jon. 4:11). Why, even the prolific sparrows are cared for by God (Matt. 10:29). Thus, while there is not a massive amount of material on the subject of animal care, there is enough to suggest thoughtful usage of the animals.

Distorted Views of Animal Life

In most Oriental religions, however, an overemphasis on animal life has gotten so out of balance that animals are almost worshiped, if not actually so. Animal life, of course, is to be treated kindly, but never at the expense of humanity. An inverted "reverence for life" can end up being more cruel than outright killing of them, as for example in the case of some animals who are diseased or who are permanently maimed. In some cases in history, and in the present time, rats and vermin are allowed to live, indeed thrive, at the expense of human life, due to a misplaced respect for animal life. It is not the length of the animals' lives that is primary, as if they too were meant for eternity; the quality and purpose of their lives now is what matters.

So strongly are some in support of animal "rights" that they have tended to put more value on the whales, and on their pets, than they have put on people. Surely that is a confusion of a major sort, for animals do not have the image of God within them, nor were they put in charge of creation or made responsible to God for the management of the created order.

Elmer Smick reminds us that when an animal acts out of character, as in the case of an ox that takes on the habit of goring people, then that animal is to be put down.[2] Furthermore, it would appear that animals are capable of being possessed of an evil spirit. Jesus allowed an evil spirit to enter a herd of pigs, resulting in several thousand jumping off a cliff and drowning (Matt. 8:28–32). This is not to claim that animals have a moral nature or purposeful conduct, for these matters cannot be based solely on activity.

The Charge of Factory Farming

Recently there has come the charge that the method of caring for animals on the larger farms has made them into machines of production. In this scenario, the new goal of farming is to move the cattle or poultry from breeding to meat or egg production in the shortest period possible in the smallest space possible with the cheapest feed possible.[3] This same opinion was expressed in an article in *Christian Century* in 2001 entitled "Farm Factories: The End of Animal Husbandry" by Bernard E. Rollin, a distinguished professor of philosophy, physiology, and animal sciences at Colorado State University in Fort Collins, Colorado. He claimed that:

> Factory farming, or confinement-based industrialized agriculture, has been an established feature in North America and Europe since its introduction at the end of World War II. Agricultural scientists were concerned about supplying Americans with sufficient food. After the Dust Bowl and the Great Depression, many people had left farming. . . . At the same time, a variety of technologies relevant to agriculture were emerging. . . . Animal agriculture beg[a]n to industrialize.[4]

Many experts in the field were discouraged by the name change from "Animal Husbandry" to "Animal Science" in agricultural schools in most state universities. The point is well taken, for "to husband" is to care for the animals. The change to "Animal Science," it is thought, makes it possible to look on animals as specimens that we can manipulate. Accordingly, the claim is made that the larger proportion of hogs and chickens raised for human consumption are grown in factory farms that are owned and operated by multinational corporations. Over against this trend, the western cattle rancher is praised as the last practitioner of husbandry because of the use of extensive pastures in which the cattle freely roam and graze.

The Issue: Confinement Agriculture

The charge is that confinement agriculture violates biblical principles. The texts used to support this charge, however, seem to deal more with the general care and well-being of the animals, and the estimate of confinement as a negative principle must be assumed in every case. Bernard Rollin gives six biblical mandates where we are told to avoid deliberate cruelty to animals: (1) We are to help raise back on its feet an animal that has fallen under its load, even though it may belong to our enemy (Exod. 23:12; Deut. 22:4). (2) We are warned not to plow with an ox and an ass yoked together, for that would impose a hardship on the weaker animal (Deut. 22:10). (3) As already noted, we are to rest the animals on the Sabbath day (Exod. 20:10). (4) We are not to muzzle an ox that is trampling (i.e., threshing) the grain, but let the ox take a swipe of grain as it goes round and round (Deut. 25:4). (5) We are to rescue a son or an ox that has fallen into a well, even if we must violate the Sabbath (Luke 14:5). (6) We are not to boil a young goat (a "kid") in its mother's milk (Exod. 23:19; 34:26; Deut. 14:21), though this practice was forbidden because this was a pagan ritual as borne out by the discovery in the Canaanite Ugaritic tablets.[5] All of these speak of the care that is to be given to animals, but the issue of how much space each animal must be given is not a direct objective or directive of any of these texts.

The argument, therefore, must move on to the case for animal suffering. Can a case be made for the fact that animals can experience pain and suffering? Certainly an animal suffers when it is not given the proper amount of water and feed. And an animal can get sick when any disease breaks out due to lack of proper management of housing conditions or standards of cleanliness. But there does not seem to be a way of demonstrating that debeaking chickens that are involved in cannibalism of other chickens is a source of pain to the chickens so altered, just as there is no evidence that castrating swine or cattle leaves the creature suffering. Others cite the cutting off of pigs' tails to cure tail-biting among hogs as another source of pain and suffering to the animals. And even if suffering could be proven in some, or all, of these cases, would the suffering be any less necessary than the suffering experienced by humans in some necessary operations they must go through? There is no guarantee in this fallen creation that there will be no pain as humans or animals go through life.

It is true, of course, that in 1988 Sweden banned high-confinement agriculture and Britain and the European Union (EU) banned sow confinement.[6] Even though food at the turn of the century cost over 50 percent of one's income, up until recently it had cost only 11 percent of one's income—a decisive downturn! Many of the savings found in food costs of a family in the US, some contend, are paid for by decreased concern for animal welfare. But it may equally be attributed to the enormous advances in technology in everything from fertilizers to the mammoth combines and tractors now in use that cover vast amounts of acres. Parallel to what has been achieved in the advances in farming grains are the gains that have been matching in raising poultry and cattle in confined pens.

Vegetarianism: A New Way of Solving the Problem

Matthew C. Halteman has argued in his essay "Compassionate Eating as Care of Creation" that the way to act Christianly is to refrain from, or at least reduce, our eating of meat and to eat only, or mainly, vegetables. He points to others who "maintain that compassionate eating should be exclusively plant-based, since the production of eggs and dairy causes significant animal suffering and death as well."[7] Halteman frequently mentions "the peaceable kingdom," apparently alluding to Isaiah 11:6–9 and 65:25. For example, he claimed that "the goal of compassionate eating in summary, is not some this-worldly utopia. . . . Rather, [it] is this: . . . to live [as] faithfully as we can toward the peaceable kingdom in which the harmony among human beings, animals, and the natural world will be restored."[8]

We will return to this passage later, but for the moment this passage of Scripture, which has been the subject of some famous painters and Quaker theology, reflects more of what is called in theology a postmillennial view of life, in which things are to get progressively better as God's rule and reign comes in the historic flow of history rather than in any sort of divine in-breaking at the second coming of Jesus, as premillennialists hold.

Those who resist confinement agriculture are ready to accept the increased food costs that they believe the abandonment of confined poultry and cattle agriculture must involve. However, this has not proven to be the case in all aspects of farming. Take for example the doom-and-gloom scenario predicted two centuries ago by Thomas Malthus, the population explosion expert.[9] He forecasted the fact that exponential population growth in human population (doubling every twenty-five years), if left unchecked, would overwhelm food supplies, which he calculated would only grow arithmetically. This would lead to widespread starvation and mayhem, in his opinion. Malthus did not foresee the advances in technology that involved everything from fertilizers to tractors. Maize, or what Americans call "corn," is the benchmark grain of the commodity markets. Its price has climbed to more than four times what it was just a few years ago. Despite bumper crops, grain stockpiles were lowered in 2004 by 18 million tons to 104 million tons, the lowest in three decades. Now the newly rich in China are consuming large quantities of both meat and grain. China is a nation with almost 23 percent of the earth's population, but it has only 7 percent arable land to produce its own grain and beef. But the world's capacity to produce more in the area of grains keeps increasing each year despite the lowering of the grain stockpile and the prohibition against cattle confinement in the European Union. The Earth Policy Institute, a think tank, estimates that the remaining grain stockpiles could feed the world for fifty-nine days, while most would be happier if it were seventy days' worth of stockpiling for food security. But it is noteworthy that the way this increase has been met in the area of grains should also lead the way for us to consider how it might be done in the area of cattle and poultry.

The Future Peace in the Animal World

The prophet Isaiah first described in Isaiah 11:1–5 the righteous conduct of the Son of David, then he followed this in verses 6–9 with the peace that will prevail under his future government, indeed, "the peaceable kingdom." Verses 6, 7, and 9 are repeated in Isaiah 65:25, but in a more abbreviated and condensed form.

But how are these verses to be interpreted? Calvin and many ancient interpreters take these verses in an allegorical or spiritual sense, in which the animals represented various spiritual conditions and states that are found within human beings. The Rabbis, and many premillennialists, however, take the passage literally or realistically, looking for a literal fulfillment and a change in the animal and created world from one of violence and cruelty to one of total peace and harmony in the coming millennium of Christ's thousand years of ruling and reigning on this earth.

Text: Isaiah 11:6–9; 65:25

Title: "The Future Peace in the Animal World"

Focal Point: verse 9, "[The animals] will neither harm nor destroy on all my holy mountain."

Homiletical Keyword: Actions

Interrogative: What actions will secure the future peace in the animal world?

Outline:

I. The carnivorous and the domestic animals will lie down together (11:6)

II. The carnivorous and the domestic animals will all eat hay and straw (11:7)

III. The viper will not harm the infant (11:8)

IV. The peace and security of the created order will be restored (11:9)

I. The Carnivorous and the Domestic Animals Will Lie Down Together (Isa. 11:6)

When our Lord returns as the reigning Seed of David, the rest of creation will be restored to what it was originally intended to be. Just as evil will be eradicated from society, so all ferocity will be removed from the lower animals as well. Peace and harmony will be the rule of that new day.

If the cause of Noah's flood was that "all flesh [i.e., both man and beast, I take it] had corrupted its ways" (Gen. 6:12 NRSV), then the prospect of peace would signal the peace and harmony of both humans and animals in the coming age. While nothing is said here of the products of the earth in this passage, it must be assumed that to heal one is to signify the healing of all of creation.

It is important to notice that the healing is never envisioned to be completed in this age. The context for this passage is the second coming of the King of Peace, who brings with him the peace and harmony that he had originally invested in all of nature and creation.

It appears as if the independently strong of the species will become dependent on the weak, or at least they will be concessive to one another. These otherwise wild animals will yield their leadership to a "little child," if not in fact, then at least in surrendering control of their voracious appetites.

II. The Carnivorous and the Domestic Animals Will All Eat Hay and Straw (Isa. 11:7)

No longer will the lion and, presumably, the bear be thirsty for blood, but they will content themselves with hay and straw as the domesticated ox has for all this time. This prophecy will be realized, as we have said, at the juncture of the conclusion of history leading into the entrance into eternity.

Some cannot accept a literal interpretation of this verse, for this would require a basic alteration of the lion's nature. But to reinterpret it simply for this objection alone is to diminish the power of God. Surely the one who made the gastronomical processes of the lion in the first place is able to retrofit the lion to enjoy the produce of the land rather than the blood of other animals or humanity.

III. The Viper Will Not Harm the Infant (Isa. 11:8)

In one more picture of a changed ecology, the weaned child can stretch out his hand as boldly and fearlessly as the child pleases, even if the child's play area is over the hole of the viper itself. Normally, one would want to snatch a child playing over the den of poisonous snakes away from that danger as quickly as possible. This is a changed world indeed, but it does not represent the kind of world we are currently living in. To call for the so-called peaceable kingdom (represented par excellence here in Isa. 11:6–9; 65:25) now, in our day, is to miss the fact that these conditions will not be realized until the Messiah returns again.

IV. The Peace and Security of the Created Order Will Be Restored (Isa. 11:9)

The reference to "they" in verse 9 continues to refer to the animals. The promise is that there will be safety and security. All anxiety will be removed because "the earth will be full of the knowledge of the LORD as the waters cover the sea" (v. 9). With the prevalence of the knowledge of God, the destructive hostility between the animal world and humanity will be vanquished.

The references to the "holy mountain" and the "earth" have primary reference to the land of Israel, where the dominion of the Son of David will originate. From that time forward, that site in Israel will be the paradisiacal center of the whole earth. This knowledge of God will be an experiential knowledge that can be personally known by all who live and move under the regime of the newly arrived Messiah.

Conclusions

Scripture does call for a kind and generous care of the animal world, but the full healing of the created realm is not promised until the time when the Messiah returns. This is no more a loophole that allows for outrageous maltreatment of animals than the dominion of humans over the earth is an excuse for abuse of the environment. Balanced thinking and acting is required in any case. In the meantime, "We know that the whole creation has been groaning as in the pains of childbirth right up to the present time. Not only so, but we ourselves, who have been the firstfruits of the Spirit, groan inwardly as we wait eagerly for our adoption as sons, the redemption of our bodies" (Rom. 8:22–23). Certain things in the created order, as in the realm of humans, sense that something is out of order. We wait for our Lord to fix what the fall badly damaged, without using it as an excuse for abuse of the created order or of animals. Scripture does not speak of animals as if they had certain "rights"; therefore, it is a misnomer to speak of animals as having "rights" similar or parallel to those that mortals, who have the added advantage of being made in the image of God, possess.

God has given many of the animals as food for humans. Only Eastern religions, up to most recent times, had leveled out all of life to be similar and without any distinction, whether human or animal. This is a confusion as well. Vegetarianism is not mandated by Scripture, but those who choose this path and wish to supplement their diet by vitamins to make up for the absence of protein and the like are not to be condemned; Scripture does not have a dog in that fight.

On the issue of confinement of animals, much depends on what sort of conditions exist for the health of the animals, but it cannot be assumed that all forms of confinement necessarily imply the worst sort of health conditions for these animals. Here again, the farmer, like all mortals, is answerable to God alone at the final day when we see him face to face.

Bibliography

Fabre, Jean-Henri. "Air, Necessary to Life." Translated by Michael Attias. *Chicago Review* 51 (Spring 2005): 125–31.

Halteman, Matthew C. "Compassionate Eating as Care of Creation." Washington, DC: The Humane Society of the United States, 2008.

Johnson, Dan. "Defending the Rights of Chickens." *Futurist* 52.4 (May 1998): 11.

Linzey, Andrew. *Christianity and the Rights of Animals.* New York: Crossroad, 1987.

Rollin, Bernard E. "Farm Factories: The End of Animal Husbandry." *Christian Century*, December 19, 2001, 26–29.

Smick, Elmer. "Animals." In *Baker's Dictionary of Christian Ethics*, edited by Carl F. H. Henry, 21–23. Grand Rapids: Baker Academic, 1973.

Vantassel, Stephen. "A Biblical View of Animals: A Critical Response to the Theology of Andrew Linzey" (a privately circulated essay, Newburgh, IN).

Zee, Leonard Vander. "Also Many Animals." *Banner.* April 2008, 1–3.

Discussion Questions

1. In order to demonstrate proper kindness and husbandry, to what extent must farmers care for animals headed for slaughter?
2. What is the difference in the views of an Eastern religion on the care and rights of animals vis-à-vis those of a Christian?
3. From the verses in Scripture that talk about the care of animals, what counsel would you offer to Christian farmers on the proper care they are to give their animals? Should all forms of animal confinement be disallowed?
4. In what ways could the teaching gathered from this chapter affect the way we keep and treat our own pets?

18

CARE FOR THE ENVIRONMENT

Psalm 8:1–9

The classic, and much-reprinted, essay that became famous for laying the blame for the ecological crisis in our day at the feet of Christians because of their biblical teaching about "dominion" in Genesis 1:28 was written by Lynn White Jr.[1] White, an American historian, made Christianity the "ecological scapegoat." He depicted Christianity as a destroyer of pagan animism, which in turn made it possible for Christians to exploit nature with an air of indifference to the feelings of natural objects—at least those Christians who took Genesis 1:26 and 1:28 literally.

Less temperate, but just as condemnatory, was Ian McHarg, a professor of landscape architecture and town planning at the University of Pennsylvania. He commented that Genesis 1:26, 28 (which reads: "Then God said, 'Let us make man [i.e., humans] in our image, in our likeness, and let them rule over the fish of the sea, the birds of the air, over the livestock, over all the earth, and over all the creatures that move along the ground' . . . and God blessed them and said to them, 'Be fruitful and increase in number, fill the earth and subdue it' ") is

> one [biblical] text of compounded horror which will guarantee that the relationship of man to nature can only be destruction, which will atrophy any creative skill. . . . [It] will explain all the despoliation accomplished by western man for at least these 2000 years; you do not have to look any further than this ghastly, calamitous text.[2]

In our contemporary world, a pantheistic view of nature and the world has risen to the ascendancy. Christianity, it is charged, has separated humans from nature rather than linking us with the rest of nature. Pantheism views human intervention with nature to be wrong because it breaks up our oneness with nature. Therefore, trees must not be cut down for lumber or firewood nor must animals be killed for food. Christians would be well advised to follow the pattern of St. Francis of Assisi, it is contended, for he was appointed by the pope as the "Patron Saint of Ecology." St. Francis is known for his preaching to the birds and his talking to the flowers. But other than his personal regard for the created order, he did not help us by setting down any biblical or theoretical guidelines as to how mortals are to be separate from nature yet careful in our care and regard for the natural order.

How shall Christians respond to such charges? Is the teaching in Genesis 1:26, 28 responsible for all that is now put under the "greenhouse effect" and the environmental imbalance described so frequently? If the dominion view of ecology states, from a Christian view of the environment, that humans have a right to use creation for their own needs, yet without vandalizing or raping it, but using it as persons responsible to God and sensitive to nature itself, must it be judged wrong and inferior by those who take a deeply spiritual approach to ecology from a stance of pantheism or a nature mysticism?

A Christian view of the environment begins with God. He is the Creator and Sustainer of the whole universe. As will be seen in our key text in Psalm 8, he designated the moon and stars to rule over the heavens, and he likewise made men and women to rule over the earth. This mighty duo was commanded to till the earth and to keep the garden (Gen. 1:28; 2:15). The clear inference is that God is the owner of the universe (Ps. 24:1, "The earth is the LORD's and everything in it, the world, and all who live in it"; cf. Job 41:11, "Everything under heaven belongs to me"). The psalmist expressed the same thought when he told Israel that it was no favor to bring God bulls and goats as a sacrifice, for "every animal of the forest is mine, and the cattle on a thousand hills. I know every bird in the mountains, and the creatures of the field are mine. If I were hungry I would not tell you, for the world is mine, and all that is in it" (Ps. 50:9–12).

Moreover, God not only owns the world, but he sustains it as well. This he does by his "powerful word" (Heb. 1:3). "In him," Paul teaches in Colossians 1:17, "all things hold together." Without God's sustaining power, the universe itself would possibly crash and implode on itself. Its regulation is so perfect that we adjust our watches and even our atomic clocks by the dependable movement of the heavenly bodies that are also part of God's management and preservation.

It must also be recalled that God made a covenant with the world following the flood in Noah's day (Gen. 9:16). The divine word was made with both humanity and all the animals. The "sign" God set in the sky affirming his covenant was the rainbow. The promise was that never again would the waters mount up in such a way as to destroy all life (Gen. 9:12–15).

God placed human beings in the garden to exercise dominion and to subdue the earthly creation (Gen. 1:28). They were not to bully, violate, or rape the land and all its inhabitants; they were to take care of the garden (Gen. 2:15). The word for "take care of it" is the Hebrew word *shamar*, "to guard, to keep, to preserve." This gave no license to abuse the land and to plunder its resources without tenderly replacing and restoring it to its former state—or even improving what it was when individuals first came upon it.

Even apart from the creation narrative, God made a direct connection between the people's obedience to his specific commands about exercising a proper stewardship of the land and the blessing that would come to the people and the land (Lev. 25:1–12). The Israelites, for example, were to conserve the trees of the land (Deut. 20:19–20), bury their human waste (Deut. 23:13), treat their domesticated animals generously (Deut. 25:4), and respect their wildlife (Deut. 22:6).

When all is told, there are no grounds for apathy toward the environment. To casually declare that the world and all that is in it is corrupted by sin and is therefore evil and to be used with abandon (since the Lord was to return soon), is to earn divine judgment upon ourselves and the work of our hands. We, the body of Christ, cannot steer away from teaching and preaching on care for the environment; our doctrine of creation and our view of God will not allow it. Nor can we fall into the pantheistic trap, in the absence of biblical preaching and teaching, and conclude that we and the environment are the same. Technology is a wonderful gift from God, but it must be used properly.

Technology is neither good nor bad in itself, but the worldview behind it sets the value it will have for good or for ill. The fact that we *can* do something is no basis for why we *should* do it. Accordingly, fertilizers, herbicides, and pesticides can be of enormous help, but each must be carefully evaluated as to what side effects it brings along with its intended use. Technology must not be the shaker and mover of our society, but we the people of God must be the controllers of technology if we are to be keepers and managers of the earth where God has placed us. It is worth remembering the inscription I saw over the old Cavendish Laboratory of the Physics Department in Cambridge, England. It reads:

> Great are the works of the LORD,
> pondered over by all who delight in them. Psalm 111:2

Extolling God's Majestic Sub-contract with Humanity

The Christian action proposed here to help us keep humanity's true stewardship in focus comes from Psalm 8:1–9.

Text: Psalm 8:1–9

Title: "Extolling God's Majestic Sub-contract with Humanity"

Focal Point: verses 4, 6, "What is man that you are mindful of him?
. . . You put everything under his feet."

Homiletical Keyword: Evidences

Interrogative: What are the evidences that God has put humanity in charge of everything on earth?

Outline:
  I. See the majesty of our Lord radiate from his work (8:1b–2)
    A. God is king, governor, and ruler
    B. God is majestic in all he does
    C. God is glorified in his deployments

II. See the interest God takes in his mortals (8:3–4)
  A. There are two spheres of rule
    1. Heavenly
    2. Earthly
  B. The sphere given to humans
III. See the glory conferred on mortals (8:5–6)
  A. The gifts conferred on humans
    1. Made a little lower than heavenly beings
    2. Crowned with glory and honor
    3. Made ruler over the works of God's hands
    4. Everything was put under their feet
  B. Explanation of the gifts
IV. See the rule placed in mortal hands (8:6–8)
  A. Mortals exercise dominion and subdue the earth
  B. Post-fall position over creation reinstated

Psalm 8 is a hymn of praise. It is nicely bracketed in what is known poetically as an "inclusion," for verse 1 and verse 9 both emphasize "O LORD, our Lord, how majestic is your name in all the earth." This Lord is deliberately called "our Lord." The psalm forms what could be called a "lyric echo" of Moses's account of the creation of the universe. Our joy in the created order could not be possible if it had not been for the work of our Creator. With a living and acting Creator and Sustainer of the universe, it is possible to distinguish between humanity and nature. Pantheism, on the other hand, deifies and glorifies nature (not the Creator) and cannot ultimately distinguish between nature and the pantheist him- or herself.

I. See the Majesty of Our Lord Radiate from His Work (Ps. 8:1b–2)

The Coverdale translation of the Bible in early Europe reads, "O Lorde, oure Governoure," for to speak in this manner was to name him king. One day the "name" of our God will be praised on all the earth, but for the moment, sadly, that is still not yet so! Nevertheless, the "name" of our God acts as a sign, an impress on nature itself, which we see in all God's works in the created order.

It is for this reason that God is also seen as "majestic." This word is also a royal attribute, for it is seen in God's victories (Exod. 15:6), in his judgment (1 Sam. 4:8; Ps. 76:4), in his law (Isa. 42:12), and in his rule over creation at large (Ps. 93:4). This same glory has likewise been set far above the heavens; thus a double acclamation comes to our Lord from the earth below and from heaven on high.

To be more particular, the praise that emanates from the earth matches the heavenly praise offered to our Lord. Psalm 19:1 makes it clear that "the heavens declare the glory of God." But from the earth a paean of praise comes from the lips of suckling children as well as the older kids. No matter how unruly and obnoxious the wicked have become on the earth, they cannot silence the praise that even children raise instinctively to our great God. This praise from little children is celebrated in Matthew 21:15–16.

Indeed, this praise of our God is "ordained," and it is itself a "fortress," a "bulwark" and a "fortification." The words "ordained praise" in Psalm 8:2 (the Hebrew word the NIV translates as "praise" is 'oz, "strength") depict the strength of a fortress and the like. No wonder such words of praise "silence the foe and the avenger."

II. See the Interest God Takes in His Mortals (Ps. 8:3–4)

God rules over two large spheres: the celestial heavens and the planet earth. God made the two great lights on earth (the sun and the moon) "to govern the day and the night, and to separate light from darkness" (Gen. 1:18). Even though our Psalm 8 may have been written as an evening hymn, omitting the sun in deference to "the moon and the stars," it is still clear that the celestial bodies were given their spheres of governing directly by God. But the governance of the earth was likewise directly designated by God and delegated to the man and the woman (Gen. 1:28).

Surely the wide range of celestial space revealed the glory, wisdom, and power of God (Job 36:29; 38:33; Ps. 89:11). All of these bodies in the heavens had their appointed places in the "work" (Ps. 8:3, Hebrew, ma'aseh; note singular, not plural "works") God has given to them. Indeed, they were the work of God's "fingers." So tiny was the huge celestial universe in comparison to God that it was viewed as an entity that could be pushed into shape by the sculptor's divine digits, his "fingers."

Over against that mind-boggling, huge celestial universe, God stooped to place the care of his earth under the oversight and protection of mere mortals such as ourselves. Even the word he used for "man" in verse 4 (Hebrew, 'enosh, coming from 'anash, "to be frail") pointed to humanity's "frailty," "mortality," and "impotence." Humanity certainly was not divine, nor were they in their own nature an obvious choice for this role. The psalmist did not choose to use the word for "man" that comes from gabar, "to be strong, heroic" (as in gibbor khayil, "a mighty man of valor" or the like), nor did he use the Hebrew word 'adam, "to be ruddy, red"; instead, it was the word that recognized the dependency of mortals on God himself.

God was "mindful" or "remembered" (Hebrew, zakar), and he "cared for" him (Hebrew, paqad, "visited" him). Rather than "visiting" humanity with the judgments their sin deserved, the goodness of God dealt gently with them and showed them care, apparently the same care he wanted them to show for the other parts of his creation that he had entrusted to them.

III. See the Glory Conferred on Mortals (Ps. 8:5–6)

Men and women in and of themselves were weak and frail. Nevertheless, God endowed men and women with the "image and likeness" of God (Gen. 1:26–27). Yes, mortals were "less than God" or even "less than the heavenly beings" (Hebrew, 'elohim). While no other creature in all the universe had such high endowments as the image of God, still mortals were made "lower" or "made to lack" (Hebrew, khasar, "to be short of something, to lack something") what was found in God and possibly even found in the angelic beings, if that is how we are to understand the "Elohim" in this difficult passage. Surely the dignity of men and women is a gift from God. The image of God involved the following characteristics: the man and the woman were dominion-havers, who also possessed the ability to show and give love and to communicate, and they were beings who had knowledge (Col. 3:10).

As if to top it all off, it is this evening hymn that celebrates the fact that God has "crowned [the man and the woman] with glory and honor" (v. 5). In like manner, Jesus was crowned as fully man (along with being fully God) in Hebrews 2:7. The "glory" of mortals notes the weightiness and fullness of the tribute given to humanity while "honor" speaks of the beauty and brilliancy of God's gift. Accordingly, mortals made in the image of God are adorned, as it were, with a royal crown; humans were to be lords of all things that dwell on earth.

There were four gifts that God conferred on each mortal: (1) they were made a little lower (or the alternative reading: for a little while lower) than the heavenly beings, (2) they were crowned with glory and honor, (3) they were made rulers over the works of God's hands, and (4) they had everything put under their feet.

IV. See the Rule Placed in Mortal Hands (Ps. 8:6–8)

The privileges and responsibilities assigned here are very reminiscent of Genesis 1:26, 28. The verb "to rule" or "have dominion over" (Hebrew, *radah*) occurs twenty-two times in the Hebrew Qal stem in the Old Testament. It is true that the verb is connected with the idea of force and having mastery over, yet in Leviticus 25:43, 46, 53 its use in the role of the master over a slave is qualified by a strong prohibition against harshness and violence. The verb reflects the language of royalty, yet it also carries the requirement of being compassionate in its use without any exploitation associated with it.

In a similar manner the Hebrew verb for "subdue" (*kabash*) has an element of force in it too, but it likewise is regulated by its semantic parallel, to "till and keep the land" (Gen. 2:5, 15). There is not any excuse here for running roughshod over nature in an abusive and self-ish way. After all, as God's managers and stewards, we must render to God an accounting both in the here and now and in the final day. Since some will nevertheless exploit the land and all creatures on it, it is no wonder that "the whole creation has been groaning as in the pains of childbirth up to the present time" (Rom. 8:22). But of that too we must all, where guilty, give an account at the final day of reckoning, if not before (2 Cor. 5:10).

If our crowning is in the present tense, and it is in verse 5, as is our being made rulers over all the works of God's hands, then it may also be inferred that the reason some businesses and farmers suffer losses is due to the fact that they are acting as tyrants over the created order and squeez-ing everything they can get from the ground and materials of creation without one thought of returning anything back to that same source. How thoughtless and how arrogant of us to act as if we are the masters of our own fate and of the possessions we use. Whatever happened to the fact that "the earth is the Lord's and the fullness thereof"?

What had been originally given to mortals prior to the fall in the garden is amazingly still offered after the fall of humanity into sin; it was not taken away (Gen. 9:1–3, 7). Therefore, mortals are still God's appointed keepers of creation on earth. We, together and individually, must maintain order in nature, care for and nurture the creation in all its forms, and finally, we must answer to God for the way we used what he put us in charge of.

Conclusions

It is clear then that we mortals are God's resident managers of the earth with all its creatures and resources. We must render a careful audit of how we kept all that was within the purview of our ownership and management. The final audit will be on the day of our Lord Jesus Christ when we shall give an account of all the deeds done in the body, whether good or bad (2 Cor. 5:10). This is not to say that in this present day our Lord cannot also judge any ruthless abuse of his creation, for he can do that now as well as in the final day!

Therefore, just as the heavens are ruled by the sun, moon, and stars, so we humans are to rule and care for the earth in place of God, who created and who also sustains all the created order.

Finally, it is amazing that we who are crowned with glory and honor should also be kept in the memory and care of so loving a heavenly Father. He does think about us and the sphere of responsibility he has given to us. He likewise visits all the work of our hands to see how we treat that which he has made and has left to our charge. Does not such oversight call for added attention to the details of exercising dominion and subduing all things great and small on this planet? May our Lord grant us his special help and carefulness!

Bibliography

Beisner, E. Calvin. "Managing the Resources of the Earth." In *Readings in Christian Ethics*. Vol. 2, *Issues and Applications*, edited by David K. Clark and Robert V. Rakestraw, 387–96. Grand Rapids: Baker Academic, 1996. Originally from E. Calvin Beisner, *Prospects for Growth: A Biblical View of Population, Resources, and the Future*, 155–68. Wheaton: Crossway, 1990.

Berry, R. J. "Christianity and the Environment: Escapist Mysticism or Responsible Stewardship." *Science and Christian Belief* 3 (1991): 3–18.

Reidel, Carl H. "Christianity and the Environmental Crisis." *Christianity Today*, April 1971, 6.

Schaeffer, Francis A. *Pollution and the Death of Man: The Christian View of Ecology*. Wheaton: Tyndale, 1970.

Stott, John R. W. *Issues Facing Christians Today*. Basingstoke: Marshall, 1984.

White, Lynn. "The Historical Roots of Our Ecological Crisis." *Science* 155 (1967): 1203–7. Reprinted in *The Environmental Handbook*, 1970.

Discussion Questions

1. Does the Bible command or even allow Christians to use the environment any way they please just so long as they make a profit from it before the Lord comes back again?
2. Is work an evidence of sin and the fall of man, or was there a doctrine of work both before and after the fall?
3. What are some of the ways you and I can manage the environment of the earth in the limited areas where we have access and control? If we own any property, such as the lot our house sits on, no matter for how brief or lengthy a time, in what ways are we to leave it in better shape than when we first owned it?

NOTES

Introduction

1. As described to me by my student Francis Graham.

2. The word translated "*company* of the righteous" here is literally the "*generation of the righteous*," i.e., a moral notion of the group (see also Ps. 24:6).

3. Franz Delitzsch, *A Biblical Commentary on the Psalms*, trans. Francis Bolton, 3 vols. (Grand Rapids: Eerdmans, 1955), 1:213.

4. See Derek Kidner, *Psalms 1–72*, Tyndale Old Testament Commentaries (London: Inter-Varsity, 1973), 81.

5. On the topic of interest and usury, see Walter C. Kaiser Jr., *Toward Old Testament Ethics* (Grand Rapids: Zondervan, 1983), 108–9, and especially the section entitled, "The Question of Interest and Usury," 212–17.

6. On ethical theory and bribery, see Bernard T. Adeney, *Strange Virtues: Ethics in a Multicultural World* (Downers Grove, IL: InterVarsity, 1995), 142–62.

Chapter 1 The Poor, Oppressed, and Orphans

1. "Hunger Facts: International," Bread for the World, http://www.bread.org/learn/hunger-basics/hunger-facts-international.html.

2. Quoted in Helen Harris, *The Newly Recovered Apology of Aristides* (London: Hodder and Stoughton, 1893), as cited by W. Stanley Mooneyham, "Orphans," in *Baker's Dictionary of Christian Ethics*, ed. Carl F. H. Henry (Grand Rapids: Baker Academic, 1973), 477.

3. John H. Scanzoni, "Poverty," in *Baker's Dictionary of Christian Ethics*, 519.

4. Robert D. Linder, "Oppression," in *Baker's Dictionary of Christian Ethics*, 473.

5. This double use of the word "fast" is a figure of speech called *Synoeceiosis* (Greek) or *cohabition* (Latin), as a subset of the figures known as *Antanaclasis* or

"Word Clashing" in E. W. Bullinger's *Figures of Speech Used in the Bible* (1898; repr., Grand Rapids: Baker Academic, 1968), 294–95, where the same word is repeated in the same sentence or context with an extended meaning, as in John 6:28–29, "Then they asked [Jesus], 'What must we do to do the *works* God requires?' Jesus answered, 'The *work* of God is this: to believe in the one he has sent' " (emphasis mine).

Chapter 2   Racism and Human Rights

1. The main statistics here came from J. C. Gutin, "End of the Rainbow," *Discover*, November 1994, 71–74.

2. Kerby Anderson, *Christian Ethics in Plain Language* (Nashville: Thomas Nelson, 2005), 174.

3. The Hebrew Piel form of the verb *galah*, "to uncover" (but Gen. 9:21 uses the Hebrew Hithpael of *galah*), means "to commit fornication," as does *seeing* in Lev. 18:6–19; 20:11, 17–21; Ezek. 16:36–37. But these all seem to be heterosexual, not homosexual, acts.

4. Luke T. Johnson, "The Use of Leviticus 19 in the Letter of James," *Journal of Biblical Literature* 101 (1982): 391–401. Also see Walter C. Kaiser Jr., *The Uses of the Old Testament in the New* (Chicago: Moody, 1985; Eugene, OR: Wipf and Stock, 2001), 221–24. Citations are to the Moody edition.

5. J. A. Motyer, *The Tests of Faith* (London: Inter-Varsity, 1970), 51.

6. Ibid., 53.

Chapter 3   Gambling and Greed

1. Kenneth S. Kantzer, "Gambling: Everyone's a Loser," *Christianity Today*, November 1983, 12.

2. Henlee H. Barnette, "Gambling," in *Baker's Dictionary of Christian Ethics*, ed. Carl F. H. Henry (Grand Rapids: Baker Academic, 1973), 257–59.

3. I am indebted for most of my facts in this chapter to Kerby Anderson, *Christian Ethics in Plain Language* (Nashville: Thomas Nelson, 2005), 166–73.

4. Kantzer, "Gambling," 13.

5. "Gambling in America," *Gambling Awareness Action Guide* (Nashville: Christian Life Commission, 1984), 5.

6. *The Final Report of the Commission on the Review of the National Policy toward Gambling* (Washington, DC: US Government Printing Office, 1976), 65. See also the National Council on Problem Gambling, Washington, DC; and William N. Thompson, *Legalized Gambling: A Reference Handbook*, 2nd ed. (Santa Barbara, CA: ABC-CLIO, 1997), 25–31.

7. Martin Luther, *Matthew*, loc. cit.

8. Ibid.

Chapter 4   Media, Entertainment, and Pornography

1. *New York Times*, April 20, 1980, quoted in Robertson McQuilkin, *An Introduction to Biblical Ethics* (Wheaton: Tyndale, 1989), 488. Another study, the A. C. Nielsen Report for January 1984, put the daily average at seven hours a day for television watching. See the joint statement of the Surgeon General's Office and the National Institute of Mental Health entitled "Impact of Entertainment Violence on

Children," *American Academy of Pediatrics*, July 26, 2000, www.aap.org/advocacy/releases/jstmtevc.htm.

2. Neil Postman, *The Disappearance of Childhood* (New York: Vintage, 1994), 72, quoted in Kerby Anderson, *Christian Ethics in Plain Language* (Nashville: Thomas Nelson, 2005), 188–89.

3. Allan Bloom, *The Closing of the American Mind* (New York: Simon and Schuster, 1987), 68, quoted in McQuilkin, *Introduction*, 489–90.

4. Bloom, *Closing*, 73.

5. Quoted in McQuilkin, *Introduction*, 490.

6. Anderson, *Christian Ethics*, 197.

7. S. Robert Lichter and Stanley Rothman, "Media and Business Elites," *Public Opinion* (October–November, 1981): 42–46. Later published in S. Robert Lichter, Stanley Rothman, and Linda S. Lichter, *The Media Elite* (New York: Adler and Adler, 1986).

8. See Anderson, *Christian Ethics*, 195–96.

9. Irving Kristol, "Sex, Violence and Videotape," *Wall Street Journal*, May 31, 1994, as cited in Anderson, *Christian Ethics*, 190.

10. Beginning in the 1970s, the Annenberg School of Communications found in a study led by George Gerbner and Larry Cross that TV watching for four or more hours per day manipulated the worldviews and psychological frameworks of children and adults (George Gerbner and Larry Cross, "The Scary World of TV's Heavy Viewer," *Psychology Today*, April 1, 1976, 41).

11. Richard Seaver and Austryn Wainhouse, eds., *The Marquis de Sade: Justine, Philosophy in the Bedroom, and Other Writings* (New York: Grove Press, 1965), 318–20, quoted in McQuilkin, *Introduction*, 236.

12. Frank Thielman, *Philippians*. The NIV Application Commentary (Grand Rapids: Zondervan, 1995), 220n11.

Chapter 5   Adultery

1. Robertson McQuilkin, *An Introduction to Biblical Ethics* (Wheaton: Tyndale, 1989), 191.

2. Taken and modified from David K. Clark and Robert V. Rakestraw, eds., *Readings in Christian Ethics*, vol. 2, *Issues and Applications* (Grand Rapids: Baker Academic, 1996), 256.

3. Samuel Janus and Cynthia Janus, *The Janus Report on Sexual Behavior* (New York: Basic Books, 1988), 169.

4. Joannie Schrof, "Adultery in America," *U.S. News and World Report*, August 1998, 31, quoted in Kerby Anderson, *Christian Ethics in Plain Language* (Nashville: Thomas Nelson, 2005), 123.

5. Statistic cited at www.doctorbonnie.com, quoted in Anderson, *Christian Ethics*, 126, 227.

6. Ibid.

7. Frank Pittman, *Private Lies: Infidelity and the Betrayal of Intimacy* (New York: Norton, 1989), 53.

8. Much of the material used here I discuss in my article "True Marital Love in Proverbs 5:15–23 and the Interpretation of Song of Songs," in *The Way of Wisdom: Essays in Honor of Bruce K. Waltke* (Grand Rapids: Zondervan, 2000), 106–16.

9. See my discussion of Old Testament polygamy in Walter C. Kaiser Jr., *Toward Old Testament Ethics* (Grand Rapids: Zondervan, 1983), 182–90.

10. Milton S. Terry, *Biblical Hermeneutics*, 2nd ed. (Grand Rapids: Zondervan, 1950), 330–33.

11. Alvin Toffler, *Future Shock* (1970; repr., New York: Bantam Books, 1990), 251–53.

12. Charles A. Reich, *The Greening of America* (New York: Random House, 1970), 245.

Chapter 6 Cohabitation and Fornication

1. These figures come from the U.S. Bureau of the Census, Current Population Reports, Series P20–537; America's Families and Living Arrangements: March 2000 and earlier, quoted in Kerby Anderson, *Christian Ethics in Plain Language* (Nashville: Thomas Nelson, 2005), 117.

2. E.g., see Alfred DeMaris and K. Vaninadha Rao, "Premarital Cohabitation and Subsequent Marital Stability in the United States: A Reassessment," *Journal of Marriage and Family* 54 (1992): 178–90.

3. Walter Trobisch, *I Loved a Girl* (New York: Harper and Row, 1975), 8.

4. Dr. Robert J. Collins in the *American Medical Association Journal*, as reported by Jim Conway, "Cheap Sex and Precious Love," *His* (May 1976): 34.

5. William Edward Lecky, *History of European Morals, from Augustus to Charlemagne*, 2 vols. (London: Longmans, Green and Co., 1910), 1:263 and 2:303, as cited in John Stott, *The Gospel in the End of Time* (Downers Grove, IL: InterVarsity, 1991), 81.

6. *Skeyos* is used metaphorically in the New Testament of human beings: in Acts 9:15, "my chosen instrument," and 2 Cor. 4:7 (NASB), "treasure in earthen vessels." Also see 2 Tim. 2:21. But it occurs more frequently in pre-Christian Jewish texts as a reference to a wife, following the Hebrew precedent. See Stott, *Gospel and the End of Time*, 83–84n22.

Chapter 7 Divorce

1. For these figures and logic, I am beholden to Kerby Anderson, *Christian Ethics in Plain Language* (Nashville: Thomas Nelson, 2005), 132–33.

2. Diane Medved, *The Case against Divorce* (New York: Donald I. Fine, 1989), 1–2, quoted in Anderson, *Christian Ethics*, 131.

3. Anderson, *Christian Ethics*, 132–33.

4. R. C. Campbell, "Teachings of the Old Testament Concerning Divorce," *Foundations* 6 (1963): 175.

5. J. A. Fitzmyer, "Matthean Divorce Texts and Some New Palestinian Evidence," *Texts and Studies* 37 (1976): 212. This find comes from the Murabba'at Cave II of the Bar Kokebah era, dated AD 124.

6. Joyce G. Baldwin, *Haggai, Zechariah, Malachi* (Downers Grove, IL: InterVarsity, 1972), 240.

7. R. C. Dentan, "Malachi," *Interpreter's Bible*, ed. George A. Buttrick et al. (Nashville: Abingdon, 1956), 6:1136.

8. Much of what follows is a reworking in part of Walter C. Kaiser Jr., *Malachi: God's Unchanging Love* (Grand Rapids: Baker Academic, 1984).

9. T. V. Moore, *Haggai, Zechariah, and Malachi: A New Translation with Notes* (New York: Robert Carter and Bros., 1856), 362–63.

Chapter 8 Abortion and Stem Cell Research

1. Kerby Anderson, *Christian Ethics in Plain Language* (Nashville: Thomas Nelson, 2005), 38.

2. A "pessary" is defined as a small soluble block inserted into the vagina.

3. Philip King and Lawrence Stager, *Life in Biblical Israel* (Louisville: John Knox, 2001), 41.

4. Paul Cartledge, *Thermopylae: The Battle That Changed the World* (New York: Vintage, 2006), 80, as pointed out to me by my graduate student R. Ryan Lokkesmoe.

5. Flavius Josephus, *Contra Apion* 2.202.

6. *Didache* 2.2, in Michael W. Holmes, trans. and ed., *The Apostolic Fathers in English*, 3rd ed. (Grand Rapids: Baker Academic, 2006), 164.

7. Clement of Alexandria, *Paedagogus* 2.10.96.1.

8. From the Greek word *blastos*, "sprout," denoting an early time in the development of the embryo when it is a hollow ball of cells. When the sperm and the egg first join together, they form a "zygote," which grows to form an "embryo." After some seven weeks it is called a "fetus."

9. Charles Krauthammer, "The Great Stem Cell Hoax," *Weekly Standard*, August 20–27, 2001, 12, as cited by Anderson, *Christian Ethics*, 49.

10. Franz Delitzsch, *A Biblical Commentary on the Psalms*, trans. Francis Bolton, 3 vols. (Grand Rapids: Eerdmans, 1955), 3:350.

Chapter 9 Homosexuality

1. These figures are often cited by public speakers, but they are very difficult to verify. No one has, to my knowledge, come up with a verifiable set of figures on exactly what percent of the population is homosexual.

2. These characteristics come from Peter C. Moore, "Homosexuality and the Great Commandment" (Ambridge, PA: Trinity Episcopal School for Ministry, 2002), an address given at the annual Convention of the Diocese of Pittsburgh on November 1, 2002.

3. Ibid.

4. Derrick Sherwin Bailey, *Homosexuality and the Western Christian Tradition* (London; New York: Longmans, Green, 1955).

5. John Boswell, *Christianity, Social Tolerance and Homosexuality* (Chicago: University of Chicago Press, 1980), 107–17; Virginia R. Mollenkott and Letha Scanzoni, *Is the Homosexual My Neighbor? Another Christian View* (San Francisco: Harper and Row, 1978), 61–66.

6. John Murray, *The Epistle to the Romans* (Grand Rapids: Eerdmans, 1968), 44–45.

Chapter 10 Crime and Capital Punishment

1. William F. Willoughby, "Crime," in *Baker's Dictionary of Christian Ethics*, ed. Carl F. H. Henry (Grand Rapids: Baker Academic, 1973), 150.

2. "Cost of Crime: $674 Billion," *U.S. News and World Report*, January 1994, 40–41, quoted in Kerby Anderson, *Christian Ethics in Plain Language* (Nashville: Thomas Nelson, 2005), 142.

3. Anderson, *Christian Ethics*, 143.

4. John Dilulio, "Getting Prisons Straight," *American Prospect* 1 (Fall 1990), quoted in Anderson, *Christian Ethics*, 144.

5. Anderson, *Christian Ethics*, 144.

6. Cal Thomas, "Programs of the Past Haven't Reduced Crime," *Los Angeles Times*, January 13, 1994, quoted in Anderson, *Christian Ethics*, 147.

7. Edwin Zedlewski, *Making Confinement Decisions* (National Institute of Justice Research in Brief, 1987); Edwin Zedlewski, "New Mathematics of Imprisonment: A Reply to Zimring and Hawkins," *Crime and Delinquency* 35 (1989): 171, quoted in Anderson, *Christian Ethics*, 145.

8. See Walter C. Kaiser Jr., *Toward Old Testament Ethics* (Grand Rapids: Zondervan, 1983), 90, 164.

9. Cesare Beccaria, "On Crime and Punishment," in *An Essay on Crimes and Punishments*, trans. E. D. Ingraham (Stanford: Academic Reprints, 1952), 104–5, quoted in William H. Baker, *On Capital Punishment* (1973; repr., Chicago: Moody, 1985), 27.

10. This view is developed by Rousas John Rushdoony, *The Institutes of Biblical Law* (Nutley, NJ: Craig Press, 1973), 358–62.

11. While the earliest and best manuscripts do not contain John 7:53–8:11, it has generally been received as a real event in the life of Jesus.

12. The best discussion of this episode, which is followed in the main here, is from John W. Burgon (1813–88), *The Woman Taken in Adultery*, 239ff, quoted in Rushdoony, *Institutes*, 397–98; 702–6.

Chapter 11   Suicide, Infanticide, and Euthanasia

1. John Donne, *Suicide: "Biathanatos,"* transcribed and edited from the original 1608, 1647, 1700, and 1930 reprints for modern readers by William A. Clebsch (Chico, CA: Scholars Press, 1983).

2. John Jefferson Davis, *Evangelical Ethics: Issues Facing the Church Today* (Phillipsburg, NJ: Presbyterian and Reformed, 1985), 160.

3. Herbert Hendin, Chris Rutenfrans, and Zbigniew Zylicz, "Physician-Assisted Suicide and Euthanasia in the Netherlands: Lessons from the Dutch," *Journal of the American Medical Association* 277 (June 1997): 1720–22, as cited in Kerby Anderson, *Christian Ethics in Plain Language* (Nashville: Thomas Nelson, 2005), 58.

Chapter 12   Genetic Engineering and Artificial Reproduction

1. Lee M. Silver, *Remaking Eden: How Genetic Engineering and Cloning Will Transform the American Family* (New York: Avon, 1998), 13.

2. Craig W. Ellison, "The Ethics of Human Engineering," in *Modifying Man: Implications and Ethics*, ed. Craig Ellison (Washington, DC: University Press of America, 1978), 3.

3. John Naisbitt, *Megatrends: Ten New Directions Transforming Our Lives* (New York: Warner, 1984), 74.

4. Francis S. Collins, "Shattuck Lecture—Medical and Societal Consequences of the Human Genome Project," *New England Journal of Medicine* 341, no. 1 (1999): 28. On June 26, 2000, the completion of the working draft of the HGP was officially announced at a joint press conference by Francis Collins and Craig Venter, who represented a private corporation called "Celera Genomics" (CG).

5. As reported in David K. Clark and Robert V. Rakestraw, eds., *Readings in Christian Ethics*, vol. 2, *Issues and Applications* (Grand Rapids: Baker Academic, 1996), 61.

6. As reported in detail in James C. Peterson, *Genetic Turning Points: The Ethics of Human Genetic Intervention* (Grand Rapids: Eerdmans, 2001), 7.

7. As reported in Kerby Anderson, *Christian Ethics in Plain Language* (Nashville: Thomas Nelson, 2005), 64–65. Also see Kerby Anderson, *Genetic Engineering* (Grand Rapids: Zondervan, 1982), 16–19.

8. Anderson, *Christian Ethics*, 66.

9. Ibid., 73.

10. Ibid., 68; testimony by Ethan Singer before the subcommittee on Health and the Environment, House Committee on Interstate and Foreign Commerce, *Hearings*, March 15, 1977, 79.

11. Gerhard von Rad, *Old Testament Theology*, trans. D. M. Stalker (Edinburgh: Oliver and Boyd, 1962), 1:146–47.

12. George Bush, *Notes on Genesis* (1860; repr., Minneapolis: James and Klock, 1976), 1:67.

13. Ibid., 1:68.

Chapter 13   Alcoholism and Drugs

1. Kerby Anderson, *Christian Ethics in Plain Language* (Nashville: Thomas Nelson, 2005), 153–65.

2. Other passages that conclude that drunkenness is a sin include: 1 Sam. 1:14; Isa. 5:11–12, 22; 28:1–8; 56:12; Hosea 4:11; 7:5; Joel 1:5; Amos 6:6; Hab. 2:15–16; Luke 21:34; Rom. 13:13; Eph. 5:18; and 1 Thess. 5:7–8.

3. Elizabeth Tener, "You Can Help Kids Resist Drugs and Drinking," *McCall's*, August 9, 1984, 92. For this citation and the general collection of facts in this chapter, I am once again indebted to Anderson, *Christian Ethics*, 153–65.

4. Craig Horowitz, "Drugs are Bad: The Drug War Is Worse," *New Yorker*, February 5, 1996, 22–33, quoted in Anderson, *Christian Ethics*, 154.

5. Anderson, *Christian Ethics*, 155.

6. Quoted in Peggy Mann, "Reasons to Oppose Legalizing Illegal Drugs," *Drug Awareness Information Newsletter*, September 1988, as cited in Anderson, *Christian Ethics*, 155–56.

7. There are two especially helpful sources that I used heavily in creating this section of the chapter: M. E. Andrew, "Variety of Expression in Proverbs XXIII 29–35," *Vetus Testamentum* 28 (1978): 102–3, and Bruce K. Waltke, *The Book of Proverbs: Chapters 15–31* (Grand Rapids: Eerdmans, 2005), 262–67.

8. Waltke, *Book of Proverbs*, noted that *zarot* may come from a Qal feminine participle from the third root of *Zur*, "to be loathsome," (pp. 262–67).

Chapter 14   Civil Disobedience

1. Kerby Anderson, *Christian Ethics in Plain Language* (Nashville: Thomas Nelson, 2005), 205.

2. Francis A. Schaeffer, *A Christian Manifesto* (Westchester, IL: Crossway, 1981), 103–4, quoted in Robertson McQuilkin, *An Introduction to Biblical Ethics* (Wheaton: Tyndale, 1989), 478–79.

3. Anderson, *Christian Ethics*, 209.

4. John A. Kitchen, *Proverbs: A Mentor Commentary* (Ross-shire, Scotland: Christian Focus Publications, Inc., 2006), 545.

Chapter 15   War and Peace

1. Jerram Barrs, "The Just War Revisited," in *Pacifism and War*, ed. Oliver R. Barclay (Leicester, UK: Inter-Varsity, 1984), 160.

2. These figures all come from David K. Clark and Robert V. Rakestraw, eds., *Readings in Christian Ethics*, vol. 2, *Issues and Applications* (Grand Rapids: Baker Academic, 1996), 489.

3. T. Raymond Hobbs, *A Time for War: A Study of Warfare in the Old Testament* (Wilmington, DE: Glazier, 1989), 226, quoted in Hetty Lalleman, *Celebrating the Law? Rethinking Old Testament Ethics* (London: Paternoster, 2004), 94.

4. Christopher J. H. Wright, *New International Biblical Commentary: Deuteronomy* (Peabody, MA: Hendrickson, 1996), 231.

5. Ibid., 230.

6. Arthur F. Holmes, "The Just War," in *War: Four Christian Views*, ed. Robert G. Clouse (Downers Grove, IL: InterVarsity, 1981), 117–35; James Turner Johnson, "The Utility of Just War Categories for Moral Analysis of Contemporary War," in *Can Modern War Be Just?* (New Haven: Yale University Press, 1984), 11–29.

7. Kerby Anderson, *Christian Ethics in Plain Language* (Nashville: Thomas Nelson, 2005), 212.

8. I am beholden for most of my ideas in this outline to John MacArthur, *The MacArthur New Testament Commentary: Romans 9–16* (Chicago: Moody, 1994), 205–40.

9. To substantiate these points, see Exod. 9:16; Ps. 75:7; Jer. 27:5; and Dan. 4:17.

10. Robert Haldane, *The Epistle to the Romans* (London: The Banner of Truth Trust, 1958), 585.

11. Ibid., 586–87 (emphasis original).

Chapter 16   Wealth, Possessions, and Economics

1. John MacArthur, *Whose Money Is It, Anyway? A Biblical Guide to Using God's Wealth* (Nashville: Word, 2000), 3 (italics his).

2. John White, *The Golden Cow* (Downers Grove, IL: InterVarsity, 1979), 67–68 (italics his), quoted in MacArthur, *Whose Money?* 7–8.

3. Brian Griffiths, *The Creation of Wealth: A Christian's Case for Capitalism* (Downers Grove, IL: InterVarsity, 1984), 21.

4. Here and in what follows my analysis is dependent on David K. Clark and Robert V. Rakestraw, eds., *Readings in Christian Ethics*, vol. 2, *Issues and Applications* (Grand

Rapids: Baker Academic, 1996), 339–80, especially for their section beginning on p. 343 that deals extensively with different types of market economies.

5. Adam Smith, *An Inquiry into the Nature and Causes of the Wealth of Nations* (London: W. Strahan and T. Cadill, 1776), especially book 5, chapter 2.

Chapter 17 Animal "Rights" and Factory Farms

1. I am beholden to Professor Elmer B. Smick for many of the ideas in these opening paragraphs from his brief article on "Animals" in *Baker's Dictionary of Christian Ethics*, ed. Carl F. H. Henry (Grand Rapids: Baker Academic, 1973), 20–23.

2. Ibid.

3. Rev. Leonard Vander Zee, "Also Many Animals," *Banner*, April 2008, 2.

4. Bernard E. Rollin, "Farm Factories: The End of Animal Husbandry," *Christian Century*, December 19, 2001, 26–29.

5. Ibid., 27.

6. Ibid., 29.

7. Matthew C. Halteman, "Compassionate Eating as Care of Creation" (Washington, DC: The Humane Society of the United States, 2008), 12. Mr. Halteman is assistant professor of philosophy at Calvin College, Grand Rapids, Michigan. He is a graduate of Wheaton College, holds a PhD from Notre Dame, and serves as faculty advisor for Students for Compassionate Living at Calvin College.

8. Ibid., 38–39.

9. This section comes largely from the paper "Against the Grain," in *The Economist*, June 12, 2004, 75.

Chapter 18 Care for the Environment

1. Lynn White Jr., "The Historical Roots of Our Ecological Crisis," *Science* 155 (1967): 1203–7.

2. Ian McHarg, *Design with Nature* (New York: Natural History, 1969), 28, quoted as a top illustration of a secular attack on Christianity in John R. W. Stott, *Issues Facing Christians Today* (Basingstoke: Marshall, 1984), 109–21.

Name Index

241

Scripture Index

23:17   196
27:5   238n9
28:9   196
29:7   174

Ezekiel

13:10   196
13:16   196
16:8   100, 101
16:36–37   232n3
16:44–50   119
18:8   16
44:22   94
45:8   21

Daniel

3   175
4:17   238n9

Hosea

4:10–11   33
4:11   237n2
7:5   237n2
9:14   113

Joel

1:5   237n2

Amos

2:6   201
4:1   21, 201
5:7–15   21
5:11   201
6:6   237n2

Jonah

4:11   212

Micah

3:5   196

Habakkuk

2:15–16   237n2

Haggai

2:8   200

Zechariah

7–8   23

Malachi

1:6   96
1:7   99
1:10   96
2:10   96, 97, 98
2:10–16   95, 96, 97
2:11   97, 99
2:11–12   96, 97, 98
2:12   99
2:13   97, 99
2:13–16   96, 97, 99
2:14   70, 97, 100
2:15   96, 97, 98, 100, 101
2:16   97, 100, 101
3:3   99
3:8   47, 205
3:11   113
3:16   48

Matthew

5   94
5:3   37
5:31–32   94
5:33–37   16
5:39   186, 191
5:43–48   130
5:44   186
6:1–18   48
6:14–15   39
6:19–20   47
6:19–34   47
6:21   47, 48
6:21–22   48
6:22   48
6:22–23   47, 50
6:24   47, 50, 51
6:25   51
6:25–34   47, 51
6:31   51
6:33   52

6:34   51
8:28–32   213
10:29   212
13:22   47, 205
14:6–11   16
16:27   179
18:23–35   39
19   94
19:3–9   94
19:8   95
19:9   94, 95
21:15–16   226
25:27   16
26:52   194
26:52–53   191
27:3–10   143

Mark

4:19   47, 205
10:1–12   94
10:14   20

Luke

8:14   47
10:40   51
10:41   51
12:13–14   136
12:16–21   204
14:5   214
16:9   204
16:18   94
21:34   237n2

John

2   71
6:28–29   232n1
7:53–8:11   236n11
8:1–11   134
8:2   135
8:3   135
8:5   135
8:6   135
8:7   135
8:10–11   136
10:35   9
12:47   133

SUBJECT INDEX